CW01628273

YOU ARE MY ROCK

PAMELA HODGE

AND YET

ABOUT THE AUTHOR

Pam Hodge is an entrepreneur from Grimsby in North East Lincolnshire. She gave her life to God as a child and has followed His leadership ever since. In 1996 she was one of the first single parents in England to adopt a family of four children. In 2008 she founded Rock Foundation to help young people and adults with learning disabilities. Since then, Rock has impacted the lives of thousands of people. This book is her life story.

First published in 2024 by And Yet

www.andyet.live

All rights reserved

Copyright © 2024 by Pamela Hodge

The right of Pamela Hodge to be identified as author of this work has been asserted in accordance with Section 77 of the Copyright, Designs and Patents Act.

Contact Pamela Hodge: pam@rockfoundation.org.uk

All rights reserved. No part of this book may be reproduced in any manner whatsoever without written permission except in the case of brief quotations embodied in critical articles and reviews.

ESV: Scripture quotations marked ESV are taken from the ESV® Bible (The Holy Bible, English Standard Version®). Copyright © 2001 by Crossway, a publishing ministry of Good News Publishers. Used by permission. All rights reserved.

MSG: Scripture quotations marked MSG are taken from THE MESSAGE. Copyright © 1993, 2002, 2018 by Eugene H. Peterson. Used by permission of NavPress. All rights reserved. Represented by Tyndale House Publishers, a Division of Tyndale House Ministries.

NIV (2011): Scripture quotations marked NIV are taken from the Holy Bible, New International Version®, NIV®. Copyright © 1973, 1978, 1984, 2011 by Biblica, Inc.® Used by permission of Zondervan. All rights reserved worldwide. www.zondervan.com. The "NIV" and "New International Version" are trademarks registered in the United States Patent and Trademark Office by Biblica, Inc.®

NKJV: Scripture quotations marked NKJV are taken from the New King James Version®. Copyright © 1982 by Thomas Nelson. Used by permission. All rights reserved.

READERS' COMMENTS

'Challenging … Moving … Elating …!'

'Faith and endless stories of everyday miracles'

'A story of how God can take frailty and turn it into strength and blessing.'

'An inspirational journey while clinging to the Rock of God.'

'A journey of faith that proves there is supernatural provision when the natural fails.'

'A journey with God during the high and lows, showing how God is always there.'

'An excellent read!"

EDITORIAL SUPPORT

Thanks to Philip Gladwin for supporting me in the writing and editing of this book. He helped me find my voice and guided me through the publishing process.

If you'd like him to help you tell your story, you can find him at www.philipgladwin.com

ACKNOWLEDGEMENTS

Thank you to all the people I worked with at Shoeboxes. All the knitters, all those who collected all the dolls, the sewers, all the preppers, the packing team, the craft ladies, the filling team.

The same goes for Rock Foundation— there have been many hundreds of people involved, so I sincerely thank all the staff, volunteers, parents, and of course our amazing students.

I thank all those who have supported us with their time, abilities, and money. It has been humbling to be just a small part of such an outpouring of pure love over so many years.

To my family and all the friends who walked this journey with me

PREFACE

To write a preface to a book which testifies to the work of the Lord Jesus Christ in the life of anyone is a humbling experience. How can I be anything other than positive when I read how Christ has divinely intervened in the life of Pam Hodge, to the extent that the call of God to lay her life down, having been received in the deepest recess of Pam's heart, was answered many times over by a glorious Yea and Amen?

Through the trials and tribulations of life, relationships, heartbreak, adversaries raising their heads to thwart, when God seemed far away but never was, Pam always returned, and continues to return to that place, that every true Christian knows, on her knees before her Lord. The Lord never failed.

This tome is about the divine call of God on a person's life, His Grace, His Love, and His desire to work through a person to embrace others less fortunate, and in difficult circumstances. The call to which Pam continues to say YEA and AMEN. It's the story of a vessel made fit for the Master's use.

Ken Smith - General Manager, Rock Foundation, 2010-2014

A LIFE IN AN HOUR

Around me and above me and beyond me were the children's voices. How beautiful they were. All squabbles of the day forgotten, all tiredness left behind, they chattered as they went. They marched hand-in-hand in twos, a loose column curving through the trees, on walkways up through the gardens, past the lanterns littered through the bushes in the soft green dusk. As they marched, they sang songs of worship. All around me, their young voices chimed out. For an entire hour, I could hear their praise for God rising through the warmth of the evening, winding up and on into the deep of the darkening sky. For an entire hour, joy overwhelmed me. I knew then: this love in action, this shepherding of the young and the frail, this guiding of new hearts to the Lord—for all this I was made.

1

What will happen to John?

It was September 2007, and a beautiful Lincolnshire day. The autumn mists had arrived. The sun was lower in the sky and the shadows were lengthening. The dew lay on the spider webs among the hedgerows and the trees were giving up their fruit. The first leaves were brown, yellow, and gold and beginning to fall.

I'd left Dunholme fifteen minutes earlier. I was part of a two-vehicle convoy carrying a carload of shoeboxes, packed by the generous people of the village for our Christmas appeal. This was our first collection of the year, and these thousand filled shoeboxes, along with 15,000 others, would soon be sent out in lorries to Romanian orphanages. There had been much excitement in the village hall where they had been loaded. Sincere thanks and big congratulations all round for the generosity of people and the provision of God.

I should have been happy. But I was far from that.

As the trees and hedges of North Lincolnshire whipped past the window and I handled the bends of the quiet roads, all I could feel was a growing anxiety. I immersed myself in the great problem that had been worrying me all summer.

What will happen to John?

John, my beautiful, adopted son, would soon be sixteen. Soon he would have to leave the safety of his school and face a much more complex, and, frankly, much less sympathetic, world. John, who had suffered such trauma as a baby that he only spoke in grunts till he was seven. John who had special educational needs and had the sweet—and sometimes headstrong—naïve vulnerability of an eight-year-old child. What place was he going to find in the outside world? Who would look after him in the coming years? Let alone in those later years, the years when I was gone.

I drove, and I prayed.

Please Lord, please help me here. Please speak to me. Please guide me. Let me know. What can I do with John?

I heard no answer.

The road went on; the hedges turned to houses as I wound through the streets of Market Rasen. There was no comfort here. I passed a garage and saw a group of young mechanics working on a car. They were laughing and having fun as they teamed up to lug a trailer along, but fear was getting hold of me and it twisted things. I'd seen in the past how good-natured banter could quickly turn to bullying when people met John. How could the tough working world ever fully accept someone like him?

It was the old mother's worry—will my child be safe in this rough old world? In John's case, this worry was well-founded. He'd been happy when he was younger, but at the moment between primary and secondary school, his teachers had warned me he had additional educational needs. In secondary school, it had become obvious that he couldn't handle many of the children around him, and many of those children couldn't handle him.

I drove, and I worried, and I prayed, and the sun shone, and the trees blew and bent in the breeze. I was slower now, lost in this conundrum, and the van ahead pulled away, vanishing out of my sight.

I was alone, just me and God.

The miles went past, and I worried, and I prayed, and God stayed silent.

I was at an age where I could see myself providing for John for another twenty-five years. Recently I had realised that would not be enough. John would be just forty then, with perhaps half his life still ahead of him. How would he cope?

The miles passed. The injustice of it all upset me. If I was having this worry, if I could see this trouble ahead for me and my son, then there must be thousands of mothers and children in the same situation. How could this be the way of the world? Hadn't God created John? Didn't He knit him together in his mother's womb? Wasn't he fearfully and wonderfully made? Didn't God have plans for John? Plans to prosper him, not to harm him? Well, where were they?

I climbed the long road up to Cabourne and there, at the very top of that hill, God spoke.*

In that subtle, gentle, lightest possible way that God has, like leaves fluttering from the trees, He spoke directly to me.

He said to me, 'All is good. You've done so well. You're doing so well.'

---

* *'God spoke to you? How can that work?' Trust me, when it happens, you know it. It can be a change in the outside world that carries an infinite charge of truth. A smile on the face of a passer-by that opens the door to a new direction. The impulse to cry which comes as I consider a fresh path, and which lets me know the Holy Spirit is in that direction. Or, like this day on the road to Grimsby, when a blast of new ideas arrived fully formed after prayer.*

I received that with gratitude and (I'm ashamed to say) a touch of my usual impatience. What was the point of doing well when I couldn't provide for my son?

Then, with the greatest, most grace-filled, most all-devastating touch, God told me what He wanted.

'It's time for that second dream.'

I couldn't help it. I gasped. I couldn't believe it. Surely, He couldn't mean ...

'What are you saying, Lord?'

No answer.

'Please God. Don't leave me to work it all out alone. Give me more.'

He was silent.

In a flood of dread, I drove on. I wrestled fear, thrown back decades. Back to when I was sixteen, when I'd been given two dreams. Vivid, uncannily real, impactful dreams. Dreams that had the shape and the weight of prophecy. Dreams that had stayed with me ever since.

The first dream had been fulfilled nearly fifteen years before and had changed the course of my life as it did so. As it went from dream to real life, it brought me the greatest joys and the greatest challenges I'd ever experienced.

That God was calling in the second dream made me weak. This could only mean hard times ahead. Harder times than I had ever faced before.

'Surely not now, God? After all I've done already? I don't have the strength.'

Four more miles. God was silent, and I wrestled my doubts and fears and loyalties, and then He spoke again. Not in words, but in symbols.

I came over the hill at Irby, and the road dropped away to the coastal plain. There, six more miles ahead, towering over the town, Grimsby Dock Tower broke the horizon. The Dock

Tower, over three hundred feet high, one hundred and fifty years old. A giant replica of a Renaissance Italian tower, such an unlikely sight in this isolated corner of North East Lincolnshire. The Dock Tower, built for the glory days of the fishing industry. The Dock Tower, that, whenever you drove back to Grimsby, was your first sight of the town.

Today there was something different about it. It looked taller than usual. Today it looked like a signpost, like a finger pointing straight up to heaven.

I considered this second dream. It was a simple picture, but it was charged with complex emotion. A big old house. A doorway framed with two pillars. There were people gathered in and around the house, and I was looking after them. Somehow, I was in charge, and I was ministering to them.

I had obsessed about this dream for years, worried about what it meant. I had known for years that a house like this would play a huge part in my life but had never understood how, or what, I was to do about it.

Eventually I had parked the dream, tidied it away into a bottom drawer in my mind. I was confident that God would make it clear when He wanted to. That I would understand everything in His time.

Now God had pulled the drawer open. Wide, wide, open. Grimsby was my adopted hometown, and it was in Grimsby, God was saying, that I should step into this second dream, this second part of His will for me. It was in Grimsby that I could bring great blessing to so many who needed it so much.

I still didn't know how. Then God dropped a sudden, flashing sequence of pictures into my mind. I finally understood what He wanted me to do, and I saw the implications of it all. The scale of what He was asking me was terrifying. Far bigger, far more difficult, and far more costly, both financially and emotionally, than I had ever imagined.

I'm not ashamed to say that I instantly rejected it. What God was asking was too immense. I couldn't possibly do it. I was too weak, too shy, too useless, too fearful.

I said, 'Not me, God, not me. You've got this wrong. You don't mean me.'

But God insisted.

I said, 'Please, not me. I can't do this. It's too big. I'm too small.'

But God insisted.

Ahead of me the Dock Tower pointed to Heaven, and I had no choice but to accept the truth.

I gave in. I said I would step into my second dream under one condition: that God would help me. That I would do it if—and only if—God was the absolute Lord of it all. That I could surrender all my control to Him and that He would accept it. That He would lead me, and I would follow Him in everything that lay ahead.

My dread melted away and changed into a deep upwelling of excitement.

This is the future. God invites me. I will take this leap of faith.

Suddenly, as He so often does, God instantly rewarded that blind jump. He confirmed I was right, with a flooding sense of His love. He let me know I should never doubt him, and so my last doubts left me. There and then I vowed I would step forward and do what He asked me. With God, and through God, I would begin this next work.

Peace fell on me, and I drove down the hill to the Laceby roundabout. The road into Grimsby and this new future lay smooth and wide. An empty dual carriageway. Clear tarmac straight and wide and clear ahead of me for as far as I could see. Just for the moment, there were no boulders ahead. I felt reassured; God could remove every boulder. And those He didn't remove, well, if He wanted them to be there, then I would accept the challenge of getting through.

I'll tell you all about this second dream, and how it is coming true, and about my first dream and how that came true, and what happened before, during and after, all later in this book. It's a story that has great happiness, great growth, and a growing ministry for good. It also has great shadows, years of suffering and pain. These pages may surprise many people who know me well. I only hope that this mix of joy and lament fulfils my deepest desire—to testify to the glory of God, and, by showing how God rewards faith, to lead more people towards the Kingdom.

For now, let's go back to where I came from, so that you can understand what was being asked of me.

2

Green pine needles, tinsel, candles. Cold pavements, games at school, the party at church. My mother bent over her sewing, making me a new party dress. My dad banging and hammering, making secret things in his shed. The excitement growing every morning, building as every evening took us closer to Christmas Day.

The road to Christmas was so thrilling when I was a child. School changed, and became more relaxed, more fun. There'd be carols in morning assemblies, and a carol concert at church, and the choir would sing the descants which made me feel like I wanted to laugh and cry at the same time. There'd be a nativity play in which we'd all play our parts. We'd spend a whole craft lesson cutting out paper snowflakes from cleverly folded triangles of paper, and share our amazement at how, just as with the real thing, each design was one in a million, one in a billion. Our teacher would stick them to the windows. We'd peer up, out through the icy flakes of paper and wish for the grey sky to give us actual snow. (Some winters we even got it. One year back then, maybe two, the pond froze in the big People's Park, and people actually went skating on it.)

There was always a big Sunday School Christmas party. Dad and the church would hire the Scout Hut. It had a vast hall and dining room ideal for a big event. There could be one hundred children there, and, of course, Father Christmas always came.

As I got older, one Sunday afternoon in Advent we would go around the streets visiting some of the elderly members of our church. We'd wish them a Merry Christmas and sing them carols, and they would treat us to mince pies, cakes, and hot drinks.

On Christmas Eve, my mother would wait till we were asleep. A little bell would ring downstairs, and a deep voice would laugh a jolly 'Ho, ho, ho' at the bottom of the stairs. (Was that Mum putting on a different voice? Surely not.)

We'd hear footsteps coming up the stairs and our excitement would build until we felt sick. The door handle would turn, and the door swing slowly open. We would try to be good and pretend so hard to be asleep. Soft footsteps in the room were unmistakable, and finally, we'd peek through our fingers so, so careful not to be caught. And there he'd be. There in the dim light, a grown-up figure in a red robe. He'd bend over the foot of our beds, leaving us the stockings, before looking back at us, and walking away silently, closing our bedroom door with a gentle click. (Was this magical figure actually just Mum, in her long red dressing gown? Definitely not.)

We'd lie there and try to sleep. We had a stocking each (well, Dad's old socks) and sometimes, if the light from the street came in, we could see them bulging at the end of the bed. It would be such a long night. Mum and Dad had forbidden us to open our presents until the morning, and we had to stay in bed until they fetched us in the morning. We tried to be good, but first light would always find us, crouched at the foot of our beds trying to prise open the corners of our presents so we could get a good look ahead of the official unwrapping. Sometimes we could see what was in there, sometimes not. Agony, and yet so, so exciting. Unforgettable moments.

Christmas Day went along wonderfully. First, to church in the morning, where Dad would lead a peaceful, joyful service. Then home for stockings, presents, dinner and fun. Dad would have bought a crate of satsumas, and some of them, along with a few nuts, and maybe some apples, would end up in the socks. Then we'd go onto the other presents. There always seemed to be more, and always one really good, enormous gift for each of us.

Dad was very capable with his hands and very good at woodwork, so he'd make my brother a garage, or a fort, whatever it might be that year. Once he made me an entire doll's house.

I loved baby dolls and everything about them, so when I was eight, Mum and Dad bought me a doll's pram. It was secondhand, but they'd worked hard on it, and it was beautiful. I saw it standing there, and took one hesitant step towards it, then another. I looked inside, and there was a baby doll smiling back up at me. Mum was a very gifted seamstress. She'd made beautiful bedding and lining for the pram, and she'd dressed the doll in a sweet little outfit. How amazing that it was for me. I thought the world of it, and I loved that baby doll.

Christmas Day would finally end, always such a sad moment. Boxing Day would be a little calmer, and then we'd have a quieter time until New Year's Eve, when all the church would get together again. My mother would arrange the food and get people baking hot cakes and pies, and they would also cook in the church. It was nothing for her to be in the kitchen at home baking a hundred mince pies and more beyond.

After the party, Dad would lead another service, and we'd close the old year and welcome the new with Holy Communion at midnight. The bells would ring out around us and the ships out on the Humber would sound their foghorns.

Christmas was the happiest time of all. Mum and Dad made a fuss of Philip and me. They made sure that we never missed out, even if they had to improvise. It was a magical time. We felt loved and special, and as the year went on, memories of Christmas gave us something to hold on to.

Because, as the year went on, we really needed something to hold on to. First there was January, and back to school. All the dark evenings and wintry mornings. Wet, grey days and soggy coats, damp shoes and socks and boring school lessons, and hard, hard homework. Before long, we'd forget the candlelight and the fun and the excitement of Christmas, and things would be back to normal at home.

Which wasn't good.

Because normal at home wasn't good at all.

3

Even as I write these words, I feel a sadness. Troubles in childhood can put a shadow on the rest of your life, and troubles we had by the barrow-load.

My mother was called Edith. She was born in 1924 in Bridgend in South Wales. She was the youngest of seven children and her brothers were all coal miners and local pastors. Growing up, she had attended chapels that leaned towards a Pentecostal background.

In the first part of the century, there had been a massive revival in Wales, which led to many seeking a deeper relationship with God. This revival eventually led many people to Pentecostalism, which was strong on the back of the 1905 Los Angeles Azusa Street revival. The Crosskeys Full Gospel Mission in Newport became a centre for Pentecostal activity, and the Apostolic Church, Assemblies of God, and the Belfast-founded Elim Church all had their roots in the Welsh revival.

Edith fell in love with God very early on. She gave her life to Jesus and was saved as a child. She was a dutiful little girl, and she wanted to be a nurse. She studied hard to get there, and throughout her career she always worked hard, always tried to get experience of every kind of nursing she could manage.

She was very clear minded, very intelligent, and her faith grew until she took a break from her nursing career to study at the Assemblies of God Bible College in Surrey. She felt God wanted her to go onto the mission field in Africa, but she discovered she had contracted tuberculosis while nursing TB patients. The doors to the missionary work closed, and she had to spend some years in a sanatorium.

Eventually cured, she came out and worked in tropical nursing in Liverpool. She met my father—and promptly discovered she had contracted TB again. The doctors told her it was serious, and that she'd need to have part of her lung removed. Mum wasn't having that. She refused the surgery and simply kept praying until God healed her.

Raymond Hodge, my father, was nine years younger than Mum. One of five children, he was born in Liverpool in 1935 and had been brought up attending the Plymouth Brethren Church.

He left school and finished his time as an apprentice armature winder, but he didn't look for any more work in that field. He felt God was calling him into ministry. He had a problem in that he felt he needed to worship in the Pentecostal style. His church was of the Plymouth Brethren denomination, and they disapproved mightily of that, because they took issue with the Pentecostal idea that you could have close experience of the Holy Spirit.

Things got far worse when Ray met the Holy Spirit directly, in an experience common among Pentecostals known as a 'baptism of the Spirit'. He felt that God's Holy Spirit had reached him personally and filled him directly. He began a much more intense relationship with God, and his prayer life grew stronger, and much more vivid. Like many Pentecostals, he received the ability to speak and to sing in the Spirit, also known as 'speaking in tongues'.*

Aware that the revivals in America and Wales were full of people sharing the same experience, Ray felt glad, happy to be equipped to serve God all the more fully. His old church disagreed. They knew exactly what to do. They felt this was not a gift from God, and they asked him to leave.

Shocked, betrayed, but free to go even deeper into his revitalised faith, he went to study the Bible at the Elim Church college in London. His years there were a blessing but left him with a lifelong thorn in his side.

The blessing was to be filled with a deep knowledge and true love for the Word of God.

The thorn came in the shape of a serious back injury. One day, he and his friends were fooling around on a staircase, and Dad got kicked in the back. It was an accident, but it needed surgery. His wound got infected. It didn't heal properly, he needed more treatment, and thus began the health problems that would attack him for the rest of his life.

Ray graduated from college in the end. He became a minister and met Edith in Liverpool. They married in 1956, when Edith was 32 and Ray was 23.

They became parents in 1958, when I was born in Wells in Somerset, and then we moved to Holyhead in Anglesey. My brother Philip was born there in 1960, and we moved to Belfast in 1962. Then Dad got a job at a church in Grimsby. We uprooted again, coming back over the Irish Sea, heading east to

---

* Tongues are strange, new languages given by God directly that manifest the Holy Spirit being poured out upon the recipient, just as on the day of Pentecost. Sometimes they are foreign languages that were previously not known to the speaker, sometimes they are strange utterances which may, some say, be only fully understood by God and His angels.

Lincolnshire. As we passed Liverpool, we broke our journey and stayed with my dad's extended family for a few days.

We would go back to visit them occasionally, and many years later, I realised how a few days spent in Liverpool around that time had changed my life forever.

We'll come back to that.

4

We arrived in Grimsby, in 1965, when I was seven.

I noticed the welcome first. How friendly everyone was. Everywhere we went, people had a curiosity, an openness, and a warmth that felt honest and generous. Very early on, a couple from church invited us out for tea. They owned a sweet shop and, before we left, they took us into their bedroom. There, under the bed, were piles and piles of glittering boxes of chocolates. Philip and I stared at the piles, stared at each other, and stared back at the piles. Could this really be real? We'd seen nothing like it. Laughing, the couple told us to take a box each. Our welcome was complete. We loved our new town.

Mum and Dad had a different perspective. Dad's church was serving a tough, lower middle and working-class community not too far from the epicentre of the docks, and that came with many darker realities. Mum and Dad were far more aware of wider issues. Domestic violence was common. There was a hard drinking and fighting culture, and much crime. The biggest thing was the fallout from the gold rush at the docks.

Grimsby was a town just coming down from the golden

years of the fishing industry. No-one had fished the North Sea in the Second World War, so in the late 1940s the fish stocks were high. The fishing industry had seized the opportunity, and by the time we got to Grimsby, the town was at the summit of a long slow boom. By the late 1950s, some people called it the Klondike of the East.

The area of the town around the dock gates felt just like the Wild West. There was heavy drinking, big spending, fights, garish clothes, and men mistreating women; everything out of proportion. The seamen had pockets full of money, but no time to spend it; there was the glamour of taxi rides, big gambles, flamboyant suits, living it up and dazzling the girls. Everything was overdone; too intense as they made up for what they suffered at sea. Men had made small fortunes and wanted to spend them, and the whole town had benefitted. One skipper, a top earner, had come home from the sea to start his own fishing business. He had made a name for himself as a tycoon by installing a personal refrigerator in the boot of his Bentley to carry his choicest fish around with him. He had not long since built his own skyscraper as the centre for his multi-million-pound empire.

This was just one of many stories of success. A tidal wave of money had flooded down the Humber from the North Sea and the North Atlantic, the Barents Sea and the White Sea. It hadn't stopped at the dock gates but had lifted many ships in the town.

With Mum and Dad both coming from very simple, very devout church backgrounds, the way so much of the town centred on getting and spending this wave of new money made them uneasy. They felt the place had a very materialist mindset. This unease went deep. In fact, in later years, they told me that their first impression was that they'd never seen a town so spiritually dead.

This feeling seemed to seep into our house, numbing and breaking everything. Almost immediately, their relationship soured. They argued. About money, about jobs around the house, about almost everything. Worst of all, they argued about God. Later on, I understood that with two parents who had gone to two different Bible colleges, disagreements about the finer points of Christian doctrine were inevitable. All I knew at the time was that our house felt dangerous. That explosions could happen randomly, and that once a bomb had gone off, there would always be a battle.

Things fell apart fast. I got used to going to bed each night with cotton wool in my ears to block out the sound of battle. I'd lie in bed in the dark, praying to God, asking for the anger and the banging to end. Begging Him to please stop them fighting. Every night, I'd drift off to sleep hoping God would do something. He loved us, didn't He? He wanted Mum and Dad to be OK, didn't He? Surely, surely, He would help them sort things out. But He didn't, and the fights grew worse, and slowly Philip and I got more and more unhappy.

Church was a refuge for a while, but not for long. I soon noticed how Dad didn't seem to have so much time for me. He was so loved at church, and he loved everyone back. He loved his children's work most of all. He was gentle, and patient, and fun, and all the little children thought the world of him. And yet he ignored me, even belittled me.

One day, I was walking along the street with Dad. We were on our way to the shops. I saw ahead of us a little girl from church. Everyone called her Curly because of her beautiful hair. Something rose inside me. A desperate need was born, and everything collapsed at once.

I grabbed at Dad's hand, tried to get his attention. I pulled hard at him to get him to look away. I dragged at him to turn left, or right, or into a shop. Anything to get him away from

Curly. I tried so hard, but I wasn't strong enough, and he was confused, then irritated. He shook me off, and then it was all too late.

Curly saw us and broke away from her mother and ran up to my dad. I looked at her coming, and I realised how happy she was to see him. I looked up at him, and I saw how he smiled to see her. How his face was loving. I saw how he bent down to her, and made such a fuss of her, how he stood to greet her mother with smiles and questions about how the family was doing, and once again I saw how I had been left behind.

As Curly took his hand and dragged him off to say hello to her mummy that day, as she'd hold his hand as they walked into church on Sunday mornings, that all hurt me so much. I couldn't understand how he could hold this little girl's hand, yet not hold mine. I was so young. Why didn't he show me any love? Was I so awful?

I don't believe he ever held my hand or gave me a cuddle or a kiss after we arrived in Grimsby. In fact, as time went on, he turned away from me ever more clearly; when he looked at me, his face grew ever more blank.

5

The rejection and the loneliness I felt, no one will ever know. A pastor has many problems, and each one fuelled more arguments at home. Dad's ongoing health problems just poured petrol on the fire. Every day, every mealtime, they argued, and it never seemed to stop.

Money was tight for us, and many in the church saw that as a good thing. There was a common saying at the time of 'Keep the Pastor poor, keep him humble'. If ever there was a lie from the devil, that was it. Some weeks, Mum wouldn't even have enough money to buy a tin of peas for Sunday dinner. One week, Dad went out and bought himself a fresh cream cake. Oh boy, the row that caused, and the frustration Mum felt when she was struggling to make the food budget stretch.

Of all the arguments, the ones about doctrine won out. Both Mum and Dad loved their Bible, but they had learned different things in college, and they each thought their own views were right. Dad's upbringing in the Brethren church certainly made things worse. He had the attitude that women were fit for nothing better than the kitchen sink. They most certainly shouldn't have opinions of their own.

In the end, they would argue over anything. I couldn't count the times Mum would be in the kitchen with the door shut, closed tight, locked, the taps running to drown him out. I couldn't count the times Philip and I would cry upstairs, or stand terrified in the front room as Dad told us we had a wicked mother.

Things closed in even outside our house. Cleethorpes wasn't far away, and the summer brought thousands of day trippers to throng the seafront. I wasn't allowed to go there. At one end of the seafront was an enclave of the devil. The Wilkie family's Wonderland was one of the biggest amusement parks in Europe at the time and would stay busy until 10 or 11pm in the summer. There were dodgems, a ghost train, an exotic fortune-teller, a cafe at the end of the prom, clowns' heads which moved side to side as you threw balls into their mouths. There was a laughing policeman, Penny Falls, slot machines, and a mirror maze. There was a Big Dipper which looked like an entire city to me, and all the candy floss you could dream of eating.

To my parents, this was the purest symbol of the world, in the sense that the 'world' was that evil way of life, the demonic system of godless pleasure-seeking that existed among people who didn't know Jesus. They wanted to shield their children from it. They wanted our family to lead a different, a better life. A life that honoured God.

So, they did their best to keep us out of the world. Forget Wonderland. I could never even go to the pictures as a child. The most I could manage was to go on a swing. Though I had a few friends at school, I wasn't allowed to see them after school. The only friends I could have round were people from church; the problem was that there was no-one my age in the church.

Church ruled everything. Sundays was three times a day. We had the morning service, Sunday school in the afternoon, and the evening service. At home, we weren't allowed to run around, or even play with a toy; we had to sit down and read Bible story books.

Dad put us to our first work in God's service. He would type all the details of upcoming church events on huge stencils, and Philip and I would use a Roneo machine to produce all the leaflets. We would stay up until bedtime working on this. We'd spend hours cranking that handle, keeping on until we were falling asleep standing up.

For the first few years in Grimsby, this was how Philip and I lived. Quietly, modestly, as calmly as we could, no matter that we had glimpses and intuitions of a vivid outside world for which we yearned.

There was one oasis: Miss Robinson.

6

Miss Robinson was an older lady in our church. We appreciated her so much. She was kind and nice, and she liked Philip so much that she invited us both for a meal at her house every Thursday. Philip loved it, as did I. In fact, nobody knew how much it meant to me.

Every Thursday, Mum and Dad would pick us up from school and drop us off at Miss Robinson's house in Ripon Street. There were no arguments. She had a standard little terrace house. Spotless and tidy with old-fashioned furniture. She would cook a proper meal, traditional food, and she always made sure she had a nice dessert for us. Philip and I looked forward to it so much. It was so lovely, and it was clear Miss Robinson wanted to bless us.

Those afternoons were a precious time for us. A peaceful time. We could just be us. She had a proper sense of fun—there was one bonfire night party when she let us burn some of her old furniture. Philip and I stood open-mouthed in the back garden as she directed some men in the party in throwing old chairs out of an upstairs window to put on the fire.

We loved Miss Robinson, and one afternoon a week was never enough.

At home, the arguments got ever worse. One day, Dad hit Mum and caught her ear with his fist. This was unusual. Overall, he wasn't a violent man. More usually, he'd focus on proving our mother was mad. She wasn't mad, of course, she was saner than anybody, but one day I overheard him trying to ring the doctor, trying to see if he could get her put into an asylum. I was distraught. I couldn't live without my mum; life was hard enough as it was.

Thankfully, the doctor didn't grant him his request, but that didn't stop Dad. He used to get me alone and tell me,

'Your mum won't be here long, but don't worry, I'm going to marry again. You haven't got to worry.'

All this made me a very fearful girl.

No-one outside our family knew my family was having trouble. Mum said nothing, and nobody knew what she was going through at home. She knew her place as pastor's wife, and she had a saying that expressed it:

'As the pastor's family, you're friendly with everyone but friends with nobody.'

I realised she was speaking the truth.

I realised that conversations with other children would end as I approached the group.

'Oh, we can't say anything now she's here. The pastor's daughter.'

If someone in the church had anything against my dad, and they couldn't get him because he was the pastor, what did they do? They got the pastor's kids.

This all hurt because I was so shy. I had no confidence whatsoever. I realised there was always going to be a barrier, that I could do nothing fun or naughty. I realised I was set aside. To this day, I have a soft spot for pastors' kids. Nobody knows what goes on behind the scenes.

This isolation was so hard because I always wore my heart on my sleeve. I was very open and emotional, and this was a sign of weakness for both my parents. Dad was increasingly cruel to me, but even Mum had been trained through her nursing to hide her emotions and so she wasn't very affectionate at the best of times. I never doubted that she loved me and Philip, but it was hard to tell. She would give us a peck on the cheek at bedtime. We might get a hug. Nothing more. For someone as emotionally open as me, this wasn't good.

Around this time, my grandmother died. Mum went back to South Wales for the funeral. I can remember the fear of being left at home with my brother and Dad. My brother was two years younger than me, and they had kept a lot of things from him so he had less reason to be wary of Dad. They had a close relationship, and sometimes I would find myself as the odd one out.

I was developing a genuine fear of men by then, so going to church on that Sunday Mum was away was terrifying for me. I coped for a while, but then an older gentleman sat down next to me. I froze and cried. People came to comfort me, of course, but I sobbed and couldn't stop. No one could understand why. They decided I was missing my mum. I was, of course, but I felt that there was so much more that no-one outside our family knew about. I felt everything I'd been through at home was all piling up on me and I just couldn't cope with it.

And then it peaked.

7

The day began quietly enough. At the breakfast table, I noticed my mum was clicking her jaw again. She had done it more often recently, and it used to drive me crazy. I tried to ignore it for a while, but I couldn't help it. It really got to me.

And then I noticed Mum give me a sideways look as she did it, as if she realised how it was grating on me. I couldn't believe it. Was she really doing it deliberately? Didn't she like me either? Was I really so alone?

We all went on eating our breakfasts. The clicking and the clinking of knives and forks were the only things that broke our silence. I didn't mind. I was only grateful that no-one was arguing.

Then I realised my dad had stopped eating. I risked a quick glance at him. I saw how the jaw clicking was irritating him, too. I noticed how he held his knife and fork so still, how coldly he looked at my mum, and suddenly I was terrified.

We finished, and, oblivious to everything, Philip asked to be excused. He got down from the table and ran off upstairs to get his school stuff ready.

CHAPTER 7

Mum gathered up the breakfast pots and took them out to the kitchen. She closed the door behind her, and I could hear the taps running as she began the washing up. She began to sing a hymn. One she loved, and, of course, one which my dad thought contained bad doctrine.

Dad looked at me, serious. I wriggled in my seat, uneasy to be held in his gaze like that.

There was a silence that went on and on. I asked if I could be excused. He didn't answer.

Unease turned to fear. Why was he looking at me like that? What had I done?

Finally, quietly, calmly, he spoke.

'I want to let you know that I'm going to kill your mother. I've got a plan. Soon, when we're out driving, I'll stop the car. Your mother will open the door, and I'll wait until she's half in and half out. Then I'll rev the engine up hard and drive off so quickly that she gets dragged underneath.'

I stared at him, trying to understand these strange words of his. He smiled, obviously wanting to comfort me.

'But don't worry. I really don't want you to worry. There's lots of other ladies at the church. It won't be hard for me to find someone else very quickly. I'll definitely get married again, so we won't be on our own for too long. You'll have another mother very soon.'

My mum sang on in the kitchen. The room around me faded. Did he already have a replacement in mind? My mind raced. Was it Miss Robinson? How could that be? Was that good? No, it was awful. Terrible. I stared at him. Speechless. Helpless.

I was there a week or two later when he tried it.

We pulled up outside our house and I saw the look in his eye. I knew what was about to happen. I waited, frozen in the same sick agony I had felt all week. I was still too scared, too timid, too small to say anything, even to Mum, even as I saw it happen.

The car stopped moving. She looked back over her shoulder, checked the path was clear, and opened the door. As she got out, and he slammed his foot down on the accelerator.

The engine roared, and the car leaped forwards. She screamed, and the car stalled, and I covered my eyes and dived into the back seat well.

'Ray. What are you doing?'

Mum's voice. She didn't sound too hurt.

I dared to peek.

I saw her sitting in the front passenger seat. She looked flustered, but unharmed.

He realised he had failed, and he covered instantly.

'I'm so sorry. My foot slipped. I'm so sorry. Are you OK? Are you OK? Love, are you OK?'

In the back of the car, I struggled up. I stared at him through the gap in the seats, aghast. What was he going to do now? What could he possibly say?

'You could have killed me,' she said, amazed.

His face was so, so sad. So upset, so remorseful, so distraught.

He had mistimed it. He had lost his nerve and misjudged everything and acted too soon. Mum wasn't far enough out of the car when he began, and as the car moved forwards, instead of knocking her out, the back of her seat had caught her up and scooped her back in. She was startled, but completely OK.

She saw the look on his face and calmed.

'What on earth were you doing?' she said, a little more gently. She adjusted herself in her seat, checked herself in the rear-view mirror.

'I'm so sorry. My foot just slipped.'

'I can't believe it.'

'I'm so sorry. I really am.'

'You could have killed me.'

She sounded half-hearted. She was already moving on. She really hadn't realised that it had been deliberate.

'It's OK Ray. Don't worry. I'm OK,' she said, much more gently. She put her hand out on his knee to comfort him.

I watched, incredulous. Was he crying?

I believe he was.

8

The biggest surprise of all that period is how such great good came out of it. The Apostle John writes how the light always shines in the darkness, and this was certainly true in my case.

Life went on. I don't think Mum ever realised what had happened. The arguments vanished for a while, but within weeks they were back. More subdued, but more intense, and somehow more desperate.

Because of the rows, I was always in bed early. This put me alone in my bedroom, ears muffled against the raised voices. With no-one to talk to, I had no choice but to turn to God.

I didn't seek God in a formal, written, scriptural way. With so many arguments about the Bible going on around me, with so much emphasis at home given to that grim, grey, joyless sense of religion, and most of all, just being a child, I found I couldn't sit down and read the King James Bible. Besides, what I read in the Bible confused me, because what I found was so different from what was going on around me.

We were a poor family. I was told that every day, and it was certainly true. But my parents also obviously thought that was right. They both agreed. Dad was a pastor, and he needed to be kept poor so that he would stay humble.

But I was realising how God had blessed so many wealthy people in the Bible. King David and King Solomon were the richest men in the world. I had heard how Joseph was so wealthy when he commanded Egypt, how God blessed Abraham and Isaac. I knew how Job lost his wealth at one point, but when he proved he was a good man, God gave it back even more so.

It confused me then, and it still confuses me all these decades later. Why couldn't we be like that? So long as we didn't make money an idol, why couldn't we have healthy finances? Why did we have to have this mentality of poverty? Why did we not have enough money to get new school shoes? Why did we always have to scrape and scratch for our food?

Right at the heart of my family's faith, I detected something that felt like a lie.

God is a wonderful father, and a wonderful teacher and, if we ask Him, He will always speak to our need. In my case, instead of speaking through the written word, or in doctrine, the Holy Spirit broke through to me directly, and I met God in a personal, healing way.

Night after night I'd talk to Him. Shorter, faltering, childish prayers at first, but over time becoming longer, more direct, more intimate conversation, until God became my only friend.

Nobody knew this was going on, but by the time I was ten or eleven, I must have given my life to the Lord twenty times. I wanted to be sure.

9

It was a Thursday morning, and I was sitting at my desk watching the teacher write on the board. I was feeling more anxious as each minute passed. I looked at the other children, who were copying the teacher's writing into their exercise books. I was struggling to read what was on the board, and I turned to my exercise book. I was way, way, behind, and needed desperately to catch up. I struggled to read the teacher's handwriting, but it was no good; the chalk letters were blurred and faint.

Surreptitiously, I looked at the children around me. They were all concentrating on their work. Perhaps I'd get away with it.

I lifted my desk lid a little and slid my hand in. Reaching about, I found the little case, and prized it open. I pulled out the brand-new pair of dreaded wire-frame NHS glasses and nursed them out of sight in my lap for a moment.

It was no good. I simply couldn't see what was happening on the blackboard. I had no choice. I slipped the glasses on, hooked them round my ears, and waited.

CHAPTER 9

No-one said anything. I had been scared for nothing.

I looked forward.

Bliss. Every letter on the board jumped into focus. I bent my head and began writing fast. It was going to be OK.

Until people noticed.

One boy at the back began. It was such a quiet, innocuous comment, but it came with a devastating sting.

'I can't read the board. It's hard to see past Pam and her *goggles*.'

The children around him spluttered in laughter. I looked at him, shocked. He was a boy I'd thought was a friend. He had put his head back down now, and was pretending to concentrate on his work, but I could see him struggling to control a sly smile.

The other children were quick to follow. They were careful to keep under the teacher's radar, but they jabbed hard.

'Old Four-eyes, you mean?'

'I can't see Pam. Where's she gone?'

'Hey, Pam. Are you OK—or are you an *owl*?'

My cheeks were on fire. I continued to write, although I was dying inside. But I was too shy, too scared to stand up to this bullying, and it didn't take very long before the other kids had won, and I had stopped wearing my glasses. From then on, my schoolwork suffered unless I could get a seat in one of the front rows of desks.

What made it worse was that I was growing up, and it felt like Dad was trying to block that, too. Though my mum worked hard to dress us, my handmade dresses and other cast-off or hand-me-down clothes stood out a mile. For games at school, my dad wouldn't let me wear shorts, insisting I should always wear skirts. My mother tried to help by making me a divided skirt, but no-one else wore them and that just compounded the problem. Other girls were talking about make-up; even I knew I was too young for that, but my dad had clarified that if I ever wore any, he would lock me out the house.

I felt like I was made to look like a freak. I certainly felt like a freak. I was out on my own with this embarrassing family. I felt insignificant. I had no confidence whatsoever. Typical child stuff, in some ways, but then I realised something strange was happening beyond how awkward I was feeling.

As a school, we'd go on a lot of trips. We might go out into the country to look at all sorts of nature. We might go to splash through the tidal marshes at Tetney or look at the seabirds and the forts in the River Humber out at Humberston. Once a year we'd go further afield to the Lincolnshire Show. At the end of those days, I was always very poorly. I'd be exhausted, tired, and weak, way past where the other children were.

For a long time, no-one could understand why. My dad had no sympathy, my mum told me to buckle up and be strong, and the doctor asked whether I was getting enough vitamins. Whatever the reason, it progressed until the doctor had to take it seriously and give me some tests. Which led to more tests. And then more. Which finally showed I had a heart murmur.

Oh, how God knew what He was doing. This was the single best thing that had ever happened to me.

Calm yet serious, grave yet kind, the doctor looked into my eyes and told me I shouldn't worry. I would definitely grow out of it, but in the meantime, I should avoid anything too strenuous. I certainly wasn't to do any sport.

I heard and didn't really understand what he was saying. There was something wrong with my heart, OK. But I wasn't going to die. OK. All I could focus on was his pen as he wrote me a note for school that excused me from all exercise.

From then on, I kept out of all PE classes. I never had to go to the hated swimming pool. I could say 'No' to any physical exertion at school. And nobody could ever question this because it was all to do with my heart.

I used that note right up to the week I left school.

10

I wasn't alone with poor health. My dad was far worse. Since Bible college he'd had trouble with his health, but at this time it was getting worse, and though he was still employed as minister at the church, he was spending more and more time sick in bed.

The family finances were so tight that mum decided she would go back to work. My Dad hated this idea, and it was unpopular with some at the church, who had clear ideas that a woman's role was at home. However, my dad was worried about what would happen if he couldn't work, and how he might struggle to support our family. In the end, there was no choice but for him to break his principles.

Mum got a job as a midwife at a local maternity hospital. Her background and experience came into its own and she quickly became a night sister. It was a well-paid job, and so, for the first time in my life, with two salaries, our family had some money. My mother loved it, and we both loved the day she took me to the shops to buy me my first dress.

There was a downside. Her hours took Mum out of our house in the evenings, leaving Philip and me alone with my dad at a time when Dad and I were really beginning to fall out.

I had never recovered from that terrible day with Mum and the car. I had tried to bury it, and go on living life, but what I saw and what I knew had eaten away at me. It was all the worse because Mum was at work, so Dad would sometimes have to take me with him on pastoral visits out to the church community. There was one elderly couple who he would visit regularly. Each time we were there, he felt comfortable enough to confide in them. I would have to sit, forgotten in the corner of the room, and listen to him tell them all about his terrible marriage. He would talk for hours about how awful my mother was. I would listen in horror as he told them all our private business. He twisted what had happened until it made him into a hero, and I'd watch them nod and sympathise with him. It hurt so much.

In fact, after a while, it did more than hurt. It shocked and disgusted me. It was a final straw, and it destroyed almost all my love and respect for him. I couldn't hide that for too long, and soon he could see what I thought about him. His gloves came off, and we entered a phase of open conflict.

That came to a head during the evenings Mum was at work. Dad would look after Phil and me, and his cruel side really came out. He wouldn't physically hurt me, so there were no actual beatings. Yet it was nothing for him to push me into things as he passed. When I got in his way, he'd give me a shove, or a trip, so that I would bang into things. His verbal aggression to me was non-stop. He'd look at me, as I was on the floor, or rubbing the place I'd knocked myself on the furniture. He would throw words like knives at me, words that fell on me like curses:

'You'll never achieve anything in life.'

'You're useless.'

'If you ever get married, he'll divorce you.'

'You'll always be lonely.'

'You're only fit for the kitchen sink.'

'You should be put in a mental home and throw away the key.'

Looking back, he was ill, physically, and mentally, and in pain. I can understand some of this at least, but I still find it hard to excuse. This was my father, who should have loved and protected me. Most days, it felt like he was trying to destroy me. I still couldn't understand why. What had I done to make him hate me so much?

As the months went by, he was more frequently in hospital. I remember sitting by his bedside and looking at him. He was a big stocky man but, in those times, he was diminished; grey, pallid, sweating, and surrounded by medical equipment. There were many times I'd come out of hospital and think he was going to die.

When I was twelve, the illnesses hit a peak, and he was exceptionally poorly. Complications from the old back injury led to endless infections, which led to heart problems, and the beginnings of severe kidney issues. Once again, Mum tried to prepare us for bad news, but he surprised us by going on.

Finally, at the age of 37, he had to step down from ministry and stay at home. He lay in bed for weeks at a time, unable to get up, reliant on my mum's nursing. He grew bitter and angry, desperate for good news from the occasional doctor's visits.

Good news which never came. It became clear that Dad would not work full time as a pastor again and he would have to retire from the church. To help us out, the church gave us an opportunity. We could buy the Manse from the church. It was only a small, semi-detached house, but it would give us stability, so we wanted to do it. The problem was that losing Dad's income meant we would struggle to pay our mortgage.

What were we to do?

11

Pray of course.

We prayed endlessly as a family for help and guidance, and God gave us a way through.

A gentleman in the church heard about our troubles and stepped forward. He had been a builder, and he owned many rental properties in town. Out of extraordinary generosity, he offered my dad some of them. Dad didn't have a penny to his name, but the houses generated income, and the gentleman was giving them to us at a good price. Dad saw his chance. He went to the bank and, though he was clearly ill, with no capital or property development experience to his name, they gave him a chance. Somehow, he persuaded the bank to lend him the money to take on these properties.

That in itself was a minor miracle. The next helping hand was from the council, who were offering grants to have poor properties redeveloped.

Dad took full advantage of this. He sent the builders into the first house, got it done up very quickly, then got some tenants in. The success of this—and the fact everyone could see a revenue stream coming in—helped him to fund getting the next house modernised. We pulled together as a family. All of us—especially Mum—would spend many hours working hard on decorating these properties. I made all the light shades, and I loved doing it. It all grew slowly but surely. Some we did up and sold on, and some we kept and let out. In the end, Dad bought an amazing eight properties, and we ended up keeping five of them. Developing the houses involved long hours planning and doing the projections, and a great deal of confidence, but Dad could be very determined when he put his mind to something, and he managed all the sales and building work from his sickbed. The properties turned out to be a blessing from Heaven. After he had paid all the mortgages and all the outgoings, they gave a small return, enough to pay for our own mortgage.

I even got my first job this way. One property was a hairdresser's, and I went to work in there on Saturday mornings. I was still twelve when I started. I worked there for several years. I didn't cut; I swept and washed hair. It was a nice little shop. I got on with the hairdresser well enough, and I liked all the old-fashioned equipment. The way the customers would come in and chat appealed to me. I was the open sort myself, but some of these women amazed me—you never knew what you were going to overhear next. I earned ten shillings for the morning, gave my brother some pocket money from that, and came away with a little cash for myself.

I realised I enjoyed working for money. The same year I wanted some cash for Christmas. I had inherited some of my mother's skills for dressmaking, knitting, and especially crocheting, so, fired up by making the lampshades, I started a little business. I used to crochet and sew, and I loved it—if I was ever down, give me a piece of material. In the sixties, the fashion was for bright wool, so I made dressing table sets and took them into school. To my amazement, everyone wanted me to make them for their mums for Christmas. Even the dinner ladies were buying them from me.

I could hide myself away in my bedroom with a great excuse. I was a speedy crocheter so I could get an entire set done every evening and give it to the customer the following day. I got a little business going, and I made a small fortune, enough money to buy all my Christmas presents and a new dress for myself. I was delighted.

12

It was a hot Saturday afternoon, and our car, a blue Morris Minor, was standing still. We were in heavy traffic somewhere out in the country. We were on a narrow side road, in a queue with other weekend drivers, and the road we were turning into was jammed solid. There were high hedges around us, and the sky was a molten blue. It was hot, and I was drowsy. My parents had worked out that if they took us out, they were slightly less likely to argue than if they were sitting around at home. One of the family crisis times was Saturday afternoons. They realised it lightened the pressure slightly if we took a picnic and went for a drive in the country. We were doing a lot of driving in the country in those days.

I wound down the back window as far as it would go and tried to catch some scraps of the breeze outside the car. I was hot and sticky on the plastic back seat, and itchy in a dress that was too heavy for the heat of the day. I looked at Philip at the other end of the seat. He was happy enough, looking out of the window at a plane overhead. Things were OK in front too, and

Mum and Dad were talking away, happily enough. Maybe this afternoon really was going to be different.

I relaxed and leaned my head on the doorframe. Dad switched the engine off as we were going, and I could hear a bird singing high overhead. It really was a nice day. My mind wandered.

I found myself back in lovely Conwy, over in North Wales. We had been going over there twice a year recently to deep-clean our five caravans. Dad had bought them after the houses as another side income. He was letting them out to holidaymakers, and it was all going very well. Things were definitely a little better recently, since we had had some money coming in. Not quite so many arguments. I was definitely glad that he didn't need to be kept poor, now he wasn't a pastor. I smiled to remember how Auntie Rose, my mum's sister, would always have so many home-made treats for us while we worked.

But then I remembered the journey over there, and how, once again, the road signs I'd seen pointing to Liverpool made me feel scared. I didn't understand why, as I hadn't been to Liverpool since I was seven. That was eight years ago now, but Liverpool was definitely a dark place in my mind. I'd see the word on the map, or see the road signs, and I'd get a lurch of fear. I wrestled again with it. Was it Cilla Black? Ken Dodd? All that pop music and telly that mum and dad hated so much? Was I just feeling guilty because sometimes I'd sing along to the Beatles?

I tried to think about other things, but I felt disturbed again. Voices from the front of the car broke in on me and I came back to reality.

'But disease is indirectly down to what we do.' said my mum. 'We put ourselves in harm's way by what we do. It's right there in Augustine. He's famous for it.'

'Oh, *Augustine* she says. And what would you know about Saint Augustine?' said Dad.

Mum exhaled, long and hard. Nodded to herself. Once. Twice. Staring straight ahead, she replied.

'And why wouldn't I know about Augustine?'

Her voice was very calm, and very low. That was a danger sign, and Dad knew it.

He shifted, uncomfortable. He began to speak but changed his mind. He looked out to his right.

'Why? Oh, let me guess. Because I'm just a woman?' Mum said.

He snorted.

'No woman I know would leave her kitchen so disgusting.'

She laughed, enraged and contemptuous.

'And how would you know what a kitchen looks like? You don't even know where the sink is.'

And off they went, and on, and on, and on they kept going. I had been wrong. It was going to be a normal Saturday, after all.

Even they couldn't keep it up forever. After a while, the mood flattened, and the traffic shifted, and so did we. We even made it out into a slow flow of traffic on the main road for a little while. But we never got going.

In the end my dad pulled up on the verge, bumping over the potholes, and parking on the edge of a gravel lay by. We were rammed between an overflowing litter bin and a wall of the cars still in the jam. I looked disbelievingly at Mum as she opened up her shopping bag and brought out the Tupperware boxes.

'Aren't we going to get out of the car?' I said.

'What's the point? We'll have it in here,' said my mum.

And so we did. We ate our sandwiches, with a stinking litter bin on one side, exhaust fumes and a wall of traffic on the other. My dad's face dark and resentful. Philip scuffling and kicking me whenever Mum wasn't watching. Mum pretending everything was normal to us in the back and addressing Dad in the front (when she absolutely had to) in a voice that could cut steel.

I'd been so wrong to hope. It was just another normal, joyless, bitterness-filled battle of a Saturday afternoon, after all.

The season of comparative peace between Mum and Dad that had come with the rental income was ebbing away. Since Dad was no longer pastoring a church, his frustration grew. So did the battles around him as he took on the outside world. What's more, we had stopped seeing Miss Robinson, who was now blessing other pastor's kids, and so we no longer had that afternoon oasis to bring us some peace.

I grew to hate Sundays even more than when I was a little child. We would still go to church several times a day, but since Dad had left formal ministry, he was getting unpredictable. As far as Dad was concerned, he was right, and everyone else was wrong. I lost count of the times he would stop someone in the middle of their sermon and tell them they were mistaken. Often, he would create arguments outside the church as he argued his point. It was awful.

I had less and less time for these arguments. I was deep into my own relationship with God by then, and it was vivid, alive, and fresh. I loved the Bible. How could I not? But I didn't spend hours digging away at the obscure corners. At that point in my life, when my parents were arguing about doctrine, I'd just be getting more and more frustrated. I'd imagine them getting to heaven and finding out that neither of them was right and the truth had been something different all along.

Beyond that, it was getting slowly worse between me and Dad. I was just a woman, and women were fit only to serve him. But he was worse with me than with Mum. His contempt went deeper. I realised how, to him, I was a nobody. I might just as well be thrown away. I was damaged goods. I was just something he had to put up with.

There wasn't much light in the house at all by then. I loved my mum, and she loved me, but even she would sometimes abandon me. One tiny, thoughtless, passing comment especially had an impact way beyond the words. It was a comment that betrayed what she thought about me, tangling with what my dad would express openly. It left me with a raw wound that would not heal for many years.

I had always felt like a freak in the outside world, and this got worse the older I got. I was very tall for my age, lanky even, and I had awful teenage acne. Around this time, two of our cousins came to stay with us. We were all out walking through the woods when Mum said something about them being beautiful girls. They turned around and said as one, 'What about Pam?'

Mum looked surprised. 'What about Pam?'

That, and all it implied, cut me like a razor.

13

Whatever we think, whatever we do, time doesn't stop.

There's an old English poem which repeats the line 'That passed over, so may this'. That idea may comfort some people, but it didn't help me. I could see that time was passing, but I couldn't see anything getting better for me.

I was certainly even more fearful than ever. Now I was 16, the fear of what I would do in the future was huge. Even though I hated school, leaving to go out into the big wide world was terrifying. I felt totally ill-equipped. Though I'd had my little business success, all I could imagine in front of me was, at best, another place where I would get bullied and embarrassed every day.

In the summer of 1975, school was done. The rest of my life yawned in front of me.

It took a few months, but in answer to prayer, another gentleman from church offered me a job. I would be an office junior in the accounts department of a large local food manufacturer.

I took it on. I was much protected there but it wasn't really what I wanted to do. Someone in the office told me of another job going with more money in the sister company and I applied. The vacancy was for a punch card operator. During the interview, they told me they felt it wouldn't stretch me enough and instead they offered me a job as a data control clerk.

I loved the job, even though, when it came to the coffee breaks, I would do anything rather than actually go for a coffee. That situation terrified me. There were a lot of men around, computer operators and programmers, and my old difficulties with men came back tenfold. Slightly bored with their jobs, they were intrigued. I was a novelty: a young girl, who was obviously a little different. They would poke fun at me in that normal, work-place way. Some of them would be deliberately offensive, some of them were just trying to be funny; either way, I simply couldn't handle their comments. Every day, I was petrified. And so, so shy.

It got worse when my dad rang my boss. He wanted to know if I was doing a good job. That got out round the office pretty fast indeed, and I had to live it down for days.

With everything still as it was at home, and work such a challenge, I became very depressed. Very soon, the doctors started giving me Valium.

In all this period, there was one happy time. I went down to Coleford in the Forest of Dean, and I stayed for two weeks with my cousin and her family. It was the best time of my life, full of fun and sunlight. We did nothing special, but there was so much love—and no arguments. I realised they all really liked me. I kept laughing because I was so happy. During those two weeks, I never took a single tablet. It was a shock. Could life really be like this?

I'd had a friendship with God for many years by then, and I would pray and tell Him all my worries, and all my happiness. I would feel God with me all the time, but it was more of a casual conversation between friends. I'd tell Him how I felt, and He'd console me, and let me know I wasn't completely alone. Until that time He spoke to me in a deeper, more momentous way.

In the Summer I was sixteen, He began this process by simply showing me my future.

14

'... I will pour out my Spirit on all people. Your sons and daughters will prophesy, your young men will see visions, your old men will dream dreams.' (Acts 2:17, NIV)

God has many voices, many ways to reach us. Dreams and visions are strong and vivid, but sometimes they are just the beginning. For some people, verses of the Bible leap out into prominence just as they are needed. Some people are given prophecy by other Christians, who receive that prophecy from the Holy Spirit during prayer and worship. Many people hear God's voice internally; a few even hear an actual voice, speaking actual words from outside their body.

God has spoken to me in these ways in my life, but I've had comparatively few dreams.

Dreams are strange. We all dream, but most of what we dream is irrelevant. Sometimes, for example, we can dream about elephants, and it's simply a dream about elephants. We forget it in the minutes, or hours, after waking up.

But sometimes we have dreams that are so vivid, so powerful, so charged with emotion that they cannot be forgotten. It's not necessarily to do with the events in the dream, it's to do with the impact.

I choose to believe dreams like this are from God, and over the years, I've learned to write them down. Very often, a few months or a few years later, when I read through these notes, I can see how the dreams were prophecies, or diagnoses, of something that was coming my way.

In the summer I was 16, I had two dreams that changed the course of my life. This was the beginning of a decade of growth, with an expanding blessing that brought me some of the greatest times of my life.

The dreams are so long ago now as I write this book, and I have rehearsed them in my mind so often, that much of the detail of the dreams has been smoothed away. What is left in each case are the absolute essentials. A couple of lines in the Book of Genesis can contain a story, such as the Tower of Babel, that can live on for thousands of years. So, these dreams lived on for me. Everything that could be forgotten, I have forgotten. Everything I remember is what I needed to remember.

In the first dream, I was a grown-up woman. I was living in a detached modern house, and I had no feeling for my first husband. I'd been approached to take on four children, and I was being asked to look after them in every way. The oldest two were girls and the youngest two were boys.

In the second dream, a couple of weeks later, I saw a great building, an old house, with two big pillars. On the front face of the building, there were steps up to a huge front door. A lot of land lay round about. There were other buildings on site, and there seemed to be tennis courts a little away from the main house. I never went through the door in the dream, but I knew I was doing things there. I didn't feel I was any age in particular, but I was looking after people with additional educational needs, and people who were disadvantaged.

I knew, at the very core of my being, that these dreams were prophecy rather than random scribblings from my subconscious. I knew they were gifts from God, that they would be fulfilled later in my life. I held each dream to me, each one a secret treasure.

Neither of these dreams has ever left me. In fact, they have guided my life ever since. Let's go on for now, but I'll come back to both. You'll notice them when they manifest in my life.

15

In the Book of Exodus, God tells us to honour our parents (not love, interestingly)* and in his letter to the Ephesians, the Apostle Paul tells us to obey them. Nowhere in the Bible are they given total ownership of our lives. Nowhere in the Bible does it say that we must remain prisoners in an abusive family. So, it can be good to move away from our parents and begin walking our own path. If the relationship is healthy, that can be a simple separation. More often, I've noticed it can be a struggle. One side or other gets hurt at some point.

I knew that if I was ever to live rather than exist, then I had to get out from under the shadow of my dad. The problem was that I couldn't see how. I couldn't see anything more than a future of depression, frustration, and endless bullying as he got more and more ill and mentally unbalanced.

The first gap in the wall came when I was seventeen.

It happened at the Assemblies of God church spring

* 'Honour your father and your mother, so that you may live long in the land the LORD your God is giving you.' Exodus 20:12, NIV.

convention in Grimsby. Every Easter AOG would run a big event at their base in Pasture Street. This was immensely popular, and two hundred or more Christians would pack into the place. They'd be hungry for praise, worship, and an encounter with the Spirit.

This year I was up on the balcony with some other young people, and Dad was sitting down below, closer to the stage. From where I was sitting, I could see the back of his head as he read. He took his Bible to all these events. It was an old, black, leather-bound book, worn and battered, the pages covered in decades of notes. I'd learned to dread what would happen after he'd spent time in that Bible. My mum wasn't there; she'd been working nights, so she was in bed. Philip was there but sitting away from me with his own younger friends.

It was the middle of the afternoon service. All was going well. The music was wonderful, and I felt a proper sense of the presence of God. Until, in front of everybody, my dad got up and shouted at the stage. I crouched down in my seat in horror. I realised he was criticising the preacher. He didn't like the sermon, and he wasn't going to hold back from telling him in front of two hundred people. The Pastor tried to smooth things over, but my dad wouldn't back down, and just spoke louder. It was a very uncomfortable scene for everyone, and of course I felt it the most. Soon, my dad was up on his feet. He waved his Bible and told the Pastor that what he was saying wasn't correct. He told him he was a false teacher, and that he was leading innocent people into Hell. That Jesus had never meant this, and the Apostle Paul had never meant that, and all the prophets had said the other, and the Preacher should get off the stage immediately and we should all pray for his forgiveness and for the Spirit to fill our ears with God's holy Truth instead.

I listened in horror as the nightmare built in front of me. Surely this couldn't be happening. For my dad, who was no longer a minister, to speak out in challenge like this in our church was bad enough, but for him to do it in front of so many people? At the Easter convention? Was he going mad? Had he totally forgotten about his family?

I couldn't contain myself anymore. First, I cried, and then I sobbed. Why was he like this? I folded up on my chair, trying to become invisible, trying to remove myself from the room.

An older lady came along the balcony. I noticed her sit down next to me and I felt her look at me. I couldn't bear her gaze, so I turned away. She wouldn't be deflected.

'That's your father, isn't it?'

'Yes', I nodded. My voice was so small, so weak. It took me all I could do to reply. 'Yes, it is.'

'This isn't the first time he's done it?'

I was crying so much I could only nod.

'That's my husband he's shouting at. He's the preacher.'

I was horrified. I sat up straight and blurted out an apology, but I was in such a mess my words got tangled up and faded away.

She listened carefully and then spoke to me.

'I just wanted to say, my husband is completely OK. He won't mind. And I wanted to let you know that this has nothing to do with you, sweetheart.'

I looked at her in confusion.

'What your dad's doing down there? That's nothing to do with you. And everyone knows that. Look around and you'll see. No-one blames you.'

I looked around and I could see that no-one was blaming me. One or two of those around me did glance at me, but all I could see in their eyes was a gentle sympathy, and absolutely no mockery.

The lady was so kind, and she was so, so gracious. She sat next to me to comfort me, and I sobbed into her shoulder until

I stopped. She stayed with me until I felt better, and she got me through it all.

That afternoon was a watershed in my relationship with Dad. After that, I point-blank refused to go to church if my dad was there. What surprised me was that my mother also refused to go with him. Lost in my own misery, I guess I'd never considered that his outbursts may have embarrassed her too. It was certainly the first time I saw anything in her that looked like a public move apart. It would not be the last.

16

The next time God spoke to me was a year later. It had been a period of isolation for me. Working with mostly men and older women in my job, and no friends from school or church, I had no one during these times. This forced me ever closer to God. In these late teen years, He became my constant companion. I would talk to Him about anything and everything. He was always there for me; He never let me down. Little did I know that my relationship with God would ever grow more precious as my life went on. Oh, how I needed Him.

I knew what salvation was, and I had asked Jesus into my life as a younger child, but when I told my parents, they would tell me I wasn't saved. I would ask why, and how they knew for sure, and all they would tell me was that I couldn't be saved because I hadn't received a baptism in the Holy Spirit. I think underneath it all, my dad believed that, as a man, my brother would be saved first. I expected no more than that from him, but I was surprised that Mum didn't back me more.

She didn't, and that was that. I would end up going back to God to cry out and ask Him what was happening? Why did they say all this? Was it true, or were they being cruel? Did God agree with them?

God stayed silent on this for a while, but then He finally made a move that even my parents couldn't mistake.

It was April, and the evenings were getting longer. It was during ministry time at our church. During each service, we would have a period where people in the congregation could pray for each other. I loved these times, and I knew how they went. You'd listen to the preacher, and something in their talk might resonate, coming alive in you in the most unexpected way. Or you'd feel convicted over something else entirely that had happened during the week. Or something completely random would pop into your head and nag away at you frantically. Whenever anything like this happened, you'd make it known that you wanted to be prayed for, and one, two, or a group of people would gather round, lay their hands on you, and pray for you.

At this service, just a normal weekly prayer meeting, for once I didn't have others praying for me. I stood, watching the scene, standing still, waiting in the middle of this ministry time. Then I prayed. I closed my eyes and sought God and the Holy Spirit in my usual way.

Things got strange. It wasn't a hallucination as such, more like an enhancement of what was there. An incredible intensification of what was going on around me. Everywhere I turned, there seemed to be more people. More voices. More music. The normal world around me seemed to drop away. It was as though doors to other places opened, and more and more people had flooded in. I felt that the whole place was packed, but amazingly so. It seemed there were hosts of people there praying.

I opened my eyes, and the room looked normal. Surprised, I closed them again, and I was back in that amazing hall with the sound of a host of saints. Was I with the ancient church? Was I surrounded by Christians from across the ages? Were they human worshippers at all, or had God shown me angels around me? All I could hear was prayers and praise in thousands of voices. I felt thousands surrounded me. Thousands upon thousands of those souls who have lived and died, and who shared my longing for our eternal Father. I leaned into this longing and prayed and praised like never before, for a time that went on and on, with no sign of anything ever ending.

Of course, it ended eventually, and I found myself back in my church. There were no hosts of worshippers. The room was normal-sized, and around me were just the church goers I knew —and my mother, who was regarding me.

'It felt like there were thousands of people around me,' I said.

She looked at me, appraisingly.

Uneasy, I shrugged. 'What?'

'God is doing something,' she finally said.

'He is?'

'You're close to being filled by the Holy Spirit.'

'Do you think so?'

'I do. Very close.'

This thrilled me. If she said that, I was prepared to believe her.

I didn't have to wait long.

Two weeks later, I went to another prayer meeting. They called it a 'waiting meeting'. It was a simple format. Different pastors laid hands on you and asked for you to be filled with the Holy Spirit and you waited.

This all comes from the day of Pentecost, which is written about in the Acts of the Apostles, in the New Testament. When Jesus died on the Cross, many of his followers scattered. Only the truly faithful remained. Instead of fleeing to the hills to save themselves, instead of leaving the country to a life where they could be free of persecution, they went back to the very worst place of all: Jerusalem, where Jesus was betrayed, captured, and sentenced.

Once there, these brave men and women didn't rabble-rouse, or plot, or take revenge in acts of terrorism. They simply gathered and prayed.

Then Jesus rose from the dead and for nearly a month He appeared to some of them in different places. In those meetings, He showed them His wounds, convinced them He was the way, the truth, and the life, and spoke to them about the Kingdom of God.

Before He finally ascended to Heaven to be with the Father, He promised that God would send them a helper. He told them that, in a few days, they would be baptised in the Holy Spirit.

For the ten days after Jesus's ascension to Heaven, this inner core of the most faithful would meet, worship, and pray for this helper to arrive. So, some forty days after Jesus died, on the Day of Pentecost, those most faithful followers gathered together in a house somewhere in Jerusalem.

I've often thought about how scared and defiant they must have been by then. Were they still hopeful, or were they beginning to feel defeated? Were they hanging on by a thread, ready to give up? Whatever their emotions, suddenly the entire world changed. A sound like a mighty wind from Heaven filled the house. Each person experienced holy flames that billowed and divided in tongues and came to rest on all of them.

All of them felt themselves to be flooded with the Holy Spirit. They all spoke in different languages, or tongues. It was a tumultuous, joyful outcry that caused passers-by to wonder, though it was only nine in the morning, whether they were all drunk.

They were certainly intoxicated, but it was with God

Himself. People had known the Holy Spirit for thousands of years, and many had been filled and strengthened by the Spirit before, but this was new. This was the first time humans had ever been filled with the Holy Spirit in this dramatic, visible, way. This new manifestation showed how our relationship with God had changed through Jesus.

It was the desire for some of this same experience that was at the heart of each waiting meeting in our church. Each person in that room that evening longed to be filled with the Holy Spirit. Longed to be as close to God as the first disciples.

It was simple when it came. Simple and gentle. There was no mighty rushing of wind, and we could see no holy tongues of fire, but the Holy Spirit fell on me, and on the other young people there. One by one, we began singing out joyfully in our own spirit languages. We sang and spoke out in tongues we didn't know, as we found those mystical languages that few, maybe only God and the angels, can understand.

It was a truly beautiful, blessed experience, one that is still vivid in my mind so many decades later.

I went home that night filled with such peace, such love. I knew without doubt that I had been saved. That God had opened His arms of love, filled me with His Spirit, and adopted me as His own daughter. That I really was a new creation.

So, I wasn't too bothered when my parents struggled with the news. My mother wasn't with me at that second meeting, so, even after all I said about it, even with the joy and the energy I felt, my parents still couldn't accept that I'd been filled with the Spirit.

It really did seem to come down to the priority of Philip being a boy. My parents simply couldn't believe that I had been filled with the Spirit because if I had, then I was good with the Spirit and my brother wasn't.

I pondered this. At least my mum had an open mind, as she

herself had previously wondered if I was close. My dad was in flat-out denial. I was inferior in his eyes. God couldn't possibly use me or do anything with me, I was so weak. In his eyes, Philip was everything I wasn't. He was a man, an inheritor, first among the people, one day to be the head and spiritual leader of his own future household. I was just a woman, just a second-class citizen. How could God have possibly chosen me first? I must have been carried away in a hysterical reaction to the Spirit filling those around me.

Yet, something of Dad's power over me had fallen away. For the first time, I was clear on what I knew. And what I knew was different. I felt complete. I felt authority. I felt a comforter. I felt a power. I felt the assurance that there was somebody there. That I wasn't on my own. It was incredible. It was amazing.

All this nagged away at Mum, and she nagged away at me. She was on a tightrope. She wanted to believe me because she loved me. But she also couldn't lay down her beliefs about men, the God-given hierarchy in the church, and the proper order of things. And those beliefs were winning out. Despite what she had seen at the first meeting, she kept telling me I hadn't been filled with the Spirit.

I sorted this out a few weeks later. We were standing in the bookshop at the Minehead annual conference, all the way down in Somerset, along with a hundred other book browsers. Mum had pulled me in there and dragged me up and down the shelves until she found what she wanted.

She pulled out a thin paperback and waved it in front of my nose.

'This. You need to read this,' she said.

I stared at it. A dull-looking book with a drab cover, by a writer I'd never heard of.

I didn't take the book from her. God had given me confidence, and I was finally coming to believe in what I thought. I had reached the point where I felt no guilt that I'd had enough of all this.

Calmly, with deep certainty in my heart, I spoke to her:

'Mum. When will you believe I've been filled with the Holy Spirit? I don't need to read this. I don't need to read anything.'

I looked at her long and hard, as she looked deep into my face. The moment seemed to go on for minutes until I finally turned and walked away down the aisle.

Somewhere away behind me, I heard her voice, pale, and faint, 'OK, OK, I believe you now.'

It was a victory, and my mum convinced my dad that I was telling the truth, but it changed nothing at home. It appeared any growth in my life was measured out in the tiniest of grains. Even after all that I'd been through, I still wasn't allowed to get baptised in water. Despite everything, despite arguing, and insisting, and begging, even crying, I was told I had to wait until my dad could do it.

Again, this was down to his own issues. Dad had to baptise me because that would mean he had his own church again. It was important for him to have a church because he believed he was the man that God would use to begin revival. He believed God would use him to change hearts across the nation. That, just like William Seymour in Azusa Street, or Joseph Jenkins in New Quay, or George Jeffreys in Monaghan, he would be used by God to light a holy fire. A holy fire of grace and forgiveness that would sweep from heart to heart as the herald of an outpouring of God's love in waves across the nation.

This wasn't a new idea to me. In fact, I'd say I had heard it almost every day of my life. But by then I was fed up with talk of revival. I didn't want to hear another word about revival. If anybody spoke to me about revival, I would automatically switch off. There was no way such a thing could happen. I knew God could never use Dad for revival. Never. Not the way he was.

I waited for them a little while longer, a month or two, but when it became clear Mum and Dad were decided, and were digging in for the long run, I realised I had no choice. It would be years until Dad had his own church again. If indeed he ever did. I just couldn't afford to wait any longer.

One evening, I went along to my pastor and said,

'Please, I want to be baptised in water. Will you do it?'

He looked at me, surprised, and frankly a little nervous.

'Shouldn't we wait for your father? I know he wants to do it.'

I wasn't angry; I wasn't shy; I wasn't intimidated. I looked him straight in the eye.

'I am not prepared to wait for my father.'

'He's been looking forward to it. Don't you think?'

I shut up, and I waited.

A couple of weeks later, the pastor baptised Philip and me in water alongside each other. It was the greatest day of my life so far.

I was 18. I'd reached another milestone on the road of my walk towards God.

17

Something had changed in the world around me, too. Doors opened. Choices came along. I had more confidence. I was still in a deep, dark place at home, but when I was outside our house, I could reach out and find people who seemed more receptive to me. In this way, God finally sent me help.

Dorothy was my new friend at church. Well, 'friend' might be too strong a word. I hadn't known her for long and I didn't really have friends, but I was always glad to see her when I went into church. She was an older lady, in her 40s, with a lot of life experience, and I guess she could see I was in trouble. She could certainly tell that I was far too fearful for my age, and so she had tried to get close to me.

It had taken me a while to trust her, but I'd grown to look out for her. I'd sit next to her in church, and we'd have a chat. God had changed me, and I found the means to open up to her, until, over time, she understood something of what my life had been like. More importantly, what it was like now. I spoke more and more freely about what life was like at home. How my mum and dad were. How sad it made me. How I couldn't see a way out; how trapped I felt.

One day she told me that if I ever needed somewhere to go, then I could just turn up at her house. I could stay there with her while I got things sorted out.

I listened to what she said, thanked her, assumed she didn't mean it, and tried to forget it. I could never go anywhere. My life wasn't like that.

Towards the end of summer, my aunt came to stay. She arrived in the usual way, on the train second class via Manchester and Sheffield, and Dad went to pick her up at the station. Mum and I savoured our last few minutes of peace. We groaned as she came up the path, and then she barged in, brash, full of herself and intrusive as ever. We were prepared for this, and I did what I had to, saying a polite hello before escaping up to my room. I felt sorry for leaving Mum down there with her and Dad, because Dad and my aunt would always gang up on the rest of us, but I just couldn't be in the same room as her.

Over the next few days, I realised something strange was happening. This time, my aunt was different. Something had changed between us. She seemed interested in me. Maybe it was also that I'd grown up, and I was interested in her. I don't know. But I slowly realised that I could talk to her. Over the next few days, with everything she said to me, I trusted her more and more. I'm naturally inclined to be open. Even today, I find myself too open. That's because I've got nothing to hide. I don't believe in secrets. But that week felt special. At last, someone normal in the family I could talk to. I leaped at the chance. We even had a laugh together. This all rebuilt the scattered crumbs of my confidence, and the darkness began to lift. I saw how things might get better. I got more and more confident, and she noticed how I was unhappy with Dad. Frowning, with a worried look on her face, she subtly asked me to go out for a walk with her. We went down Carr Lane, all the way to the allotments. We walked for a while, then found a bench to sit and talk. We spent hours there.

That afternoon was one of those watersheds in life. I danced around the subject for a little while, but she was patient, and listened, and waited. I finally felt brave enough to confide in her about Dad. I told her the way he was, the way he was with me. I opened my heart to her and told how much he had hurt me. She listened, wide-eyed at the beginning, then solemnly when she saw how serious I was. She even talked about how she had always thought that he had mistreated me. The flood gates opened, I poured out my lifetime of pain, and we walked and talked for hours.

Later that day, Philip was out at a club, and so it was just Mum, Dad, my aunt, and me. Over the evening meal, Dad made one of his usual sarcastic comments to me. Feeling stronger, for once I wouldn't let it go, and I spoke back. This escalated quickly and ended up in a row. Even that amazed me, but then I went one further. I finally told him what I thought, all the time knowing that my aunt was on my side.

Except she wasn't. The truth was the very opposite, in fact, and I realised I'd made a terrible mistake in trusting her. Instead of supporting me, she went for me. She mocked me, then started laughing at me. Said it was all me. Said I wore my heart on my sleeve because I was 'mentally retarded'. She turned on me so viciously. She told Dad everything I'd said and laughed more and more at me. Mocking me, mocking how sorry I felt for myself. I couldn't believe it. Everything had just been made one hundred times worse.

I don't know how I did it. I stood up, left the table, and went to the phone in the hall. Aware of their amazement behind me, I scrabbled through the Yellow Pages, found the number, and made a phone call:

'I'd like to order a taxi to 41 Carr Lane.'

My aunt cackled out loud. '*I'd like to order a taxi.* Who do you think you are? Lady Muck?'

'Shhh, you'll upset her,' Dad said, trying not to laugh.

'Think you're all grand, do you Pam love?'

'You two —!,' said Mum, trying to stick up for me.

'She's not grand. She's just a little bit of nothing getting above herself,' said Dad.

'She's getting mad now. Look at the face on her,' said my aunt.

I looked round at them in the dining room as they fell about in their chairs. I could see how upset Mum was, and how hard Dad and my aunt were laughing at me. I couldn't believe it.

I reached forward and slammed the dining-room door shut. My heart was pounding in my chest. I was so angry I was shaking. I went upstairs to my room. In a wave of emotion, I grabbed an armful of clothes, threw them into a suitcase, and came down to wait.

I sat in the front room, my coat on, my bag beside me, and counted the money in my purse. I had enough. For a while anyway. And I'd get paid in two weeks. I'd survive.

I listened to their voices, muffled in the dining room. Mum was muted, but Dad and my aunt had obviously forgotten about me pretty fast and had gone on to complaining about some incident to do with the extended family over in Liverpool. I couldn't really hear, and I thought about what I was doing. Was I really going to go through with it? Could this really be the moment? It was too big a thought. My mind couldn't handle it. I was both scared and eager. The big wooden clock on the mantelpiece was so familiar I couldn't bear it. I looked away and saw the picture of Pilgrim's Progress on the wall. It reminded me of a happy morning in Sunday School in Belfast nearly fifteen years before. I'd done a big painting all on my own, and Mum and Dad had both made a fuss of me. I felt like crying. Why had things gone so bad?

The taxi was late, and I waited, and waited, staring out the window. It was getting dark. I sat, looking at the house over the road, looking at clouds, eventually not thinking about anything too much.

A knock on the front door brought me back to earth.

'Pam? Door!' shouted my dad from the kitchen. I couldn't believe it. He'd opened the dining-room door to call me but couldn't be bothered to take the extra six steps to the front door.

'It must be her chauffeur,' said my aunt.

They both laughed again, and I remembered where I was and what was happening.

I got out of the chair, put my purse in my pocket, picked up my bag.

Out in the hall, I headed for the front door.

'Aren't you going to say goodbye then?'

My dad stood at the doorway to the kitchen behind me.

'Leave me alone,' I said, my voice harsh with fear.

My aunt appeared next to him.

'Where are you going, anyway?'

'None of your business,' I said.

'Wooooh's' from both of them.

My mum came out past them both and came towards me.

'Pam, love. What are you doing?'

I shrugged her off and turned away.

'Ray. You can't do this,' said Mum behind me.

I opened the front door and stepped outside.

'Pam.' said Mum.

'She'll be back,' said Dad to my aunt.

CHAPTER 17

The taxi was waiting by the kerb.

'You'll be back,' Dad called to me as I walked down the path to the gate.

'I give her two hours,' said my aunt. 'She's a mental case. She's got nowhere to go.'

I looked back in one last moment of outrage. My mum stood to the side, looking like she was in shock.

I got in the car. Took a breath.

'Yes, love?'

'Hello,' I said. 'Cleethorpes please.'

The taxi pulled away, and I didn't look back.

18

It was dark by the time we got over to Dorothy's house. I paid the driver, and the taxi left, and I went up to the path to her front door.

I knocked on the door. I waited.

'Hello? Who's that?'

'It's me. Pam.'

Silence, that went on too long. I got scared. I should have called her. She didn't mean it. I was so, so stupid to think that—

She opened the front door. It looked like she had been getting ready for bed, and she was tightening the belt of her dressing gown. She looked at me, puzzled, then looked down at my case, and realised what was happening. She gave me the kindest, most sympathetic smile and stepped back into her hallway.

'Come on,' she said. 'Come in.'

She was surprised to see me, and she wasn't. It felt like she'd been expecting me.

She showed me to a bedroom, and I unpacked a few things,

and I lay on the bed, and I looked at the room, and eventually I went back downstairs to talk to her. All that evening, she was so lovely. She kept reassuring me I had done the right thing. I was so relieved. Unlike my dad and my aunt, she had meant what she said.

It was so quiet that night. There were no arguments. It was peaceful. I got the sense that in Dorothy's house, no one would ever argue. It was strange, and wonderful.

I woke the next morning, a Saturday, and lay in bed, wondering what I'd done. I had such trouble believing this insecure, terrified girl with no confidence and no self-esteem had just walked out. I'd no idea where I had found the strength. It was obviously God.

I had breakfast with Dorothy and talked more. Dorothy listened and then went to wash up. She refused any help from me and told me to rest. I sat in an armchair in the back room and looked out the window. Dorothy had a little garden, with a couple of trees in it. I watched the leaves move in the breeze, and the birds come and go.

I felt a great wave of peace break upon me.

Dorothy came back in to check on me and said she was going upstairs to get ready. She was going out shopping later, and I could come if I wanted, or I could stay there if I wanted. Up to me.

She smiled that gentle smile again and withdrew. I heard her go upstairs. I felt exhausted and yet not sleepy. It was as though I was floating. Could I really have done it? Could I really have broken free? Wasn't it all just too good to be true?

Somewhere far off, the doorbell went. I heard Dorothy come downstairs and open the door.

I half-listened. A woman's voice, low. Probably one of

Dorothy's friends from church. I'd probably recognise her when I met her. Maybe she would be my friend too.

'Pam?'

I realised Dorothy was calling me.

'Pam? Can you come out? There's someone for you.'

Still only half present, I got up and went to the door. I was puzzled. Who else from church would want to see me?

I went out into the hall, and Dorothy turned to me. She looked worried.

I looked beyond her. And couldn't believe what I saw.

There, outside the front door, hat and coat on, suitcase in hand, stood a familiar figure.

'Pam,' the figure said.

'Mum?'

I couldn't believe it.

'We had an almighty row. He's gone too far this time, Pam. Way too far.'

Her words were defiant, but eyes were dull, her shoulders low. She looked beaten. I looked past her out along the street. I couldn't see our car.

'Where is he?'

'How could he have done this to you?' she said. 'And everything else. I can't stand any of it any more. I've left him. And Philip. He's on his side.'

'Oh.'

I struggled to make sense of what was happening.

My mum hesitated. Her face was suddenly young again. She looked so vulnerable suddenly. So unsure of herself. She glanced from me to Dorothy, back at me again.

'I've nowhere to go. Can I ... can I stay with you here, love?'

I looked at her. Saw she meant it. I couldn't believe it. This had been my independence. This had been my freedom.

I looked at her again, saw how desperate she was.

Dorothy nodded at me. Whatever I wanted was OK.

I said 'Yes. Of course you can. Of course you can, Mum.'

I stood aside and hugged her and welcomed her in.

She held onto me tight for a moment, then walked past me, into the house. She put her case down and took off her coat.

I stared at the back of her head. The tight dark perm I knew so well. The plump curve of her shoulders. The texture of her cardigan.

I had thought I was free. How could this be happening?

19

Mum moved into my bedroom. We had twin beds and I'd lie there at night feeling like a child again, except this time it wasn't clear who was looking after who. We were both in a mess. I was spinning and exultant with the taste of freedom and crushed because it had been snatched from me. I was struggling to process how my new beginning had failed to materialise. How, after that immense effort to walk out, that I wasn't free.

The pain of trying to rip my old life away from my new beginning sometimes seemed too big to conquer. I loved my mum so much and she was so unhappy it hurt. She cried a lot. It was remorse for leaving Philip. Regret for not looking after me better. Anger and pain at all the years spent with Dad. The wasted years butting up against the fact she loved him.

We'd lie in bed and talk things through endlessly and get nowhere much. One question lay under all our anger, all our sadness—how much did he love each of us? Really?

We never dared to dissect that fully, so we went on day to day. Living in one room, working out how to live in a small house with a woman who hadn't expected or bargained for any of this. But a balance with Dorothy arrived quickly. Amazing in her patience, unwavering in her support, she was a true servant of Christ.

Dad tried to make contact, but not very hard. Not hard enough, not by a long way. Once again, he was old-fashioned. It wasn't his job to apologise. We were women who had stepped out of line, and even though I guess his heart was bleeding in his loss (he surely did feel pain?) we had both gone far beyond female decency in leaving.

That judgement was fair enough in some ways. I was certainly in no mood to receive him. Just at that time I had to harden my heart to survive. Mum went out once or twice to meet him and try to talk things through. She always came back to the room far sadder than when she went out. She took her marriage vows seriously. To leave Dad, and Philip, was excruciating to her. Especially when Philip was only seventeen and needed her still.

I hated those evenings of dealing with the fallout. She couldn't help feeling sad, and bad. Though she and Dad had always fought, over the years they had reached equilibrium, and found a path that, though conflict-filled, worked for them. Basically, they were fine until I rocked the boat, and Mum had left because of me. Sometimes that came out in her blaming me, and then Mum and I would have difficulties of our own.

Weeks passed, then months. We were in a holding pattern, waiting for some unknown resolution, not really living. Dorothy was unfailingly generous, but we knew her kindness wasn't infinite. At some point, we would have to move on. I knew I would have to find my own home. But then, what would Mum do?

We were both working, Mum at the hospital, and me at the office. We were both healing from the immediate damage. Life was turning positive. And that felt good. Of course, that ignored what Dad was going through. After his early tries, we weren't seeing him at all. There was an uneasy silence between us, and I felt something was brewing. Some resolution that would take the situation and wrench it into a new trajectory. In some ways, I dreaded that. In other ways, I wanted it to shift the balance.

And then it came.

20

Mum was working nights at the hospital, so often we would only see each other in passing. Dorothy's house was a little out of the way over towards Cleethorpes, and Mum was still doing night shifts, so we were both sharing her car. In the evenings, Mum would drive to the maternity home, and back again in the morning, just in time for me to use the car to get to work in the centre of Grimsby.

One evening, I came out of the office. I was in a strange mood. It wasn't dark yet, and work had been easy. It was a Friday and the mood in the office had been light. Overall, it should have been a good day, but all day, at the back of everything, I'd had a subtle sense of dread. I couldn't help feeling there was something wrong. That I was in danger.

Was it God speaking to me? I don't know. All I can say is that when I saw the scrap of paper, folded, and tucked under my windscreen wipers, I felt a relief. Somehow, this paper was at the centre of it all.

I took the paper out, unfolded it. There was a message:

'If I were you, I'd check your brakes.'

It was my dad's writing. I checked the back of the paper. Nothing else. Eight words that made no sense; I'd just had the car serviced, so everything should be fine. I stooped and looked underneath the driver's side. No leaks and I couldn't see anything that shouldn't have been there. I thought it through. The door had been locked; the bonnet was closed tight, and I didn't know how to open it. Even if I got it open, I didn't know what I'd be looking for.

I decided to talk to Mum about it, put the note in my bag, got in, and started for home. The traffic was light up Victoria Street and I started thinking about what I was going to do in the evening. We had a Friday night youth group at the church that I was really loving, and I was making new friends and seeing God bring fresh light to so much of my life.

I turned the roundabout and headed up onto the flyover. The docks stretched out to my left, and I could see a huge freighter moored there. Over in the distance, past the old Ice Factory building, there were the funnels of one or two trawlers. I had a flash of loving Grimsby, and then I began to wonder what we'd have for tea. Dorothy was a traditionalist, and so as it was Friday, it would probably be fish, fresh from those same docks.

I was heading down off the flyover, towards the busy road junction at Riby Square, when I realised the car in front was coming up far too quickly. I jammed my foot down harder on the brake and felt a spongy nothingness. No resistance, no power. I pumped the brakes, pulled the handbrake on, and barely slowed at all. I swerved out to my right and got round the car in front but was only getting faster. I realised I was speeding up down the flyover into a big road junction at 40 miles an hour with no way of stopping.

God was there for me. It can only have been Him. It was as if the traffic stopped for me, or He made space for me, or somehow, He guided my hands and feet. I drove through the junction, miraculously untouched, and rolled to a stop by the pavement a couple of hundred yards along. My stomach was in a knot of tension as the adrenaline flooded my system, and I sat, wondering what had just happened.

That evening, I talked it over with my mum. I showed her the paper, and she agreed. There was no mistaking my dad's handwriting.

She said he must have been trying to warn me.

I just looked at her.

Initially, I struggled to believe that Dad had tampered with the brakes, but over time, I accepted it as the only plausible explanation. But then I had to ask, what was he hoping to do? And I really couldn't answer that.

Did he really do physical damage to the brakes? Had he somehow drained them during the day? Could he really sabotage his own family's car? Or had the garage who serviced the car made a mistake and his note was just a coincidence? Even a God-inspired warning?

I remembered him trying to murder my mother all those years before. I knew what he was capable of.

So, if he had tampered with the brakes, then what was he hoping to achieve this time? Was he trying to kill me? Or Mum? Both of us? Was it just a silly threat made in the heat of the moment? Was he lashing out blindly in anger that we had left him and hadn't thought it through? Was he trying to prove that we needed a capable man in our lives to look after us?

All I can think is that he was in so much pain that he had lost his mind.

I tried to forgive him, but I couldn't. He had rejected me and hurt me so much I could find no tenderness in my heart towards him. I went to my pastor at church and told him what had happened. He listened, wide-eyed, and prayed with me I might forgive. Nothing. My heart was numb. The prayer wasn't a success, but he had more to offer.

'Right. From now on I'm servicing your car. Then I'll know it's OK, and then we'll know if anyone has ever tampered with it.'

It was a kind offer, and that was really the end. I didn't go to the police. It was such an extreme thing I couldn't make anything of it, and so I had to let it go. Nothing was resolved, and this event got buried alongside all the other complex angers in that rich dark soil that lay between us all.

21

The months went by. I was definitely beginning to look to the future, but Mum was still struggling. She felt more and more guilty about leaving my brother, but he was so taken by Dad that they couldn't talk about it. Some days, she would be overwhelmed with grief. She would say loudly and clearly how it was all my fault she had left. She would put all her guilt on me. That seemed wrong to me. I had never asked her to leave Dad. I never expected her to; I thought this would be my chance for a new life. And then she would break down and say she couldn't leave me on my own.

She needed me. I was the only one who really understood what had happened between her and Dad over the years, and because of what we had both been through with him, we were so close. However, having to take on all that guilt and seeing her so distraught was so painful.

In the next May, Mum and I, plus many people from the church, went to Minehead for the annual conference. It was there that we both heard a prophecy that God would take us back home, that things wouldn't be the same as before and God would do a work in Dad.

I heard this prophecy and immediately tried to bury it, but it played on Mum's mind. A few weeks later, Dorothy was out, and Mum sat me down around the dining room table. I looked at her and waited as she struggled to find her words. I had a sinking sense of what was coming, and I feared and dreaded it so much.

'Pam,' she said. 'Your dad's been in touch.'

'Has he now.'

'He has.'

'More grief I expect?'

'He wants us to go back home. He says things will be different.'

'He always says that. So what? You know he doesn't mean it.'

She looked into her teacup, heartbroken. She knew exactly what I was saying. Over the last few months, I'd told her a lot about what had happened between Dad and me. She had been horrified and upset. She had asked me question after question, going over old times, tugging on a thread that she had suspected but never known about. We had sat up late into the night on more than a few occasions, and I had finally, after so many years, felt vindicated. I couldn't believe her attitude now.

She tried again, gently.

'The thing is, I want to go back home. It's not right, Pam. We're man and wife. We shouldn't be living apart.'

'That's OK, Mum. If you need to go, then you need to go.'

My voice was a lot braver than I felt. Being out on your own in the world is a big deal. And I knew that, if she went back, then I wouldn't be going round. Which meant that I would end up losing her. It turned out that had been on her mind, too. She spoke again, her voice quiet. Resigned.

'I can't go back without you.'

'What? Why?'

'I can't leave you out here on your own.'

'I'll be OK. I'm nineteen. It's time I left home.'

'But also, Philip and me, we need your help. He won't be the same if you're there, too.'

'I—'

'—he really has changed, I believe that. We need you, Pam. I'll give up work, I've told him. I know you're not safe in the house with him when I'm at work...'

'Mum, I can't.' I stared at her, aghast. Had she forgotten everything I'd told her?

Her voice was low, but certain.

'The prophecy at Minehead. You remember it?'

'Of course I remember it. But so what?'

'I believe it was a good one. I believe that was God speaking.'

This was a heavy card to play. At that moment, I knew how deadly serious she was. I was heartbroken.

'Where's all this come from, Mum?' I knew my voice sounded uncertain, weak.

'I've been seeing him a bit. Since we got back from Minehead. I've been round for cups of tea. We've been out for a couple of walks. He is different, Pam, I promise you. God's really done a work in him.'

Her gaze found mine. I could see how hurt she was. How vulnerable. How much she needed me to say 'Yes'.

'Honour thy father and thy mother'. There it was again, the first of the Ten Commandments to deal with human relations. And there I was, being obedient again. I struggled and fought and battled mutiny in my heart, but in the end my desire to surrender to my heavenly father won out. A few days later, once I had convinced myself I had no choice and that God was indeed in it (the prophecy was unmistakable), we packed our bags, cleared, and cleaned our room, hugged goodbye to Dorothy, and drove back to Carr Lane.

My dad met us at the door, looking tense. He managed a hug for Mum, not for me.

I held back for a moment, watching how my mum responded. She seemed natural, and glad to be back. I was happy for her. And then he turned to me.

'Pam.'

He tried to smile.

'Dad.'

I tried to express some warmth, but I couldn't. He was my dad, but he'd done me so much wrong.

Before I knew it, I was unpacked and installed in my old room. The bedroom door closed behind me, and the sound of them laughing downstairs ebbed away. He was jolly now, but it felt like an excursion away from reality. The reality that would surely come back in an hour, or a day, or a week or two, when he was tired of the effort. On my own in my room, the fact of where I was rose in me. Was this really where the last nine months' battle was ending? Just a week ago, Mum and I had been out looking at a flat for the two of us. Now, I was back where I started. Back in the place I'd fought so hard to escape.

The walls closed in and the sudden thick familiarity of it all threatened to choke me. I held on to one thought: I was older, wiser, and I'd tasted freedom. This time, it would be different.

The old him did come back, but it was never so bad as before. There was truth in the prophecy at Minehead. God had indeed done a work in Dad, and he had changed.

Another big difference was that Mum wouldn't leave me. In previous years, she knew little about how Dad had been pushing me around, all the things he had been saying to me while she was at work. After nine months with me at Dorothy's, she knew the score, and this made a big difference. She refused point blank to go back to work, and I noticed she would never leave me in the house with him.

22

We settled down into a new season. Family life was more bearable than it had been. At the time I was getting on for twenty and I was working in data control at Imperial Foods. I was feeling more confident around all the men and was holding my own a little more.

Imperial had a big old computer, one of those massive old mainframes, and I wasn't technically qualified, but things had worked out very well. Computing was comparatively new technology in those days, and lots went wrong. I enjoyed dialling into the computer and putting things right. I discovered I had quite a technical streak, and I was amazed to find out that I had the sort of mind that enjoyed playing with the cables and sorting out the problems. If anything went wrong with the machines, I was your man. Or your woman.

One job absorbed me. In those days, the programmers would write their programs by hand. When they were sure their code would work, they'd use a machine to convert the program to a pile of cards with holes punched in them. The programmer would take the stack of the cards over to the computer and feed them into the card reader one by one. This would load the program into the computer memory. It was a slow, thoughtful—and occasionally very frustrating—process for the programmer, never more so than when the process went wrong, the cards got ruined and all the information ended up in the wrong order. Many were the times that I'd end up with a stack of giant confetti. I loved the challenge of putting the cards back in the right order, and it had the side effect of making me more and more useful at work.

Slowly, all my early lack of confidence had calmed down. I had made friends, and I enjoyed working there. The months slipped by as I got into a stable routine. I was making good money (something that continued all the years I worked in that field), and I even bought a brand-new car. Soon I realised I was the most well off in all the family and so it fell to me to support the others in little ways. That helped things at home, as well as the fact that I was doing shifts. This was fantastic because it meant I was never at home for the mealtimes, which could still turn into battlefields. In fact, I was never there for most of the regular hours of normal family life, and so we could all get along a lot better. If my parents would sometimes comment that I was treating the place like a hotel, well, I was paying my way, and living like that definitely kept the peace.

The only real cloud was the constant threats of redundancy. Imperial was going through an endless restructuring, but, so far, each time this kind of crisis had surfaced, I had been kept on. I made it through one crisis by the skin of my teeth. Then, after a year, they started talking about it again, and that time it looked like the end of the road. They were closing my part of the company and keeping a small core team on to run the entire company down over the next eighteen months to two years.

I realised I faced a new stage in life, and I started thinking about what I could do instead. To my surprise, I found that the minute I thought about the future, I got interrupted by God. He spoke to me—very loudly at times—about doing children's work.

I tried not to listen. To be honest, I hated kids. Mum had been a midwife at one point. She loved little children, but she would tell us terrible stories about what had gone wrong, seemingly in every other house. These stories could get very grim. One hung over us all like a nightmare: at one birth she had attended, they had had to keep the baby from the mother because it had been born with two heads.

That horror must have gone deep into me because I couldn't think of anything worse than children's work. I didn't see the nonsense in this position—how could the misadventures of a midwife affect me working with children? I didn't analyse it too deeply, and I never wondered about the real origin of this deep fear. It never occurred to me it was a lie. Certainly, it never occurred to me it might be the enemy knocking me off track. All that I knew was that I had no intention of having children. I believed I had no interest in them whatsoever, and so I couldn't work out why God was calling me like this.

I carried on as normal and tried to ignore God, but I kept getting flashes of what it would be like to work with children. I kept seeing myself in the middle of work that was loving, tender, and gentle. Good work, in fact. I tried to ignore that, too.

So, when I saw another office job advertised over the river in Hull, I applied, did a good interview, and they offered me the post. This put me in a quandary. Redundancy from Imperial wasn't certain, but taking this job would be my chance to escape from Grimsby and move on with my life. And I wouldn't have to engage with the idea of working with children.

However, even this simple plan to move to Hull wasn't

going well. Amazingly, I couldn't find any accommodation north of the river. In a city of a quarter of a million people, there was nothing to rent that wasn't either fantastically expensive or fantastically unpleasant. I tried everywhere and found only closed doors. Even in church, no-one had anything. There was one place miles out of Hull centre, but the new job wanted me to be on call most days, so taking that would have meant hours of extra travel every day.

Meanwhile, the day of being made redundant from Imperial was getting closer and the pressure was building into a real cycle of stress. I kept worrying about how I was going to work, and God kept on speaking to me about working with children, and I kept on saying 'No thank you I have a job now,' and God kept any places to live from me, until it got to the week before the redundancies came into effect.

One of those nights I couldn't sleep. Blazed across my mind were the facts. In less than seven days, I would have no job in Grimsby, and nowhere to live in Hull. What was I going to do?

God wasn't letting me go. He kept speaking into my heart, speaking the clear idea that, forget all those practicalities, I needed to be working with children.

I kept saying, 'No. I'm not doing this. There's no way I'm doing this.' He kept on and on and on and I spent the night praying and talking to the Lord. I got so desperate in the end.

I can remember the sun coming up, the renewed light under the curtains, and finally, I remember the moment at which I said,

'OK God, I'll do it. You've closed every door, and I understand you have a path for me. Please get off my back—I'll do it. But there is one thing: I will not go out looking. If you want me to work for children, then you need to make the people who need me come to me and ask me. Lord, I promise I'll do it, providing I'm asked.'

So, in this reluctant, grudging way, I made a grumbling acquiescence to God's plans, and without knowing, made my first step into my life's work. The work He had prepared in advance for me to do. The work which would bring me so much blessing over the coming years.

He must get so frustrated with us sometimes.

23

The invitation to children's work came from the one place I hadn't expected: my church.

I hadn't even considered this as a possibility. First, they only ever worked with volunteers, so there was no chance of a salary there. Second, it had never occurred to me they would ask me to volunteer. I didn't even teach in their (very small) Sunday school, as I hated that whole idea. Admittedly, I helped out, but it was a matter of going in, playing the piano, avoiding the five children there, and coming away as fast as I could. I thought that was it.

God had different ideas.

The Sunday school superintendent walked into the church the next evening for the Sunday School Leader meeting. He didn't look at me as he spoke.

'Recently I've been feeling God telling me we should ask Pam to take over the Sunday school.'

I heard this with surprise.

If that wasn't bad enough, a lady in the meeting leaped up in amazement.

'I can confirm that,' she said.

'What?'

'I was praying this afternoon, and God told me you were to take over the work.'

I couldn't believe what I was hearing. Of course, there was no hint of any money attached. But after the night I'd had, what could I say?

Yet still I hesitated. Talk about refusal of the call.

I hesitated and came up with conditions:

First. They would have to ask the pastor. (I knew he needed someone with good experience. That wasn't me.)

Second. I'd only do it until someone came in with a real vision for children's work. When that happened, I would step down. (This was a not-so-subtle way of clarifying that I was an unsuitable stopgap.)

They went to the pastor the next day. To my horror, he agreed on the spot.

I say horror, but that's only how I pretended I felt. When they told me the pastor had agreed, I felt something shift. Suddenly I felt His hand on the matter. I realised that if God wanted me to do it so much that He was speaking prophetically into other people's lives about it, I was in a very clear situation. I realised once again that we walk by faith and not sight, and my heart gave an involuntary 'Yes Lord.' At that, all my fears and barriers went down, and suddenly I was filled with an astonishing enthusiasm for the job.

In the scheme of things, agreeing to help out at a tiny Sunday School was such a small decision, but at that time in my life it was huge.

So, when I spoke, I spoke with true faith, and I spoke out loud:

'I'll do it.'

The day after that was the day the redundancies were

announced at my office. I waited all morning, as, one after one, my colleagues were called in to see the boss. Some would come out red-faced with anger, some with quiet resignation. One girl who worked down the corridor from me had clearly been crying. As had one of the more senior male managers when he came out.

Finally, it was my turn. I went through. My boss nodded me in and asked me to sit me down. I waited while he checked, and double checked, the piece of paper in front of him.

He looked me straight in the eye.

'OK Pam. You know what's going on today.'

'I do, yes.'

'It's a very hard day for most people. We're having to make major changes, and a lot of people are losing their posts.'

'I know. It's terrible.'

'We can't shield you from this, I'm afraid. There have to be cuts. Big cuts. No-one is safe.'

I nodded. Impatient now. Wishing he'd get on with it. I wondered about whether he'd offer me any redundancy package. Some people were getting that. A few extra pounds in my last pay packet definitely wouldn't hurt.

'Your job has to go, I'm afraid. But we'd like to make you an offer.'

Here it comes, I thought. Maybe it'll be enough to get my car serviced. I'd need my car to get round to any interviews.

'We'd like to offer you another job.'

'Pardon?'

'Most people are being made redundant, but we're putting together a small team who will stay on to close the company down.'

'I don't understand.'

'You'd be one of eight people who we think can stay on to help close the company down. We'd promote you to Computer

Operator. You'd be working three shifts a week, your wage will go up by a third, and we'd train you up for the new role as and when you'd need it. What do you think?'

It took me a minute to process what he was saying. It took me another minute to realise this was how God was going to fund the children's work, and that I really, really had no more barriers to taking that on.

Once I had put all that together, I managed to speak.

'Yes sir. I'd like to do that, sir. Very much indeed.'

What else could I possibly say? We have an amazing God.

24

There was just one problem though. I had to work in the offices at night and the guys reckoned it was haunted.

Do I believe in meeting ghosts? I certainly believe in God, and meeting the Holy Spirit, and the Bible tells us clearly that there are many spirit beings in the world. In fact, a major part of Jesus' activities was driving out spirits from the people He met. Whatever the truth is around demons and bad spirits, I experienced something strange among the computers at Imperial Foods.

The whole back of the building was a big computer room. Once a month, I would be asked to work a week of nights. There were just two of us in there in any week, but I quickly realised that management could get none of the other guys to work through the nights.

The story was that a ghost walked around the computer towers, dragging a chain. I just thought this was a pretty weak excuse for people who wanted to dodge the work. For one thing, most of the guys I was on rota with would vanish over the road to the Barge pub for a swift pint before last orders.

Once gone, they'd never come back. Even if they didn't go to the pub, they would have cleared out of the office by 2.00am. I wasn't supposed to be on my own, but sometimes it felt that I was the only one who would do a full night shift in there.

I didn't care about any ghosts; personally, I was more worried about the Group 4 security firm. They'd come in and walk around in the evenings and, still fearful of men, I was more scared of them than anything else. The police would sometimes knock on the door to check everything was OK, but I'd find an excuse not to hear them, either. The ideal evening was when I'd get into the office, lock the doors, play my music, and get on with work undisturbed. That was fine. Until one night when it really wasn't.

It was around three in the morning. That was always a strange time to be awake and working, but this evening, things took a unique turn. I wasn't a fan of chart music, or pop music, and I used to take in a bag load of cassette tapes full of Christian worship music. This night I was working away, singing away. I used to turn off the overhead lights, so there was just a pool of light around me from my desk light. It was all very peaceful until a loud scream ripped through the night. It was terrifying, and went on, turning into loud shrieking, and demonic voices groaning and chattering.

I realised it was coming from the cassette player and lunged to switch it off. My heart was racing, my stomach clenched in fear. All the hair on the back of my neck stood up, and the skin on my arms tingled with goose bumps.

I stood up from the chair and backed away from my desk. The doors were all locked, and I had checked them earlier, so I knew no-one could have come in behind me. I looked around me and realised how shadowy the room was. I scanned the corner, half expecting to see an evil figure with a ball and chain. I realised how the cupboards and the gaps in the large computer units loomed, mysterious around me. Each cupboard had a door, behind each door could hide all number of things.

But I didn't believe in ghosts. Not like this. Ghosts were just the men needing an excuse to get to the pub. And I'd seen the men leaving as usual, and I'd locked the door on them myself.

I pulled myself together and flipped open the cassette player. I expected to see the cassette tape all tangled up in the works of the machine, but the drawer opened cleanly. I pulled out the cassette and examined it. It all looked perfectly fine. I put a pencil into the centre of one spool and turned it. It rotated smoothly, rattling just a little as I spun it round. Perfectly normal.

I put the cassette back in the machine, checked the label still said, 'Worship Music', closed the drawer, and, not without a little fear, pressed 'Play'.

Instant demonic screaming. Far, far louder than the cassette player was capable of. Roaring, howling, and deep guttural groans came from the machine.

In one movement, I slammed the Stop button and leaped up, practically climbing backwards up and out of my chair as it tumbled to the floor under me. I stared at the machine in horror, then turned this way and that, checking each shadow again.

I called out in prayer. Fervently.

'Jesus, Jesus, help me. Jesus, I call on your name now. Jesus, cover me with your blood, I cover this building in the blood of Jesus, protect me Lord Jesus, Jesus, Jesus ...'

I put the overhead lights on, flooding the place with light, and prayed round the room. Finally, I went back to my desk, where I bent in prayer. Slowly the fear ebbed away, and after a while I stopped to listen. Nothing. No more voices. Certainly, no rattling chains. Faint relief took root.

I prayed a little while longer, becoming more and more

calm. My pulse got back to normal, and the grip of fear in my stomach eventually relaxed.

I even did some more work in the end, as the sun came up over the buildings outside.

I left work early that morning and have never felt more grateful for sunlight. Outside, I felt completely safe. By the time I was halfway home, I felt completely free. Surely, I had been imagining it. Surely it was a mechanical failure on the tape ...

I had to know. I pulled the car over, got the same cassette out of my bag, put it into the car cassette player, and pressed 'Play'.

Nothing. Worship music came from the speakers. All was normal.

Cassette tapes go wrong, of course they do, but I've never heard one make that noise since. I continued with the night shifts when asked, but I prayed like mad before they began, and I always kept the overhead lights on. I didn't want to leave to go to the pub at 10.30, but I quite understood the men who did.

25

The cliché is that God works in mysterious ways. The truth is, sometimes God works in ways that are familiar to those who know Him. In particular He often asks us to take our first steps into deep water on our own.

Noah builds the ark with no signs of the coming flood. David faces the giant Goliath, armed only with a sling and a stone. The priests crossing the Jordan must step into the water before God dams the river upstream. Peter has to step out of the boat and risk drowning before Jesus reaches out for him.

Over and over in the Bible, this is the way God works. So, thousands of years later, in my small situation, with a tiny job to do, I can see that this was how God worked for me. Once I took that first couple of steps in faith that He was with me, then and only then did He bless me.

First, I agreed to go against all my desires and obey Him. Then He paved the way with blessings. And such blessings they were. The job and the pay rise were obvious, but they were really only the basics. Far more amazing was what He did through me at the Sunday school.

I know it was God rather than me because I had hardly begun before things took off.

I renamed it Good News Club and told some kids from next door to the church that they should come. That's all. No advertising, no other attempts to reach anyone else. Yet within a few weeks it seemed like an endless torrent of children was pouring through the door.

The church saw something good happening, so they asked me to go to Mattersey Bible College on a youth leaders' training weekend. I went but, secretly, I was alarmed by this all-too-rapid escalation, so instead of focusing on the training, I prayed for an escape route.

'Please God, send someone else to take over the work.'

I had a sense by then of how things were going to grow, and I felt I couldn't handle it. At the age of 24, running a thriving Sunday School shouldn't have been a problem, but I was still full of self-doubt, still full of anxiety.

I wonder also if I had sensed the long path ahead which God had planned for me. God was wise to keep that from me. If I had known then what I know now, like Jonah, I would have run the other way as fast as I could.

Over the weekend at Mattersey, I did my best to present myself well, but my imposter syndrome was yelling loudly into my ear. I spent most of the weekend praying more and more fervently for God to send someone to take over my ministry.

The course closed with a service of worship and prayer on the last afternoon. At the end of the service, there was a time where someone in the congregation spoke out loudly in tongues. As is usually the way, and as is instructed in the Bible, another member of the congregation found they could offer an interpretation of this impossible language.

A young man stood up and addressed us all.

'I have an interpretation. I feel God is saying to someone in this room, "You feel inadequate, but I will make you adequate."'

That got my attention. Straight to the heart of the matter, and exactly what I wanted to hear.

'There's more.'

I listened, keen not to miss a beat, as the man spoke one of the greatest prophecies of my life.

'Your work will grow rapidly and be very demanding, but you will only be there for two years. Then you will go through an awful time. A real living hell. This will last for three years. After that will come a season of healing. Finally, God will do greater things in your life, and in those around you, than you could comprehend.'

I listened, trying to hide my growing alarm. When he finished, I sat there, my mind spinning. I was a young woman with no big plans, who had just wanted some advice on how to manage Sunday School in a tough part of a small northern town. This prophecy was way beyond that—and it sounded absolutely terrifying.

Of course, stage by stage, over the many years to come, every part came true.

26

Sometimes in life you can work like crazy on something, and give it your absolute best efforts, and nothing much happens. Sometimes you can work like crazy on something and everything aligns, and you see lovely, constant growth. Sometimes you work like crazy, and you surrender the whole thing to God and pray like mad and mysteriously you find you're aligned with God's will. At which point, God sends you a following wind that can feel more like a hurricane. The next two years were like that.

Before I'd drawn proper breath, Good News Club had a regular core of forty children on a Sunday morning, with new faces always appearing. I was surprised to find that God had given me, the person who thought she hated children, an apparently endless well of bigger and bigger ideas to keep them engaged. Any child stepping through the door was given so much to do. They weren't used to that, and they found it fun.

The flow of children meant we needed a flow of Sunday school teachers to match. When a class would grow, I'd split it, and the school would multiply.

CHAPTER 26

I never advertised for teachers. Not once. I prayed instead.

'God, I need a Sunday school teacher. We have too many children. This is your problem. Please give me a Sunday school teacher.'

Either God would speak to someone in the church about offering to help, or God would give me the name of the person who I should approach. Those fresh groups would run on for a while until they would hit the size barrier, when they would multiply again.

Of course, I taught the children Bible stories, and we worshipped and prayed, but I quickly realised there was more to be done beyond that. I felt I should do my best to give these children, some of whom came from very damaged backgrounds, a taste of 'life in all its fullness'. Alongside the scriptural teaching, I slowly added extra fun through other activities.

First, I realised children were having birthdays, and that everyone enjoyed organising birthday activities. We quickly got a little team going for that. Then one of our teens spoke to me. He was very talented, and he wanted to find some way of writing for an audience. We had the idea of producing a monthly magazine. That, in turn, needed more reporters, pictures, and people to make it happen.

I'd always played piano, so I started a music workshop on Saturday morning and taught them how to play instruments. We had the usual piano and guitar, but we also had glockenspiels, triangles, a drum, the odd tambourine. It turned into quite a group, to where Good News Club ended up with their own worship team. We created a mini orchestra in the end, and I found the children's praise book 'Psalty the Songbook' and turned it into a full musical. (That show had a real impact on me because the kids did so well. Everybody in the church was in awe of what they did; I was so proud of them.)

The Good News Club just kept on growing. I'll never forget

the first day we had a hundred children there. It wasn't just me that was proud. The minister of the church would take any visiting speakers straight down to see us because it was such a showcase. I had all sorts going on, and everyone felt a part of something. There was such a buzz around all the teachers, and everybody was so excited.

Soon enough, I felt God speak to me again. I felt I should start a Saturday night club called Youthie for 11—16-year-olds. Once again, there was a mix of scriptural content alongside special speakers. We'd have fun, organise trips out, and there'd be an extra emphasis on sports. We played football and netball. Once a month, we hired a local swimming pool, and I rented football pitches and their sports facilities from a local secondary school. The kids were very competitive, and we'd take on other clubs.

In among all these activities, on Saturday night we never missed turning our attention to Jesus. Every week they would come and be encouraged to share what God had done for them since last Youthie. I had some of them preaching, giving little sermons, and they too loved the music. The combined Youthie/Good News Club orchestra was something to behold.

It wasn't long before I had a visit from the police, who wanted to see for themselves what was going on. Every Saturday night for many years, there had been police on the corner of Pasture Street. They were there to deal with problems with the kids in the area, and they were often very busy.

Within six weeks of Youthie opening, the police had left that pitch: the troublemakers were all in the club, and I never had a problem with them. The only possible downside was that some of them got so keen on the clubs that they started knocking on my door on their way home from school to see if I was in. I needed a rest sometimes, so I confess that sometimes I had to pretend I wasn't there.

CHAPTER 26

To be fair to myself, I was busy. I was doing forty hours a week plus all the overtime I could at my new job, as well as working with the children and teenagers at the church, or preparing for the club times, let alone all the usual church prayer and home groups. It felt like every moment of my time was taken care of, and so even though I didn't see any friends outside this world, didn't really see anybody in those years, I still felt I was pouring myself out into life in the most wonderful way. And God gave back so much. It was all so much fun. We had such a lot of laughter. My whole life became fulfilled and there wasn't an hour to spare.

There was one dark place still; my father found this new life of mine at the church very hard. After all, I was a woman. He couldn't understand why God preferred to use me rather than my brother, and he wasn't shy about letting me know that. Yet, for the first time in my life, he wasn't able to crush me. Though no-one was more surprised than me that God was working through me. I was learning there was a gap between what I'd been told and the truth. That girl who was told she was fit for nothing but the kitchen sink. Who should be put in a mental home and the key thrown away. It turned out she was so, so capable.

The lifelong shadow his views had cast over me faded. Not only was God blessing me in his ministry at church, but He was also blessing me in my job. I spent all day with men. I was the only woman in the entire office building, but my anxiety and my fears were leaving fast. God had showed me that not all men were like Dad. I was becoming confident, whilst simultaneously deepening my conviction that I couldn't do any of this without my Lord.

A lot of the foundation for Rock was built then. I knew overwhelmingly that God had asked me to do all this, that this blessing on the children and youth was nothing to do with me and we could lose it all if I let myself get in the way. I understood that all this amazing work was only given to me by His grace, and so I was absolutely petrified of stepping out of God's will. That began a lifelong habit of taking no major decisions without praying about it first. Every decision I made, every new teacher I invited in, everything we did in fact, we prayed and sought God first. It was all God—and what a privilege to be a part of the great work that God was doing.

27

The scope of the children's activities expanded. I started day outings across Lincolnshire, and we quickly moved to weekends away. We would invite other youth groups from other churches in places like Rotherham and Sheffield and end up with 50-60 children and youth there. I'd lead our youth in doing all the food and showing them how to host our guests. There'd be a big match in the afternoon, football, netball or similar, and the guest church would take a service for us in the evening. Then we'd go back to see them at their church, and they'd do the same for us. As my confidence grew, I began to arrange longer camps in the countryside around Grimsby, and we ended up going as far away as Wales.

Throughout it all, I was always looking to lead everyone in fun, and so I'd be the one doing these most stupid things. There would be great mischief, with me being the instigator. I was always a practical joker because a lot of the kids had come off the council estates and they'd never had much. Maybe there was more than a touch of me compensating for my childhood;

I certainly didn't want anybody to go through what I went through. I just wanted them to have good memories.

I got even bigger ideas and started bigger camps further away from Grimsby. One, at a place called Skendleby Hall, almost an hour's drive away, was agreed by all to be the best.

Skendleby Hall was an old, Grade Two listed Victorian house with fifteen bedrooms and a big clock tower: perfect, I had to admit, for a fantastic spooky prank.

On these camps, we would have a big party every evening. We'd begin with a service of worship and prayer, then move into a big disco, and games. I organised it, but the children actually did everything. I saw it as my job to get things in place, get the excitement going, and then stand back and watch them go.

This time I got to the hall first and scoped the place out. I found just the place I needed: a darkened corridor behind a heavy wooden door. While the kids were getting all the food sorted out, I went back up there and pinned up my best-ever prank: a luminous cardboard cut-out skeleton. I dressed it up a little, added cobwebs and a bat, and left it for them to find.

The Friday night service finished, then the games began, and the children gradually spread out over the house. I watched, and I waited, and, sure enough, after half an hour, some of the more intrepid of the children discovered the skeleton. Oh, the screams! None of the helpers could believe the noise ringing out down the corridors.

That wasn't the end. Our pastor was coming down for the Saturday and we had found out it was his birthday. My friend and I asked the kids, 'What can we do? It's going to be a big secret. He mustn't find out.'

We had the kids making an Old Father Time costume. We got a big birthday card, and some half-moon glasses, and a can of shaving foam. The pastor arrived, and we dressed him up.

We sat him in his throne, and very quickly he was swamped in shaving foam. The poor guy really got it. It ended up with him chasing us up and down the stairs as he tried to get his own back. People ended up in the bath, some beds finished up down at the base of the clock tower. There was shaving foam over everything, and it just went wild. It was such fun!

When everyone had settled down for the night, I nudged my friend.

'Let's get into the boys' room and get back at them. We need to give them something to remember.'

So, we dressed up as ghosts and tiptoed into their bedroom. Covered in sheets, 'Woooohing' as we went and waving our arms like ancient spectres of doom, we made quite an impression. An impression which was doubled when we pulled out our squeezey bottles full of water. We absolutely drenched them. It was brilliant.

It backfired on us both when we were running out. My friend tripped on the stairs and sprained her ankle badly. I ended up spending the rest of the night at the hospital. That calmed us down good and proper.

All this was something I'd never done before. I had no idea I could be so mischievous. In amongst a group of children, I discovered that I was the biggest kid of them all. We had such fun and excitement.

The greatest moment in all this time, an hour I'll never forget so long as I live, was one evening in the last summer of all this work.

28

It was a long, hot month, and I'd taken a group from Youthie away to join in with several more churches on a vast camp in Scarborough. It was a huge event, for once not one I'd organised, and I welcomed the chance to relax a little.

I loved spending time with the children, teaching them about Jesus, and seeing how their hearts would be open to the truth. That week, the stories really caught alight, and so many of them stepped forward to offer their lives to Christ. Things were light, fun, decorous, and God-focused, and things slowly built, until the mood became that of a mini-revival. It built all week, with joy rippling through them and the singing of the songs of worship we'd taught them, breaking out more and more spontaneously.

So many of them were baptised in the Holy Spirit and given the gift of tongues. So many of them got saved. At night I would think back over the day, and over what I'd seen, and my eyes would fill with tears at the impact of the Holy Spirit on the lives of these children.

Towards the end of the week, we took them from the camp for an evening outing to Peasholm Park. After our evening meeting, as the sun went down, we took them up into the trees to go on the woodland walk.

It was August, and it had been a hot day. There were winding paths in the woods, and raised walkways up among the trees, with many little sculptures and tableaux for us to look at. Dusk came down and the lanterns on the tree trunks came alight. There were loudspeakers among the trees playing pop music, and the teenagers sang along to that as they walked. Soon they ignored the pop music, preferring to link arms and switch to songs of worship.

We came out into a part of the walk where there were no speakers, and the pop music faded away behind us. The night-time proper fell on us, and the lanterns shone their soft glow among the trees. The teenagers, still children, really, went on singing the songs of praise we'd taught them during the week. For one priceless hour, all I could hear around me was their voices, ringing out, ringing upwards, all singing together in wave after wave, all praising God in a holy chorus that ebbed and flowed up to the skies.

It was a truly amazing evening and its memory lifts and sustains me even now, four decades later. God was doing such great things, and I felt the privilege of being a part of His work.

What an incredible season that entire period was. I had never been so happy. I poured everything I had into it, and I made many friends amidst it. God gave me back my childhood, and I'm sure I enjoyed what we were doing even more than the children. There were so many kids and they all got involved and everybody appreciated it. Everybody involved experienced so much joy. No-one who went on those camps will forget them.

Yet, like a beautiful bubble, floating, fragile, that time was short-lived. More than anything, through these years God was teaching me I could always depend on Him. All He requires is that we love Him, and we obey Him. I was soon to need that comfort, more than I could ever have expected.

29

Nothing here on Earth lasts forever. Change is a constant. The Psalms tell us all human life is like grass. We flourish like flowers in the field; then the wind blows, and we are no more. I feel that so keenly sometimes. Sometimes I see life as like mercury. It slips and slides, a silver thread constantly flowing, constantly changing. Even as we observe the beauty, it slips through our fingers and takes a new shape.

My time was ticking on. Though I'd nearly forgotten the prophecy, my two golden years were nearly up. It would soon be time for the three years of horror. Looking back, I can see how God wove my desire to do good into this overall plan of his, as I inadvertently took the steps that would end it all.

At one point, sometime into the second year of this season, I spoke directly to the Lord.

'Father, thank you for all you are doing with me. I'm only sorry I can't do more to build your Kingdom, but I am only human. I have a big ask for You. I don't want an ordinary life. I don't want to be married with two point four kids. I want my life to be meaningful. After everything I've been through in my childhood, I want my life to bless people. I want good to come out of it. I don't want to be the victim. I want to minister to other people.'

Shortly after this, God moved.

My mum and dad's neighbour died, and the family asked if I would like to buy the house. I was horrified. I didn't want a mortgage. I felt blessed already. I had done well at work and was on a good wage and I enjoyed being able to buy new cars and have the freedom to do what I wanted with my money.

God had different ideas.

I started to feel so guilty for not wanting to buy this house and I simply could not work out why. I felt like I'd committed the worst sin. I felt absolutely awful because again, I thought, I'd rejected the Lord.

'You need to get that house,' I felt God saying.

Me being me, all too flawed, all too human, I dared to disagree.

'I don't want that house,' I'd say. 'Why do I want that house?'

'My will is that you buy it.'

'No. Why do I want to be burdened with this house?'

Of course, the Lord won. I surrendered in less time than when we argued about the children's work. I was, at least, learning something.

'Alright, Lord, I'll go for the flipping thing. But you'll have to help me with the money.'

I took a trip to the building society. I needed £15,000 for the house and I thought I needed another £3,000 to have it modernised. I got that completely wrong. I had a look round and realise it needed more than a little work.

I took a builder round for an enlightening afternoon. He prescribed almost everything: solid floors, rewiring, new kitchen, bathroom, electric, gas central heating, pebble dashing and new windows throughout. Even in those days, it was clearly going to cost a lot more than £3,000. But God told me £3,000 and so I obediently fixed my mind on £3,000. Even then, I thought £18,000 was way above what I could get. I couldn't imagine that anyone would lend me that amount. Somewhat to my horror, the building society offered me the lot.

The purchase went ahead, and the house was mine. (Or, the bank's, with me a willing servant of the debt.)

We started to do the house. At which point, Dad amazed me. He wanted to help.

He had always been very good with his hands, but all his experience with the houses he had developed had left him with proper expertise in many relevant areas. He arranged all the tradesmen, all the right builders, and supervised them all. Bit by bit, the house took shape.

The Lord was providing. Another house down the road had brand-new windows put in, and then a few months later they sold it. The people who came in wanted to alter it all, so they took all the windows out. They gave me all those brand-new windows. Then someone else gave me a good quality bathroom. And someone else gave me the kitchen.

Then it came to furnishing it. I got carpets and found wonderful deals, so everything was the best. I realised I needed a three-piece suite. A factory was closing down, and this suite was the last one in the place. I got it so cheap, and it was fantastic quality. I had it for many years. God's provision was amazing. After we got the decorating done, and bought all the brand-new furniture, the price for everything came to exactly £3,000. I took that as another lesson about how wonderful God is. He just needs us to be obedient.

I had needed somewhere to work at home for a long time, and so when we found a room up in the loft of this house, I saw my chance. It must have been created in the Second World War and never redecorated. It was up some stairs, along a tiny passage, and had clearly been used as a model railway room. It had been boarded out in tongue and groove and was finished in dark green paint. It was fabulous. I set that up as an office for me and did all my Good News Club work up there during the six months we were doing the house up. It was a great place for me to hide away.

Finally, the house was finished. All the work had been done and, just as I could have predicted, then came the curve ball. God had blessed me with a lovely home. You would have thought I would be eager to get out of my parents' house. Yet for some reason, I was reluctant to move in.

30

I was getting wise to the way God works. I was learning that, with God, there is always a reason. The cause of my reluctance would probably not be one that I would expect, and perhaps it wouldn't be for me to know, but I was now a firm believer that God always knows the bigger picture.

During this time, an older couple had come back from the mission field abroad and joined our church. The man, Malcolm Smith, was older, in his late fifties, but he had taken on the role as assistant pastor. I'd never spoken to him apart for a hello in passing, so one Sunday evening he and his wife invited me back for supper. As we were getting to know each other, we got talking about what I was doing with the children and the youth work, and all about my job. I started talking about my testimony and how my house had taken shape with God's help.

As I was leaving, I thanked them for supper and they both agreed that I had no idea what I'd said tonight. I went away wondering what could have been so significant, but quickly forgot it and planned for the week ahead.

There was a prayer meeting two nights later. Malcolm and his wife both came over after the meeting and asked if they could see me, so we arranged a time for me to go over again. This was getting mysterious.

Over the next few days, I spent time with them both. They told me how Malcolm was expecting to lose his job at the church. They told me how they had big problems coming. Eventually, they admitted these problems meant they wouldn't be able to afford their house and that would leave them homeless. Mrs. Smith was a lot older than Malcolm and found this prospect very alarming.

Finally, they got to the point. They wanted to know if I would be prepared to loan them my home for a while until they got themselves sorted out.

I said I would pray about it and get back to them.

I felt God was challenging me. He wanted to know whether I would be prepared to give up the house for him. I realised this was probably why I felt I couldn't move in. But everything was brand-new. Could I really give this up to someone else? After all our work on the house, I couldn't think of someone else using all my things before me. I stood still and agonised. Could I really do it? Was I really prepared to give it all up and let this couple use my home?

I was so involved in my work that I hadn't been involved in church politics, preferring to keep my head down and get on with doing what God had called me to. I found out the problem that had caused this couple to run out of money came because there was tension between the two pastors, and this older one was about to lose his job. When this happened, they couldn't pay their mortgage, and they'd lose their own house.

It made sense when I heard about all this, and it fed into my thinking. Late one night, I was praying in my bedroom when I had a breakthrough. I realised God was making me let go of the house. I needed to realise that it wasn't mine to keep hold of. In fact, God was confirming an ongoing teaching that nothing was mine.

It felt similar to what I'd been learning from the experience of building the Good News Club. Over the time there, I had realised that I was walking a very fine line. I had to be very careful at all times because God could take all that we had built away at any point. Sunday School wasn't about me, and it wasn't me making it happen. God was in charge of this whole thing, and I was just an instrument that He was using. God could put another instrument there anytime He wanted to. Alone in my bedroom, I realised God was also teaching that same thing about my home. It wasn't for me to hang onto. He wanted to know whether He could trust me. Was I prepared to let it go for Him?

I decided I would let the couple move in, but first I should see the main pastor of my church to pass it by him. I told him what had happened and said I felt this was what God was asking me to do. He thanked me for being up front with him, said he was fine about it, and I left.

I formally gave the house to the couple for six months. Almost instantly, I understood how deeply God's hand was in this. We soon saw that every item of furniture I had, they didn't. Everything I didn't have, they had. It went so far it seemed funny in the end, but it was a big thing between us. God and I could allow them to have the best of everything. I'd never actually used my new furniture. I'd never even had the joy of having anything new and being able to use it. God was asking me to give the whole thing new to them. I didn't charge rent either. They paid the bills, but I paid the mortgage.

I hope God saw and approved, but I wasn't sure. He certainly moved. Almost immediately, I was called into the vestry at church. The pastor looked calm, confident, and we chatted a while before he told me that a children's evangelist had now come into the church. I nodded, expecting more, but he had fallen silent

'Are you asking me to step down?'

He had fallen silent.

'OK. I will do.'

He nodded, accepting. And that was that.

It was a terrible feeling. I kept my hurt hidden and pressed for details. It became clear the new children's leader was starting the next week. I gave up my role and left the vestry, dazed.

Over the next few days and weeks, I processed it. On the one hand, it was clear I'd walked into the middle of a political minefield. With my head in my work, I had missed the fact there was tension between these two pastors, and by offering my house to the junior pastor, I had placed myself into the middle of a battlefield. I, an innocent bystander, was just collateral damage.

On the other hand, well, right at the beginning of all this, God had said I would only be there for two years. I just hadn't quite believed Him. Silly me.

I told the team and the children, and stepped down as cheerfully as I could. The new evangelist took over, and I was done.

Left on my own, I could admit how I felt I'd been left high and dry. In the same few weeks that I lost the children's work, my two-year redundancy contract at the office ended and I'd soon be out of work.

I knew I was going to find it very difficult seeing the children each week, and it was going to be equally hard for the person who took over from me so, when I realised that some people in the congregation disapproved of me giving the house to the pastor, this was the last straw. I found another church and tried to move on.

There was a strange epilogue. When people in other churches across town knew I had left my youth work, one by one they approached me to do the same for them.

Even though I knew I was no longer needed, I tried to help my own church out. I took a youth group to an event in Lincoln. We got trapped by heavy weather and our van got snowed in on a steep hill. The local church stood up wonderfully. Some in local homes, some on the floor of the church hall, we bedded people down for the night. It felt like something of a disaster, however, and it confirmed to me that the anointing had gone from my youth ministry.

This came to a head when the pastor at my new church got hold of me. Every single leader in the church had already tried me, every single one of them had invited me to their home to persuade me. Every single one of them was telling me that God had told them I was to go there and be their children's and youth pastor and take over. The pressure was intense and painful. I finally snapped.

'Sorry. No. That won't be happening.'

'What do you mean?' the pastor said.

'You're telling me that God has spoken to you. But God hasn't spoken to me. He will speak to me first and then He'll confirm it through other people. He doesn't do it the other way around.'

Praise God, my paid job was saved, and I was moved sideways, to a sister company, but my heart was sore. I felt I had gone from being so busy working at the heart of God's will to having nothing. It was a very hard stage of my life as that season ended.

It appeared God was intent on disrupting things and shaking

the foundations of my life. At this exact time, Dad had an attack of severe chest pains. We called an ambulance, and though he looked OK, they took him into hospital for observation. Mum went to visit him after lunch and came home in a state of terrible distress. She was a nurse, so as soon as she had got onto the ward and saw him, she recognised he was in the middle of a powerful heart attack.

31

Dad had been in bed in the middle of a busy ward, but the staff on the ward hadn't noticed. Incredibly, it turned out that he'd been like it for a couple of hours. No-one had seen anything and nothing had been done. Because he had been left so long, it had affected his kidneys. The consultant's opinion was that his only hope was to get him to Sheffield and get him into dialysis. However, the consultant also felt he wouldn't make the journey, so they were waiting to see if he stabilised before taking any more decisions.

We went back that evening to visit, and they said the situation had clarified. Dad's only hope was to go to the Renal Unit. We looked at them expectantly, but they shuffled papers and looked uncomfortable. Finally, they admitted they hadn't been able to get hold of the Renal Unit in Sheffield because their phone was engaged. They said they would try again later.

I was so mad. There was nothing more we could do that evening, but the following morning I went back with my mum. I walked into the consultant's office. I stood in front of the receptionist.

'I want him in Sheffield, and I want him there now.'

I found a seat, took it, and folded my arms. I wouldn't move until they got an ambulance and had him on his way to Sheffield.

Within 30 minutes, things were moving. I followed him in the car with my mum, but it was an agonising trip. The ambulance went at twenty miles an hour, all the way from Grimsby to Sheffield. What's more, it kept on pulling over. We realised he was so poorly they had to keep on stopping to see to him.

They got him to Sheffield, and as they were taking him out of the ambulance, they realised he was heading into another heart attack.

They intervened and stopped that one in its tracks before taking him down to theatre. We were told the outcome was uncertain, but he came through. They finally got him on dialysis, and eventually he was discharged to go back home. We were given all the equipment we needed to do the dialysis at home, and we even built a room in the back of the garage to hold all the supplies. From then on, his constant companion was the bag on a stand on one side, dripping liquid into his body through tubes. The liquid would flow into him as I watched, and a tube on the other side would take a darker fluid out. This was all a hard sight. However, Mum became his carer, and things stabilised for a while. *

. . .

* Dad stayed on kidney dialysis for the rest of his life. He always thanked me for getting him to Sheffield. I was the only one who fought for him, and he knew that. My mother wouldn't fight for him. My brother wouldn't fight for him. Dad always believed that God was going to heal him, but that wasn't to be the case. He got infection after infection and suffered agonising pain. He ended up back in the hospital many times, until he died, ten years later. It's not too extreme to say that he went through hell on earth in those last years. God had a reason for this, but I've realised I will never know what until I meet with God myself, when perhaps he will explain to me why this happened.

CHAPTER 31

With Dad home, and stable, I finally had space to look around me. I suddenly felt so alone. It felt like I was in a wilderness, as though everything had been taken from me. Children's work, my church, the job I loved, and (my doing, this) all my friends, who I'd ignored for the last two years. I felt so isolated. It was a horrible feeling. It was awful.

Then, in early spring, at my new church, I met Jonathan, and he overwhelmed me.

32

Jonathan was younger than me. He was alive with energy and personality, and he turned it all my way. An attractive trainee pastor in his last year of Bible College, he was dazzling. We got talking, spent more and more time together, and things moved fast. He had no money or job yet, but we didn't care. He was strong, very present, and he was clearly mad about me. He proposed within weeks, and I agreed on the spot. We were married by the autumn, and then it began.

We were married on a Saturday in September 1986. The first real warning things were wrong came on the night before. I cried through most of the evening, sobbing loudly at times. I didn't know why.

The service came and went in a blur, and before I knew what was happening, we were off on honeymoon.

All I can really remember about that first week together is that it was my 28th birthday, and Jonathan bought me a gift of white lilies. I stared at them and tried to be grateful. But the truth is I hate white lilies. I cannot abide them. I find them gloomy, even sinister.

That he had picked them out of all the flowers he could have chosen felt so ominous. I found a bowl for them and put them in the corner of our hotel room, where they sat and wilted. Every time I caught sight of them, I sensed the approach of something awful.

The honeymoon ended, and the weeks passed, and we tried to learn to live with each other. The couple to whom I had lent the house were moving to Wales to be closer to their family, so they had given me my house back and we moved in there to begin our married life. We were only there for a few months, as I didn't feel it was right for us to live in a house that I had bought. I soon sold it and late that year we bought a house on a more modern housing estate out on the edge of town. This was clearly our house, and we felt in some ways this was a proper beginning. We had such high hopes, but sadly, it soon became clear we were in deep trouble.

Out of love and respect for the two poor humans involved, I won't go into many details. It's enough to say that our marriage was a living hell. My only concern in this book is to reveal how God worked throughout that time for me.

The first time I felt God speak about what was going on was towards the end of the first year. One day, a chaplain dropped by to see us. Jonathan wasn't at home and for the first time in nearly a year, I opened up and told someone just a little of what had been happening. The chaplain listened we prayed. He left me with a verse from the first chapter of the Book of Joshua.

'Be strong and of good courage; do not be afraid, nor be dismayed, for the Lord your God is with you wherever you go.' (Joshua 1:9 NKJV)

I was lost and floundering, so to be reminded of this central truth was so timely. God truly spoke to me at that moment, and I found immense peace in the scripture.

I also remembered the prophecy I was given at the beginning of my children's work. The two years of joy had come true. This was surely the three years of living hell.

For a while, that brought me hope. Though the awful prophecy seemed to be being fulfilled, at least it gave hope of an end to the period of torment. I became convinced that God would heal the situation after three years. Divorce was unimaginable, and I was petrified I'd fall pregnant, but I knew there would be an end, so I could go on.

Until one day when I had come home from work. We had moved house again and were now in our third house since getting married. I drove onto the drive, looked at the house and realised that it was the exact house I'd seen in that prophetic dream when I was sixteen. A dream in which I was alone, with no feelings for my husband.

Such was my fear of divorce, I suppressed that part of the dream in which I was alone, in favour of being metaphorically alone. However, it left another level of foreboding over my life. I did not know why God had shown me this when I was sixteen. I had such a fear of Him.

As the weeks and months went by, I got ever more desperate, in an ever-lower place. I could see no sign of God's healing. I wondered whether I was wrong about that, and, I must admit, I finally opened my mind to a curiosity about divorce.

I did my best not to pursue that line of thinking. I was helped in that by how divorce was frowned on in those days. Especially for a pastor's daughter. I would have been the talk of the town. The attitude around me would have been 'You've made your bed, now you have to lie on it.' And, though it was causing me such pain, I agreed with that. I knew I wouldn't be the one to initiate any divorce. God hates divorce.

So, we went on. I kept everything that was going on, of how badly we were doing, to myself. Philip had seen some of it, but I still said nothing to my own parents as Dad was very ill and I wanted to keep all the stress away from him.

Around this time, I had damaged a disc in my back. With all the stress, this disc became painful, and I questioned God about why we weren't seeing healing miracles like there used to be. After Jonathan had finally left our relationship, I went to a Christian's Businessman's fellowship in town. One night, a visiting speaker said he felt God wanted to heal some people. That he knew there were people in the room who had back problems. I was deeply cynical.

'Everyone has back problems,' I thought. 'The speaker is taking the biggest cop out. He's playing this safe.'

I was questioning everything badly. So, when the pastor called people forward, I didn't move.

My mother kicked my ankle.

Surprised, I looked at her.

'Go for prayer,' she hissed.

I smiled, and looked back to the front, and didn't move.

She nudged me again.

'Go for prayer.'

I sat firm and shook my head.

'Go for prayer.'

'No. I'm happy as I am.'

She nudged me with her whole body.

'Will you go.'

I looked at her. She was frowning at me. Her mouth was set, her eyes were dark and beady. I knew she wouldn't give up.

'Oh, for goodness' sake,' I said.

So, I went forward. I found a chair near the front. Gingerly I lowered myself into it, and sat, waiting to be prayed for.

'OK Lord. Let's see what you're up to. Now let's see if you can do what you say.'

That was my attitude. It was awful.

As I sat there, I had to admit I was in a tremendous amount of pain. It was worse that day, but it had been bad for a long time. I was so tired of feeling like that.

The speaker came over to pray for me. I bowed my head, closed my eyes, and held out my hands. He put his hand on my shoulder, called for the Holy Spirit, and lifted me up before God as a precious child who needed healing and restoration.

He sank into prayer. It went on for some time. My mind drifted. I felt absolutely nothing.

He said Amen, and I said Amen, and I opened my eyes and found him smiling at me. He had a kind face. I couldn't smile back; I was still hurting. I went back to my seat, though it was getting hard to walk. The pain was worse than ever. The prayer had been a complete waste of time, and I wasn't shy in telling God that.

I went home, went to bed, and tried to sleep. That night, I seemed to be in more pain than ever. There was a knot in my back that wouldn't go. I struggled to get comfortable and struggled to close my eyes.

The next morning, I woke up to a great sense of normality. I lay there and tried to work out what was different. I realised the dull ache in my spine wasn't there. I gingerly moved my legs to free them under the duvet and realised there were no twinges. I was happy about that. I'd obviously slept in the right position for once. The real job was getting up from the bed. I prepared myself, took a last breath, and tried to stand up.

There was no trying. It was simply doing. Standing was effortless. One smooth move and I was up.

I stood still for a moment, surprised. I could feel nothing wrong at all. I had no pain.

I took a step, then another, waiting for my spine to compress and it all to begin. But nothing happened, except I was two steps closer to the door.

I turned gently. Left and right. Nothing. I risked twisting further, going left and right. Nothing. At least, no pain. Just freedom of movement. In a moment of absolute mad daring, I bent over to pick up a book that had dropped off the bed.

Nothing. Absolutely no pain.

What is there to say? My pain had gone completely. My back has been fine ever since. God is kind. Praise Him.

33

Much happened in our marriage, about which I can't write. In the end, we separated and began to live apart. I was reluctantly accustomed to the idea of divorce, and so that process began. Just before I was due in court for the hearing, I was very ill. The doctor said he felt I had glandular fever. At that time God had been taking me through the book of Ruth. I was near the end and God was speaking to me through Boaz, and how Ruth had rested at Boaz's feet. I had an overwhelming sense that Jesus wanted me to rest at his feet. To trust Him with my needs, with my future, with everything. To rest in Him.

The Lord then took me to another scripture:

'Is anyone among you sick? Let him call for the elders of the church, and let them pray over him, anointing him with oil in the name of the Lord. And the prayer of faith will save the one who is sick, and the Lord will raise him up.' (James 5:14-15 NKJV)

I rang my pastor and asked if he would come and pray for me. He came with a few of the elders. When they got to my house, he took one look at me and said,

'I think we should call the doctor.'

The other elders nodded. They all looked worried. I was firm. I knew what I needed.

'No. The doctor was here last night and said I will be another six weeks like this. I just have glandular fever. It's OK.'

It wasn't OK. I couldn't even lift a kettle. I was so weak. I really needed a breakthrough, and after all that had happened with my back, I had high hopes that God could bring it.

They gathered round my bed and prayed. They prayed for a long time, in fact, and I felt a great peace fall on me. I was full of love for all these people, and so grateful that they would take time away from their day, come all the way across town and intercede like this for an hour or more.

They finished the prayers, and the pastor anointed me with oil. There was nothing magical about the oil. It wasn't a sacrament, or anything similar, just a humble symbol of how we depend on our Lord, a physical act expressing the spiritual truth: we belong to God, and we commit ourselves to Him for our care.

I thanked them all, and they left me. Once again, just as with the prayer for my back, I felt the same in that there was no obvious change. The difference was that this time, I also felt God speak to me.

'You can lie here and let this thing take its course, or you can get up and trust me.'

I took that first step of faith and forced myself up and out of my bedroom. That day, I found that the more I did, the better I felt. I knew something had shifted in my illness.

That same evening, I knew there was another evangelical meeting with a guest preacher in the Memorial Hall. I took another leap of faith: if God had healed me, then I should claim that healing. I asked my mother if she wanted to come to the meeting with me. She was very concerned about this. The last time she had seen me, I was flat on my back, practically unable to feed myself. She was convinced I shouldn't be going. But just as she had nagged me at the meeting about getting my back prayed for, I kept on at her. I just kept saying, 'Mum, God has healed me,' until eventually she relented.

We went into the meeting, and I saw my pastor was already sitting on the stage. The minute he saw me, he jumped up and came running down off the stage.

'What are you doing here?'

'God has healed me.'

'Praise God,' he said, and he ran back onto the stage. That was quite a meeting. I opened my heart to the Lord and sang songs of gratitude and praise all evening.

That was on the Friday. On the Monday evening, I went back to the businessmen's fellowship and that night's speaker arrived late. He walked in and, before he'd taken the floor, before he'd taken his coat off even, he turned to the assembly:

'There is a lady in this room who has had glandular fever. God told me on the way here that I am to pray for her.'

I hadn't time to be self-conscious. This was too direct, too urgent. I stood up.

He walked over, faced me full on, looked into my eyes.

'That's me,' I said.

He nodded, and put his hands on me, a hand on each shoulder. I bowed my head, and he spoke four simple words.

'God, meet the need.'

I instantly felt like a red-hot poker had gone right through my chest and wrapped itself around me. I gasped and stepped back. He moved with me, keeping his hands on my shoulders, praying in the Spirit. The sensation moved, and settled, and calmed, and felt like I had thousands of arms around me. I felt heat, and such love.

He prayed a few minutes more and left me to recover. Of course, I was fully healed, but I've also always wondered whether that moment was an anointing for what was to come. What an awesome God we have.

34

I was due in court with Jonathan. On the Sunday before, we had a visiting speaker at church. She said she believed God had given her a word for me. She didn't know my situation, but the word she gave me was clear enough:

"The Lord will fight for you, and you have only to be silent." (Exodus 14:14 ESV)

That was comforting, but I knew there were still big trials ahead. Full of anxiety, I went to court the following week. My pastor and my friend came with me. Amazingly, my dad turned up too. He gave me a quick acknowledgement and then took his seat in the court. He never spoke to me about it outside the court, but he was there throughout the hearing. I was so moved to see him there, to know that, for once, he was there for me, not against me.

All my anxiety was pointless. I never had to do or say a thing. The case was settled very quickly and very quietly in the corridors of the courthouse, in the last minutes before we got into the courtroom itself. Our barristers got together and negotiated it all without either of us having to testify a word.

My barrister came over to bring me the news.

'This is the worst divorce case I've ever had to work on, but you'll have no more problems.'

I don't know what happened, but we walked out of court, and in summer 1989, three years after we'd met, I was legally free. God most definitely fought for me that day.

35

Legally free was one thing, financially free another. As the financial settlement progressed, I could see I was going to be left in debt. Serious debt, that would take years to get through. The pressures and stresses around the divorce had taken their toll, and I became deeply depressed.

One Sunday afternoon, alone in our house, I hit a low. I'd had enough. I couldn't cope anymore. So, I came up with a plan. It was a good plan. It would resolve things.

I was in the Elim Church at the time, in the worship group as the main keyboard player. I loved the group, but it didn't touch the sides of my grief. My plan was to go to church and play for them that Sunday evening, but not to speak to anyone. As soon as the service was over, I'd come out of the church, I'd get in the car, and I'd drive it as fast as I could into a brick wall. I knew just the one. Tall, massive, thick, and solid, out among the warehouses in the docks. A perfect, anonymous place to dump all this pain and end this failed life.

That night I stood on stage in church, listening to the music, playing my part, being a good musician. The idea of being in a worship band is that you aren't the star. You aren't important at all. You exist on that stage only to lead people in worship. Your job as a worship musician is to remove yourself, your ego, all your pride and need for praise, and stand only as the signpost to the actual star—Jesus Christ.

That was sometimes tough, as we all like to get a response from the crowd, but that evening, that humbleness suited me just fine. I stood still, and played, cut off from my pride. In the depths of my despair, I didn't notice that I had turned myself away from God, that I was also cut off from His love, and cut off from anything but my plan.

I played through our ministry time and watched the people step forward to receive prayer. 'Good for them,' I thought. 'How nice that they are being healed. How nice that they are receiving God's blessing. Good for them.'

I had no more idea of myself. No more idea of my life, or my needs, other than my need for the evening to end.

The service finished, and we were dismissed, and I avoided everyone. I packed up my music and put on my coat. I slipped through the crowd and got out of the church. I knew no-one suspected anything.

I got into my car and prepared myself. I didn't pray. How could I, at a moment like that? God was hidden from me—or I had turned my face away from Him. Either way, I was determined. What was going to happen would happen.

I breathed deeply, once, twice, and went to turn the engine on. The blinking thing wouldn't start. I couldn't believe it. I tried again. Nothing. The ignition clicked and clicked again, then there was an electric whine under the bonnet. The engine made a whirring, grinding noise, but it just wouldn't start. I kept the key turned, and the engine kept on making noises, but still nothing useful happened.

I let the key go and sat there, perplexed.

I tried again, and the engine turned more slowly. Jumping and lurching this time. It sounded like a wounded dog.

I remembered my dad telling me about how engines would flood, and I wondered if I'd done that. Dad said if you waited five minutes, the fuel in the carburettor would have cleared and you'd be good to go.

Beginning to panic, I waited. Waiting for when I'd be good to go.

After five minutes, I tried again. The engine groaned, and turned over once, twice, three times. Then everything went dead and the lights on the dashboard all went off.

I sat there for an age. I couldn't believe how unfair things could be—I always kept my cars well serviced. I was so thwarted; I felt like crying, but I couldn't even manage that.

Eventually that frustration faded, and a numbness settled on me. Despite it all, I knew the agony of knowing I'd have to live on. I sat still, staring ahead, not knowing what to do.

After a while, there was a tap on the window. I saw a concerned face looking in. I wound down the window.

'Are you OK, love?'

It was Pastor Renshaw. He was an elderly man from church. He'd been a missionary, and he had just come back from furlough. He had a peaceful heart, and was a proper man of God, but I didn't want to talk to anyone.

'I'm fine. Thanks though.'

I reached for a tissue and blew my nose. He watched me with deep compassion.

'Having troubles, Pam?'

'My car won't start. That's a trouble alright.'

'Nothing else?'

'Nope.'

'Are you sure?'

'I'm fine. Honest.'

I dabbed at my eyes and checked my face in the mirror. He was wise enough to leave it there.

'Right-oh. Why don't you pop that bonnet open, and I'll see what I can do for you.'

This got my attention. Pastor Renshaw was a missionary, but he'd also been a mechanic for many years. Maybe he could help me get what I wanted.

He fiddled around, and tried the ignition, and went to get some jump leads from his car. He fixed them and told me to turn the key.

I did as I was asked. Nothing useful happened. The engine stayed dead. I stayed alive. My disappointment was intense.

He fiddled around a bit more, and the engine stayed dead. After a while, he closed the bonnet and went to the boot of his car to pull out a tow rope. He found the tow point under my engine, roped us together, and gave me instructions. He pulled away, and the tow rope went taut and, with a little jump, my car followed.

We set off into the sparse Sunday evening traffic. I sat in my car and steered all the way home, trundling through the streets like a child on a fairground ride.

Such was my suicide attempt.

Pastor Renshaw left the car on my drive and said he'd sort out a garage for me in the morning. I got inside my house, and, to my surprise, I found I could finally cry.

I sobbed for a long time, and something happened. The tears released me, and I discovered I wanted to live. My despair turned into gratitude. I couldn't help but see how God had intervened. I knew I had been saved by grace once again, though it would take me a good while to accept that this was a good thing.

36

I went on, but I don't think I knew where I was. My confidence was at rock bottom. I had no self-esteem, and I was desperate for an end.

There was one patch of light. Through it all I knew God had stopped me from killing myself. So, maybe He was saving me for something. Maybe He had a job for me I couldn't see. That was my comfort, even at this moment: I was precious to God.

Financial settlement finally came, perhaps a year later. The hell that was my marriage was finished.

That sounds strong, but my deepest regret in life is getting married. I went from the frying pan into the fire. From Dad at home, and then to a relationship that was even worse. Looking back, we had no chance. The path of our relationship was clear, set long before we ever met. We were innocent, inexperienced, and under-equipped. I had come from a fractured battlefield of a childhood, with aggressive confrontation and humiliation being the preferred mode of communication, and a father who had tried to kill my mother. I was starved of genuine affection and had no real idea what proper love was. In his turn, Jonathan suffered from severe mental problems, anger management issues, and unrealised layers to his desires.

People in pain seek other people who can understand and validate that pain. It's therefore not so surprising that we found each other in the first place, or that we clicked when we did.

It's also not surprising that our three years tangled up together were bitterly painful for us both. Many couples are surprised to find that, when they marry, they can't help repeating what they learned about marriage from their parents. If what they learned was bad in the first place, then the stage is set for trouble. We were no exception.

The last time I saw Jonathan was over twenty years ago. I'd just come out of seeing my dentist, and I was parked in the carpark at Asda in the centre of town.

I heard a familiar voice.

'Pam!'

I went cold. Slowly, I turned.

Jonathan was standing a couple of rows of cars away. We stood and gazed at each other for a long moment. He looked older. I'm sure I did too. He was still slim, but his hair was greying. He was so, so familiar to me.

'I know what I did to you, by the way.'

Just like him. So direct.

'And so do I,' I said.

I waited for him to apologise, but he shrugged. As though it was all long gone and forgiven already. Was the apology implicit? How did that make me feel?

As I wrestled with this, he took a step towards me. I lifted my hand. In peace, not rebuke.

'I don't want to know, love. Do go back,' I said, as kindly and as gently as I could.

I turned and walked away.

A banal greeting in a busy supermarket carpark, and a final parting. A ragged way to end, but no less poignant for that. I'll remember that moment, and our marriage, and Jonathan, forever.

37

My two years of joy, and my three years of hell were over. Now the prophecy promised me a season of healing. I needed it so much. I was free, but I was in pieces.

After my divorce, God took me through nearly three years of healing. It was just me and God and it was the most painful season I'd ever go through, but it was the most precious. God taught me so much and built so much confidence in me.

It's amazing how gentle our Lord was. He would take one thing at a time and say, 'How do you feel about it?'

So, I would tell Him.

I'd experienced so much hurt, pain, and rejection in my life, and I needed to deal with it. Very clearly, the Lord showed me it wasn't wrong to release all those pent-up feelings, whatever way they needed to come out.

I went all the way from early childhood, right through to everything that had happened in my marriage.

First, something new would come to mind. I would let God know how I felt about what had happened or what people had done to me. There were so many emotions. Sometimes I'd be screaming at Him, blaming Him outright. Sometimes I'd be blaming others, and I'd be screaming at them. Wherever it took me. At other times, I just cried.

After I'd finished, God would say to me: 'Right. Now I want you to forgive that person for what they've done to you.'

The only way I could forgive some people was to see them as someone who was sick. Then I could do it. Because the truth is they really were sick.

I would forgive them. Then I'd to say to the Lord, 'Come and heal me just now while this hurts so much.' And God would.

It was hard in one way, because for three years I was reliving pain and being healed. I always knew I had been healed when I could talk about a matter, and it didn't bother me. If I had any emotional reaction, I knew I wasn't free, and I had to go back to the Lord.

Alongside it all, God was blessing me through what He was showing me through the scriptures. In fact, He opened up the scriptures to me like no other time in my life. It was like everything in the Bible was coming alive to me.

I questioned a lot of what we had been told as kids. God showed me the truth for myself. One prime example of that, which I was glad to leave in the dust behind me, was that I realised how wrong it was to "Keep the pastor poor to keep him humble". There were many more such false ideas which I realised were imprisoning me, and from which I broke free.

In time I realised everything about me, all my thoughts, were challenged, even my faith. God was getting a lot of questions from me, as was my pastor.

In the end, what God was doing became so clear. He was ripping everything away from me completely. Not only was He healing me of all the hurts, but He was healing me of all the doctrinal things that I was involved in, everything that had been pushed into me through the years. Doctrine's not wrong, of course; it's good that we have doctrine, but for me it had been a problem. I was left knowing that from now I should forget doctrine, just know it was just me and God walking a path together.

From that time onwards, I became confident that I would listen to nobody else but God.

38

Another area for healing was my self-esteem, and there was one event that symbolised the whole thing. At one point, when I was seriously doing my best to stall, even halt the divorce, my father had been to my solicitor behind my back. He wanted to get the divorce moving. When I found out, I couldn't believe it. I went to see the solicitor and told him to stop the divorce in its tracks. As I was leaving the office, the solicitor said, 'You don't need to worry, you know. An attractive young lady like you, you'll soon be married again'.

That hit me for six. I couldn't believe he was talking about me. Three more people that week then said the same thing to me.

This had such an effect on me because of how I'd been led to think about myself. My mum, my dad, Jonathan, had all told me I wasn't attractive, in all directions, repeatedly.

It had been like that all my life: if they could have pulled me down, ripped any more out of me, they would have done. It had been Satanic really; they couldn't have been any worse to me.

It's strange how that single comment from the solicitor really ministered to me, but it did. I prayed around it, and in that process, God spoke to me. Loudly, He said to me, 'I will lift you up before them all.'

That phrase rested on my heart and gave me strength. It too was prophetic, and many years later I was to see it made real.

39

More healing came in my relationship to money.

The divorce had left me in a lot of debt. I had never been in debt before, and I'd always had a good job with good money. Now I was looking at having to sell the house to pay for all this.

I felt so bad. I had no money to buy food, none of the small things. When I look back at my diary, I see brief comments and little things I've written. 'Oh, praise God, I've got some overtime today. That means I can get my hair cut this month'.

I did feel God was moving around me, sometimes in the most trivial of ways, with the lightest touches of comfort. For example, I can remember some friends coming around for a Saturday evening. All afternoon I'd been thinking I'd love to eat some grapes, but I was saving every penny, so I didn't buy any. I remember mentioning it to God in passing, just a simple comment: 'God, I really fancy some grapes.'

Of course, when my friends arrived, they had brought me a bunch of grapes. Coincidence? Sure, maybe, but there were so many silly little things like that. Coincidences or not, they all helped.

I realised that it all felt familiar to me. All my childhood, I'd seen my parents live like that. They'd never had money. On top of my new poverty, I felt socially disgraced. Divorce wasn't common like it is today, and it was worse because I was a pastor's daughter.

I'm not a believer in the prosperity gospel, but as part of my healing, God started to really deal with what was really my strong subconscious desire for poverty. Praise God. He always vindicates.

I've always been very determined and so I started working three jobs. I continued at my main job. I set up a party planning business, and I started making dry flower arrangements.

God blessed me and I met a gentleman from church who had his own shop. He sold them for me.

Still, it wasn't enough to pay everything that I owed.

I'd put the house up for sale, but I had a strong sense I shouldn't be selling the house.

I prayed about it. God asked me a direct question.

'Tell me, what would you do if you kept this house?'

I reeled off a list of all the things I would do. Repairs, decorating, the garden, everything.

'Trust me and get on with that work,' God said.

'But Lord, I have no money.'

'Trust me, just do it. Don't waver. Don't look to the right or the left; look only straight ahead.'

So many times do we let our circumstances dictate to us. In the obvious way of things, the house needed to be sold, but, praise God, He knows the bigger picture and He wants the best for us. So many times do we miss out on what God wants for us. We give up and think it's impossible, or times get hard, and we feel we can't go on. But that's the time we need to press in all the more; our victory is just around the corner.

40

One day, while this was going on, I had a dream. In this dream, God gave me £300. It arrived in three anonymous envelopes and came through my door via the post. Two envelopes contained money, and one envelope had a cheque. The cheque was for double the amount of the cash. I was to give the envelopes to my pastor. I wasn't to ask questions, and I wasn't to know the reason why. It was one of those ultra-vivid dreams that have a prophetic feel to them.

A week or two later, I came downstairs to find that someone had put an envelope through my front door in the night. I had no idea who had put it there, or why, but I thought it was great because I was in debt up to my eyes.

'Thank You, Father. This will help pay for some of my debt or my bills. I'll finally have some relief.'

Then I remembered my dream, and I thought, 'Oh, hang on...'

I wobbled. Even though I was in such debt, I felt I was working very hard, and so I had been determined not to shut my life down entirely. Accordingly, I was supposed to be attending a Christian concert that weekend. I had decided to go, but I had been worrying about paying for the tickets.

I looked at the money in the envelope, and I said to the Lord,

'If this is part of the dream, then let me know. When I go to buy the tickets, please make it clear. If this is you now giving this money, if this money is part of the dream, then let them tell me I can pay by cheque. Otherwise, I'll use this cash to pay for my tickets.'

It was a simple enough request and could easily go either way. I wondered if I could really trust the result, but I was losing my belief in coincidences. I'd seen too many of them.

A day or so later, I went to the concert venue to buy the tickets. Sure enough, they said to me,

'You can pay by cheque if you prefer. You don't have to pay by cash.'

'OK,' I thought. 'God is in this.'

I paid by cheque, came home, and put the money back in the envelope, the envelope in the drawer, and settled down to see what would happen.

Another week went by, and some more money came through my door, double the amount of the first lot. I wasn't too surprised. There was no question now, God was at work. I put the money in the drawer next to the first envelope. Another week went by, and a cheque came in, double again. It was following the pattern of the dream, and so I knew what I had to do.

I took the lot and went to the pastor's house. I told him what had happened, and I said, 'I'm not to know the reason, but I've got to give it to you.'

I gave every single penny to him. It was a gigantic step of faith on my part, and I needed courage to do it. It totalled many hundreds of pounds, which could have paid a lot of my bills, and even helped with my debts.

The pastor looked at the money.

'You'll never know what you've done,' he said. 'You'll never know what this means.'

'I'm not to know,' I said, and I walked away.

The following day, one last envelope was put through my door. It was packed with banknotes and was for double the total so far. I believed this gift was for me. I used it to pay so many of my bills. I never knew where it came from.

From there, God took me through decorating the entire house, room by room. The way He provided was amazing. One example was when I was working on the kitchen. Sometime earlier, I had seen some wallpaper that I had fallen in love with, but it cost a small fortune and I knew there was no way I could ever afford it. I shouldn't have doubted. God wants to bless us with the best. You know how we love to give to our loved ones? How much more does God want to bless us?

One Saturday morning I woke up feeling that I needed to go to Marks & Spencer. I kept saying to the Lord 'Why? I have no money,' but the prompting wouldn't go away.

Off I went into town.

I said to the Lord,

'I'm confused. I've only a few pounds in my purse.'

No reply. I pottered round the shelves some more, but then I got cheeky.

'Lord, I don't want just anything. I want something I would choose if I had the money.'

I went around the shop and saw nothing. But as I was about to come out of the door, there was a box with the wallpaper. It had been reduced by about 80%, and there were the exact number of rolls I needed. I checked what money I had in my purse. There was enough, with just a little left over. It was all very tight.

'Lord, if I buy all this wallpaper, it will take all my cash. What about buying food this month?'

'Trust me.'

So, I did. I bought the wallpaper and took it home. Then, when I went into work on the Monday, they asked me to work overtime. This overtime payment came to the exact cost of the wallpaper.

41

God had told me to decorate, not to hold on to the house, and so the house was still on the market. I was still doing three jobs and people were still coming to look around the house. Yet my sense of conviction only strengthened, and I felt even worse. I talked to Mum about it and told her how guilty I felt.

'I know I'm not meant to sell this house and when people come to look around, I feel awful. I know it won't sell, and I'm wasting everyone's time.'

Unusually for Mum, she had no advice.

'I've been praying,' she said, 'But I think you're on your own with this one. I've no witness to this. I think this is between you and God.'

A couple of days later, my friend's husband came around to see me. He was very concerned about my financial troubles. He told me it needed to sell. I cut in:

'I believe God wants me to keep this house.'

'But God hasn't told me that,' he said.

I can remember being quite sharp with him.

'Do you know I don't care? God has told me and that's that.'

He was surprised, then thought about that for a moment, then nodded, uneasy.

'That's fine. I'll come in agreement with you then.'

I couldn't believe it.

'I don't care whether you do or don't,' I said, even more sharply. 'I know God wants me to keep this house and if God wants me to have it, so be it.'

Not that I wasn't prepared to move. I was. But I was sure by then that God was active in this, and He always knows the bigger picture.

The weeks went by. I had been working part time and had not long gone back full time. I had paid off my debts to the bank, but I still needed to give Jonathan the £6,500 for his share of the house. The mortgage had been in both names, and the mortgage provider had been reluctant to let me take over the mortgage on my own, so I needed to buy him out completely in a lump sum.

God spoke to me and told me He was going to provide for me, but the money was going to come from someone I wasn't expecting, and I wouldn't be happy about it.

I discussed it with my mum, and once again she said that I was on my own with God on this.

One morning I woke up and I felt the Lord telling me I was to call the mortgage provider again. I couldn't see why, there was nothing left to say, but again I just went with it.

I spoke to a lovely lady, explained my situation to her, and she said she didn't know why, but she felt she had to give me a chance. She agreed to take Jonathan's name off the mortgage and let me continue alone.

At which point Mum arrived on my doorstep with some unbelievable news.

She and Dad had taken out extra on their mortgage; enough for me to pay off Jonathan. I was devastated and told her I couldn't do that. Mum reminded me that God had said it would come from someone I wasn't expecting, and I wouldn't be happy.

After a while, I accepted it, and said I would pay them back. At which point Mum exploded. She told me that if I paid it back to them, it would be like giving God his gift back.

Within a couple of weeks, the house was off the market, and, as God promised, it was mine. But, you see, you can't out-give God. Mum and Dad had been obedient and so it was no surprise that in the weeks after they handed me the cheque, they found out they were entitled to some money they hadn't expected. It turned out to be enough to pay all their mortgage payments. In the long term, they ended up with a lot more than they had ever given me.

Those years remained hard. Every penny was counted for, and I prayed hard. I had no choice. God was my provider and He never let me down. I learnt the importance of tithing and joyfully giving to God what is God's. But God has promised that if we honour Him, then He will honour us. I lost track of the times I would need something, and I would be offered some extra hours at work. Just enough each time. Through this, God was teaching me how to depend on Him and trust Him.

42

The journey through forgiveness was endlessly hard, and I needed to go back over it as God showed me new areas of hurt.

There was so much more than I've portrayed in this book, and it took the three years of God bringing things back to me and me coming before Him and dealing with it.

However, God is a gentleman and, just as it says in scripture, he's a great father who only does things when He knows we are ready to deal with them.

'I will instruct you and teach you in the way you should go; I will counsel you with my loving eye on you.' (Psalm 32:8, NIV)

After a time, I started feeling stronger, able to give out blessings as well as receiving them. I realised how clearly this was happening one day in a food shop in town. One freezer had broken down, and they had to get rid of all the stock very quickly. I saw a lot of meat on sale for next to nothing. I felt God tell me to buy a great amount of it and give to another couple who God had laid on my heart.

I did this, and I actually think I was more blessed than them. It turned out that they and their three children were desperate for help, and the excitement and praise on their faces was just such a joy. Even now, I want to thank the Lord for using me to bless someone else.

Another memorable blessing was on a day at a special children's church meeting out in the countryside. They wanted me to speak to the children. At the end, I gave an appeal and seven children accepted Jesus as their saviour. Praise God.

43

Through the three years of healing and afterwards my father's health was poor, and he was spending more and more time in Sheffield Hospital. I know he was in pain over me being so hurt, and the social disgrace of the divorce was hard for him to bear, but he was also getting more and more nasty towards me. He had started saying the most horrible things once again, as if somehow that was a way of showing love to me.

He went into hospital for a massive operation, and he thought he was going to die. God showed me an amazing vision. It was a cave. In this cave, Dad was laid on his bed. I saw many forms, like demons, things, spirits coming out of him and going back into him. There were lights too, at the top of the cave.

I said to Mum,

'He's not going to die. He'll be fine.'

I knew the demons would keep him alive, and that his body hadn't left the cave. Alongside this dark vision, Dad was clinging to the idea that he was going to be the man used by God to bring revival.

These contradictions were upsetting me terribly. Dad was constantly trying to tell me what to do, and it was really bearing down on me.

One day I felt God say to me:

'You will not take this.'

I wouldn't listen at first. I was very conscious of the scripture about honouring your father and your mother, and how you had to be there for them when they needed you.

God spoke again:

'You can still honour them, but you don't have to put yourself through this anymore. I'm releasing you. You can forgive your father, love him, be there when he needs you. But you don't have to place yourself in the situation where you are being constantly hurt.'

I spoke to my mum and explained to her that when Dad was there at home, I wouldn't be going around to see them. It was hard, and it meant Mum had to come to me. He was in and out of hospital at the time and she'd relied on me for everything.

'If you need me to take him to the hospital, or if you need to go and visit him, I'll help you. But I won't be alone with him, and I won't visit him in hospital. I'll do what I'm supposed to do, but no more than that. God has released me.'

So, I was always taking him to hospital appointments. He was in and out of hospital every couple of months and two or three times a week after I finished work, or at weekends, I would drive Mum over to Sheffield to see him.

We were used to him having big operations. Often, we didn't think he would make it, and then he would pull through. I was constantly in hospital with them, from my divorce onwards. He got to where he couldn't walk or even stand. One evening, I really felt he was going to pass away. That night I wept and wept. I saw him the following day in hospital. He said my name, and he was crying out in pain.

In August and September 1994, he went downhill very fast. He realised what was happening, and in the week before he died, he'd said to my mum, 'God's not going to use me, is He? I'm going to die.' That was so confusing for him.

I woke up on the Monday morning and I felt so strongly that something was going to happen. I sat up in bed wondering what it was. The post came, including a Christian magazine. I picked it up and saw the headline: 'Do not be fearful.'

I want to Mum's at 10.30. My auntie Rosie, my mum's sister, was over from Wales and staying with Mum. I showed them the magazine.

'Prepare yourselves,' I told them. 'Something's going to happen today.'

At 10.45, the phone rang. It was the hospital. The voice on the phone was calm, but firm.

'He's very bad. Can you get here straight away?'

We raced over to Sheffield. I stopped at the hospital entrance and dropped Mum and Rosie off. I parked the car and followed them in.

Mum met me halfway down a corridor. One look at her face told me the story. But there had been one last awful moment: Mum and Rosie had walked into the ward, and nobody had stopped them. They had walked on into his room and found him laid out dead in the bed. Nobody had warned them at all. It was a terrible shock for them both.

We had felt the need to keep his birth certificate on us. Thank God we did, because then we had to rush to register the death in Sheffield. The hospital had apologised, but we were all in such a state of shock I didn't feel I could drive, so we got a taxi to the registry office. All the way over, we kept saying it was amazing how God had prepared us for something to happen with the magazine.

In the days after he died, the vision of Dad in the cave with the demons came back to bother me. I kept asking 'God, where is he?'

Then, as I prayed, God showed me a beautiful beach and a beautiful sea. I could see my dad there. He was a child again, and he was sitting on the sand. There was a little girl with him. Whether that little girl was me, my mother, or someone else, I don't know because I only saw their backs. The sea stretched out towards the horizon, a miraculous blue and the colour of the sand was tawny and gold. They sat there, and I knew relief. Wherever he was, he was OK.

I shouldn't have been surprised. For all that he was like, for all the pain he lived in, for all the pain he had caused in his life, I knew he loved the Lord.

44

I've seen photographs that show a place where two seas meet, and two tides run into each other. You can see a line in the water marking the line which divides the two bodies of water. In the same way, just like two tides, my past and my future met head on in the week my dad died. Just as he passed away, ending that first era, God picked me up and began the rest of my life.

To explain, I need to go back a little way.

In the months after my healing had really settled in, God had reminded me about the first prophetic dream He had given me when I was sixteen.

I shared with Mum again what was on my mind:

In the dream I was a grown-up woman. I was living in a detached modern house, and I had no feeling for my first husband. I'd been approached to take on four children, and I was being asked to look after them in every way. The oldest two were girls and the youngest two were boys.

To my surprise, Mum accepted the dream fully. She felt it was clearly God speaking to me.

I felt the Lord tell me I should be actively praying to meet the children. A battle went on inside me for a while, but in the end, I surrendered and began this prayer work.

Almost immediately, the whole of my spirit warmed. I seemed to get so full I couldn't stop praying for them. I couldn't understand what was going on, so I went back to Mum. She said the Lord had spoken to her at the weekend and told her that she too was to pray for the children.

I wasn't sure what was happening. The more I thought about it, the more significant it all seemed. I was a grown-up woman, living in the right house. I was alone, and I definitely didn't have feelings for my first husband. How could a sixteen-year-old girl have really imagined this in such detail? I could see no choice but to believe this was true prophecy, and that God was speaking loudly and clearly to me.

Which led to an enormous idea. The other part of this dream was that I'd been approached to take on four children, and I was being asked to look after them in every way. The oldest two were girls and the youngest two were boys. Could this really be my next step in life?

It became such a big thing that I set out a fleece.

This is an idea which comes from a story in the Book of Judges in the Old Testament. The Angel of the Lord had told a warrior called Gideon to lead the army against the Midianite invaders. Gideon was fearful, and he doubted. He was the lowest in a weak family. How could he possibly be the one to win this tremendous victory?

As night fell, he got a woollen coat from a recently sheared sheep and laid it out in the threshing room where he had been working. He asked God to make it wet while keeping the surrounding ground dry. If God did that for him by the next morning, then Gideon would believe God was truly with him. God did exactly that, and in the morning the fleece was full enough of dew that Gideon could ring it out to produce a bowl of water.

Gideon was facing a huge decision, so he was still too fearful to go ahead. Just like any doubting human, he asked for another sign. The next night, he asked God to reverse things: to make the ground wet with dew but keep the fleece dry.

God did exactly that, and Gideon could finally believe that his army would have the victory that the Angel of the Lord had promised him.

So, a doubting human, just like Gideon, I too laid out my fleece.

'Lord, let me know one way or other if this is You. Please, Lord, show your hand. If this dream is from You, then send me some children's clothes by midnight next Friday.'

The days went by, and nothing happened. A week went past, and I forgot about the fleece. On the last Friday evening I went to help a friend of mine who was decorating her lounge. I had decided that the Lord wouldn't move, there would be no children's clothes, and that was great, because then things would be clear; I could just forget about the dream of looking after children and get on with my life.

We finished the decorating about half an hour before midnight. We sat down to have a quick drink. We chatted for a few minutes, then my friend looked at me strangely and said that something odd had happened to her in the week. Someone had given her a load of children's clothes and told her she would know who to give them to. She said, 'I had no idea who, but now, sitting here, I feel I have to give them to you.'

You can imagine my reaction. Literally minutes before my fleece ran out. God is full of surprises.

Unlike Gideon, I never needed to ask a second time. It was to be an incredible weekend; one I will never forget. The clothes coming in were just the beginning.

The next morning, I had guests, a Baptist minister and his wife. The minister prayed and prophesied over me. The Lord told him that all my life I'd been walking down a path that had boulders and rocks in the way. I was still on the same path, but there were no more rocks and boulders, and the path was straight and clear ahead of me. The difficulties were over, and I was stepping out into a new unknown. But I shouldn't worry. God was going to take me on from one thing to another. God's glory was going to be upon me, glory upon glory. I would also write a book, and God would use it mightily. I would be involved in a team, and God was going to use me greatly in that team. The people in the team would be oblivious to my past and be amazed how God was using me. There would be many people who would come across my path. God would also give me a greater gift of discernment and wisdom. I would be a woman of great faith, and I would receive things as I needed them, not before.

I heard all this and was stunned. Then the lady spoke. She asked me if she could wash my feet. She belonged to a group called the Dorcas Ministry, and now and then God called them to wash someone's feet. She'd only done it twice before. This was all new to me, but I agreed.

Then I too had a vision. God showed me a room. It was empty. It had been full of rubbish, but all that had gone now. All that was left was dust and the rest of the cobwebs. God wanted even this cleaned out now, as He was taking the dust of the day from my feet.

That Sunday evening, after they had gone home, I went to see my close friends Chris and Tony. They had been with me throughout the hard years and were like another mum and dad to me. They were such an encouragement and blessing.

That Sunday evening, Tony told me he believed he had

something for me from the Lord. He said that the Lord had shown him a wide stream.

'It's a stream that is low, but that will change. There isn't much in there at the moment, but it will run with silver and gold, flowing in and out endlessly.'

I knew that this was to do with my finances in my life. That it was a confirmation that I would always have my needs met. I was so shocked and eager, and yet I still didn't know what to do. Where were these children going to come from?

As the week wore on, I got more and more impatient, until I received yet another word from the Lord.

'Sit still, my daughter, until you know how the matter will turn out.' (Ruth 3:18, NKJV)

Sit still? How on earth was I supposed to do that? But I did my very best, and waited just a little while longer, until I couldn't bear any more sitting still.

I had a long conversation with my mother, in which she told me how sometimes God expects us to bring a dream into being ourselves. If God wanted me to take on four children, then perhaps I had to move some of the way towards Him.

The waiting had a benefit and things slowly crystallised for me. That confirmed an idea I'd been playing with all this time. We both agreed that the Lord wouldn't mind if I took one small step to get things going. Soon, I knew exactly what I should do, as well as how to do it.

I picked up the phone.

45

I was so naïve. I thought I could just ring up social services and say I was available to adopt some children and it would all happen. I soon realised that as a single person, it wasn't so easy.

In the early stages, I kept telling them I wanted to adopt, not foster, but they had different plans. It seemed there was a long road to walk before I would see any children at all, let alone the four God had shown me.

The first paperwork arrived, and I started getting approved to foster children. There were lots of meetings, courses, medicals and so on, but eventually I was approved. I would begin with a six-year-old girl, and she would stay with me for one weekend in four.

A couple of days after she arrived in September 1994, my dad died in the hospital in Sheffield. He was 60. He met none of the children that would come into my life, and he knew nothing about the work I would do.

So, the world turned. With him went so much of me. It was terrible, and it was painful, and I lost a stone in weight. Despite all that had happed between us, he was still my father. At the very bottom of it all I loved him, and he loved me. I was left picking up the pieces regarding the funeral and looking after Mum. All her friends had left town over the years, so wherever I went, she'd come with me. I'd feel guilty if I didn't take her, but at the end of the pain, I could step forward into a new season.

I was working full time, and I fostered on weekends. The little girl was indeed lovely. But she had her issues. Social services had forgotten about her, and she'd been left with her brother in a children's home where some teenage boys had abused her.

In time, as things settled, social services wanted to know if I would apply to be approved to take on a sibling group for the short term, to look at a longer-term placement for them. I would need to give up my day job. I really struggled with this, and in the end, I turned them down. I wanted to continue just as I was for the time being. As He does, God stepped in and dealt with me. He told me it was no good to just carry on, and that He expected me to take a step of faith, just as I did with the house. He said He needed me to do my part while He did His. He said He needed me ready to take more children.

I wasn't prepared at all. First, to really do this work for Him I would have to give up most of my social life. More than that, I would have to give up the security of my job and my income. I didn't want to be back in a place where I was wanting and wondering how to manage for basics.

I soon realised God was asking me to give Him everything. My life, my ambitions, my all. He was gentle, but persistent. He kept reminding me of many years before, how He had asked me to give up everything for two years to do the children's work, and where that had led me.

I struggled with that and stepped forward slowly.

I took the little girl's brother first, and after them, another little boy called Paul. It was hard work. All of them had been starved of affection and were very needy.

Paul came to me because his mother's partner had left her, and Paul had got meningitis. She had three other children, and she couldn't cope. Paul was frustrated because he'd lost his hearing. He was only four, but he was banging around, breaking things, even damaging walls. He kept getting hold of matches and setting fire to things.

I took him on at weekends to help both him and his mother. My Mum used to come and help us, and he thrived. It got so that, if he was naughty at home, his mum used me as a threat:

'If you're naughty, you aren't going to Pam's.'

He loved coming and we had him for years and years, on and off. It reminded me you don't give up anything for God. God always gives you so much back.

Despite the difficulties, watching these three children grow, helping them live more freely, was wonderful. I so enjoyed being a part of their lives. And yet, at the back of my mind, the thought that this wasn't what God had showed me gnawed away at me. In fact, sometimes I felt so burdened that a deep cloud of sadness would bathe me. The only way through was for me to take myself off somewhere quiet, and alone, and pray in the spirit until I felt the darkness lift. I never knew then why I felt so heavy, but it would be so deep, so grave, that I would sob as though my heart was breaking. Some years later, God would help me piece together why I was crying like this so randomly. For now, all I did was note the dates of when it was happening and wonder what the next level for God would be.

Soon afterwards, Grimsby social services rang again. This time they asked me to hand in my notice at work. They wanted me to take a 10-year-old boy Monday to Friday, and to keep doing respite care for other children. They said they would pay half of my mortgage to make this possible. I was sure this was not what God wanted for me, so I refused.

Social services came to see me again to change my mind. In that meeting, they let slip the fact that they had taken me off the adoption list. I was annoyed, but deep down I knew that, however this worked out, it was all part of God's plan for me. I had been fostering for two years, and I'd go on doing that because I knew God would do something when it was His time.

In the meantime, I went to visit my brother in Sheffield. The minister of the church he was attending asked to pray for me. After praying, he said God would now bring a dream of mine into being.

I heard that eagerly and sat down to wait, assured it wouldn't be too long. Sure enough, a friend of a friend got in contact soon after. She worked in social services in Lincoln, about 35 miles from Grimsby, and she had a question that grabbed my attention.

'We hear you're doing great work with the fostering, but that you're also looking for a deeper involvement. Is that right?'

'It is right. I feel I've got a lot more to give.'

'We wanted to know how much you are interested in adoption. How far you would go.'

'Try me.'

'Would you be interested in taking on four children at once?

My antennae picked up.

'Who would they be? What are they? Are they male? Female? Both?'

'The older two are girls, the younger two are boys.'

'Hang on,' I thought. 'God's in this now.'

This was all familiar from my dream. God had told me I'd be approached.

'They're all one family,' she said. 'Two girls, two boys.'

This was exactly what the dream had said. I knew these

were the children for me and my whole spirit leapt inside me. This was my dream, and it was actually coming to pass.

Almost instantly, the fundamentals jumped at me, and I was gripped with fear. Four children? How would I do this all alone?

'But how can I afford that?' I said. 'I've got a mortgage and bills. I need to keep working.'

'Well. Because you'd be taking on a sibling group of four, we'd be willing to fund it. You probably wouldn't need to work.'

'How do you mean?'

'We'd make sure you get a proper adoption package. It would all be paid for. All the children, and your own living expenses.'

I fell silent.

'Most people find that is very manageable,' she said, slightly aggrieved.

'It's not that,' I said, struggling to grasp what was happening. 'It's just that—oh, never mind, tell me more.'

I was truly amazed. Not at the offer, as such, though it made the way smooth. I had realised it was a fulfilment of the prophecy that silver and gold would run in and out of my life, and I wouldn't have to worry about finances while I was in God's will.

I put the phone down twenty minutes later. I was thoughtful. It all sounded amazing. Just what I had been praying for. Once again, God had opened the door wide and paved the way for me until it should have been an effortless decision. Yet I had a moment's hesitation. God was asking me for something very profound at that moment. I knew that, once I had those children, because they were so wounded, I wouldn't be free to marry for a very long time. I had felt that I wasn't free to marry anyway, as I was divorced, and that I would need God to speak to me about it directly if that were ever to change. Taking on four children would make all that theory real. What man would ever want a woman with four adopted children? Looking at it the other way, what man would ever be selfless enough to take on the challenge of serving my calling? I was still in my thirties, still a woman with the desires of a woman. The disastrous marriage, the agonising divorce, and the healing years had all stolen such a big chunk of my youth. I realised a part of me was still holding on to the hope of a proper, grown-up, beautiful love all of my own. If I took the children on, that was my life mapped out for the next fifteen years. Can you blame me for hesitating?

The answer came from afar. A church in Toronto had experienced massive revival. It had torn through the congregation, leaving worshippers with intense physical reactions to prayer. People would cry, shake, experience uncontrollable laughter, and fall to the floor in semi-conscious states. Services would last for hours, and long queues would form outside the church all day. Word spread quickly, and people flocked to visit. What was truly miraculous, it didn't stop. After a year, the manifestations of this Toronto Blessing were spreading to churches worldwide, and a church in Sunderland had been experiencing a similar outpouring. I was very weary, but I went with some friends to see what was happening.

The service was calm, peaceful, and felt reverent. We worshipped in reverence, moved deeply by a tangible sense of the Holy Spirit. Towards the end, as the mood shifted and people left, an elderly couple came over to me and asked if they could pray for me. When they had finished, they said they had the sense that I was going to be responsible for a number of lives. They spoke of the mysterious pain that had made me weep in the last year. They explained that the reason I was grieving inside at those times was because of these people. God was preparing me to minister into these lives, and that no-one else could minister into those lives apart from me. They said I was to trust God and put my complete trust in Him over the next few months. They also said God was going to give me a gentle spirit and give me far more confidence.*

We drove back to Grimsby, and all I could think about were the four children. Surely, God was talking to me about them. They were from the same family, but four children at once was a big ask. No-one else would adopt them, and it had been made clear to me I was their last chance. If I didn't adopt them, then they would be split up, and this would add so much pain and uncertainty to their already troubled lives.

Again, I felt God was honouring me with such wonderful prayer. It showed me I was stepping in God's will and doing what God wanted me to do. He was making sure I knew that.

---

* Over the years I eventually pieced together how each period of darkness for me corresponded to a period of darkness in the children's lives: when they moved out of their birth parents' home, into two different foster homes, beginning different schools, and their last contact with their parents. In some mysterious way, God was linking us before we'd ever met.

46

It was the sort of house you didn't want to go into. Inside was worse. The corridor was bare boards with stained old newspaper that stuck to your shoes. The back room was dark, chaotic, with dirty pots, empty bottles, takeaway cartons and broken-down furniture. A big TV in the corner, a ripped sofa in front of it. A cot in one corner, a full potty in the other. The air was rich with a complicated smell of something decaying, something rotten, something vile, something made in the dark.

In the dim light I saw five children dotted around the room. Three little girls, a little boy, and a toddler standing in a cot. They all looked at me, but they looked without seeing. The toddler sat down abruptly and cried, with a thin, piercing screeching. No-one went to comfort him.

A row of VHS boxes had tumbled over on a shelf near the TV. I glanced at their titles. 'The Evil Dead'. 'I Spit on Your Grave'. 'Texas Chainsaw Massacre'.

The foster mother, the woman whose house this was, was showing me round. I'll call her Jackie, though that's not her real name. She was a larger woman, a decade older than me, with grey hair. She saw me looking at the videos and had the grace to look sheepish.

'They love it when we have our Spooky Nights. Don't you, girls? It's like Halloween. We switch the lights off and I put a film on. I might dress up and we have a right bit of fun.'

The oldest girl stared at me glassily. The other two girls looked terrified. A wave of darkness rolled over me. There was something unspeakably sinister in this house.

I looked around at the children again. I was there to adopt four of the five. I hoped they would become my children and I could do what I could for them. My heart broke even then that I wouldn't be able to help the fifth, Jackie's own child.

Jackie bustled around me, picking up the dirty clothes that lay in balls over the old sofa.

'Take a seat, Pam, love,' she said. 'Did you want a cuppa?'

'I just had one, thanks. I got here too early and went to a café.'

'Keen one, aren't you?'

I shrugged. I was lying about the café, God forgive me, but there was no way I was going to have anything to eat or drink from this house.

She pulled the oldest girl to her and put her arm round her waist.

'This one's mine, worse luck.'

She waved at the other four.

'That lot are yours. If you want them.' She pointed rapidly round the room. 'This is Rebecca. That's Ruth, John, and Stevie.'

The children looked at me, aware something strange was happening. I looked back at them, taking them all in properly for the first time.

Rebecca was the oldest. A sweet looking seven-year-old, with long blonde hair, and a look of fearful rebellion. Social services were worried I would never get a connection with her because she was very traumatised. I saw she was holding a doll with a porcelain head and a long, grubby, old-fashioned dress.

'That's a pretty dolly, Rebecca. Will you show me?'

She stood still, too shy to step forward. Jackie spoke.

'Don't be rude now. Show the lady.'

Rebecca backed away, put the doll behind her.

'Rebecca!'

'No,' she said.

'You behave, young lady, or I'll tan your arse.'

Jackie meant what she said. Rebecca backed away further, bottom lip trembling.

'It's OK,' I said.

I saw the way she was clutching the doll to her chest.

'I really like your doll, Rebecca. She's so lovely. I've got one just like it at my house.'

A couple of months before, just after Christmas, all the sales had been on. I was in a shop, and I had been drawn to a pot doll. It was a Christmas doll of a young girl holding a lamp which lit up and the doll itself moved back and forth. It had been reduced in price and I couldn't take my eyes off it.

'I don't want this doll,' I thought. 'What would I do with it?'

Once again, I felt that prompting inside. I had known I was to buy this doll. Now I understood why.

'Do you know, Rebecca, my doll moves, and it lights up. Would you like me to bring it to show you next time I come?'

Rebecca thought about it, and then, slowly, gave me the slightest of nods.

'Then I will. You'll really like it.'

She smiled at me. It was like the sun coming out.

. . .

That day was when I made the first proper steps towards the children.

Ruth was four and she was totally lost. Still, shy, quiet. She was in a world of her own and I felt she could disappear into the wallpaper. It was obvious she felt no-one cared whether or not she was there.

John was three. He had stopped breathing for a time when he was being born and the social service reports worried about brain damage. He looked worse than I had expected, covered in eczema from head to toe. He was in a daze, and didn't speak, just made gruff noises. It was sad, and, in the truest sense of the word, pathetic. All the time I was there, he kept coming to stand by me. I put my arm around him. He was so slightly built it moved me deeply. All that afternoon, he looked at me and stood as close as he could get to me.

'I hate him,' said Jackie. 'He's covered in that rash, and he grunts.'

She was right. He couldn't speak at all, really. My heart melted for this lost little boy. I knew he had been taken to hospital several times recently, twice for food poisoning. My eyes fell on the full potty in the corner of the room, and I thought I understood why.

Stephen was the youngest and still very like a baby, although he was two years old. He was so thin and tiny I couldn't believe he was big enough to walk. He wore big baby clothes, which stretched and pulled at him as he tottered around.

She saw me looking at him and smiled.'

'Stevie's my little baby. He's the one I'd want to keep. If I had to.'

'You don't have to. Don't worry.'

I was trying to keep calm. Never in my life had I seen kids

so fearful. So lost. It was truly awful—but it made me determined to take them on.

I stayed for a couple of hours that first time. Before I left them, I couldn't last any longer. I had to go to the loo.

'Can I use your—?'

'Upstairs, facing the stairs, you can't miss it.'

Indeed, you couldn't. There wasn't a single door remaining in the house. I couldn't work out why, at first. Surely you couldn't sell doors. Then I remembered the open fireplace in the back room. They'd lived there for 18 months, so presumably they'd all been burned over the winter.

There was one door that I really did miss—the door to the bathroom. The filthy toilet faced straight down the stairs to the front door. If anyone had opened that door at an inopportune moment, I'd have been able to say hello to people at the bus stop.

The first thing I did when I got home was have a shower.

I couldn't stop thinking about each of the children.

All afternoon, Rebecca played with her doll.

All afternoon, Ruth just sat on my knee staring at me.

All afternoon, John stood by me, staring at me.

Stephen spent the afternoon on the floor, not sure what to make of it all.

Adoption felt like the biggest challenge of my life. But I had made that breakthrough with Rebecca. Surely the rest would follow.

47

The process of adoption had begun six months before.

The very first thing had been for me to meet with the social worker's boss. I had no idea that this was out of the ordinary, though I was surprised at how aggressively he questioned me.

He went over my house, he went through everything, and he was there for hours. It was a very heavy session, but I didn't know that was unusual.

At the end, he said, 'Can I apologise to you now?'

'Why?' I said.

'This isn't normal. I would never ever normally do this kind of interview. I'd told your social worker there was no way in a million years I'd let a single person take on these four children. Every time anyone else sees this family, they say 'No way.' So, they were going to have to be split up. But their case worker told me she wouldn't split them up until I'd met you. She can be very persistent! As it is, now we've spoken, I'm 99.9% sure you're the right person.'

I sat back, surprised, and very much relieved.

From then on, social services came to see us every month,

as they worked to get the adoptions through. There were a lot of problems because I was one of the first single mums to go through this.

The assessment process dug through my entire life until I had no secrets left. That's when I realised how much inner healing God had done. By the end of the assessment, social services knew everything about me. What I'd gone through as a child. What I'd gone through in my marriage. They'd been through the sexual side of my marriage, and all the reasons for its failure. They went through everything, and there was nothing they didn't ask.

I think they were amazed how whole I was after all that they found out. I knew that was down to my healing work with God, but I had to be so careful. I couldn't bring God into it. Common sense told me that if I'd said, 'God has given me a dream in which I was going to take four children', I wouldn't even be looked at.

Eventually, it was time for the first real-world introduction. This had led me to their foster house in Lincoln. Jackie was getting foster pay and doing very well on it. She'd already taken herself and her daughter off to America on the funds. I didn't like her at all; I could see what she was doing. But I had to make the pretence.

First of all, I went over to see them for a couple of Fridays. Then I had to visit them for an entire week every night after work.

The next stage was to stay for the whole of one Saturday. It deepened my understanding of what they were going through.

I had heard about the house where the birth parents lived. Social services had gone in three or four different times to clean the place out, but the parents had let it revert each time. All the furniture had been destroyed or sold for alcohol. It said many times in the reports that these children should have been removed, yet social services hadn't acted until very late in the day.

Jackie's house wasn't much better. The dirt was ingrained throughout, and I couldn't face eating anything from the kitchen, so I went hungry. There was no gate on the garden; the front went straight onto the main road. For these small children, it was very dangerous. I reported all this, but social services told me they had nowhere else to put them while they were looking for adoption. To me, it was bad enough that it felt like open abuse.

Every time I went to see the children, I took the pot doll. That did it with Rebecca, and so she let the other three children draw near me too. Rebecca was protective of her siblings. She had a different father to the others, and had experienced some terrible, abusive times with him. He vanished early on. The mother found another man, and they had the other three children together.

I got to hear some details about Rebecca's previous life. From the age of five, she'd had to beg for food. At 11.00pm at night, she'd be outside knocking on neighbours' doors because she was hungry.

Stephen had only been kept alive because the mother had put him to sleep in a cot with John; every now and again, John would shove a bottle in his mouth. In return, they often put John in a cupboard underneath the stairs.

Then there was Ruth. Sweet Ruth, who knew that attention from grownups brought pain, and so had learned to vanish from view so well that she had become an expert. Even I overlooked her at first.

I was told so much about the children, but not nearly as much as I should have been, and with the sheer chaos of their foster house, I didn't notice how damaged they were until later.

As well as the neglect from their birth family, they had been subject to a lot of other, much darker abuse.

Social Services were probably frightened to tell me everything in case I was put off. They privately considered them to be the most damaged children they'd had in twenty years. Every other family who had looked at them had refused them. I was their very last chance to stay together.

As the month went by, I got to take them home to my house for the day. We had a good, calm, peaceful time, and then, on the way back to Lincoln, the boys fell asleep in the car. When we got to their house, I carried them upstairs to pop them into bed. I'd never been allowed upstairs before, and I was sad to see how filthy the bedroom was. There were no covers on the quilts, there were old, threadbare curtains and damp on the walls, and the entire room was chaotic with clothes, papers and old food in mouldering piles across the floor.

Jackie showed me around their lives outside the house. I went to meet the teachers at their school and saw the places where they played. It was all strange, and I struggled to remember this was all really happening. I think I was in shock. I went through the motions of being polite and non-committal, but inside I was constantly thinking, 'Oh, my goodness me,' at each new insight.

Through it all, I noticed how the children connected with each other; how deeply they loved each other. They had been betrayed by those who should have cared for them, and now they were just lost. My heart went out to them. I couldn't help it. I felt so drawn to them it had to be from God.

Even now, whenever they doubt their own value, or whenever we go through difficult times as a family, I still say to them:

'Look, why did God tell me about you before you were born? He knew what you were going to go through. He knew what I was going to go through. But He told me there would be two girls and two boys. The girls were the eldest and the boys would be the youngest. There is no doubt that you were chosen.'

It was Ruth's birthday on the 12th of March. We had her birthday party at my house, so they'd get to know the place. The following week, they came to me for a weekend. After that, all the arrangements were put in place. Paul's first period with us ended, and we said goodbye. He went back to his family home and I wished him well and prayed blessings over his life.*

The four children came to me a few days later, on the 22nd March 1996. Stephen was two. John was three, Ruth was five, and Rebecca was seven.

* In fact, before too long, Paul would come back to live with us again. He stayed with us until he was 14.

48

The day I took them, Jackie gave me a fistful of black bin liners, full of their clothes.

When I put the bags in the car, I looked at the clothes. I saw they were just rags. That was OK. I already knew we'd have to ditch them all, and so I'd been shopping for them already.

Rebecca couldn't find a pair of shoes to wear, so Jackie threw her a pair of her own daughter's boots. Ruth's feet were crammed into shoes that were far too small, and her toes were bent and curled. John's shoes were ripped across the uppers, and Stephen's had paint all over them.

The moment of leaving was an anti-climax. We all stood in the narrow hallway, uncomfortable in the small space.

'See ya then, kids,' said Jackie. 'Be good.'

The children didn't reply. We all stood for a moment more, awkward, and silent, and then I took them down the path to the road. I put the children in the car and got in. I started the engine and looked around the car.

'Off we go.'

The children were unemotional. They just seemed to be relieved that they were going. There was no looking back.

It was about an hour's drive back, and they relaxed. As the miles passed, you could see their tension leave them, and the more eager they got. We got out into open country, and they got increasingly excited. By the time we got to Grimsby, they were bouncing up and down. It was lovely to see.

We went straight to my mum's house ('Grandma' as she would now insist on being called) where she'd cooked a meal for us. My auntie Rose was staying, and they had a big welcome planned, but we soon realised that would feel over the top. These children needed a gentle beginning; they were terrified of other people.

Mum and Rose were shocked at the clothes and the shoes they had come in, so I took them into town after the meal to kit them out. Social services gave me £200 clothing allowance, but the gap in expectation and reality became apparent when that didn't even pay for the shoes. I bought them a new pair of school shoes and some trainers each. The boys just screamed, absolutely petrified of somebody measuring their feet.

I took them to Woolworths to get pack up boxes for school. I'll never forget how proud Rebecca was to get this pack up box. She turned around to the lady and said, 'This is my new adopted Mummy.' She took my heart there and then.

Eventually, we took them to my house. They couldn't really believe this was going to be theirs, too. Rebecca and Ruth had their own rooms, which they loved. I'd had the garage made into a playroom. My friend had come and painted cartoons on it, and it overwhelmed the children. They were so happy they ended up getting everything together and throwing all the toys up in the air.

. . .

After I'd had the children a week, social services wanted me to meet all the birth parents. I thought about it and decided it was a good idea.

I had to go to the offices in Lincoln and I had to get there at a certain time. The three parents would come later, and I'd have two meetings.

My mum sat in the car outside with the children, while I sat in a waiting room, waiting to go in to meet the social worker. Eventually I saw them take a couple through.

After a while, they called me in, and we all sat in a small room together. I'd been worried about the meeting for the last couple of weeks, but when we got in the room, all that left me.

None of us knew what to say at first. The social worker gave us a little space before getting the meeting going, so I sat, and they sat, and we looked each other up and down. The two parents and me, the woman who wanted to adopt their children.

I saw the father was a stocky man, and his face was opaque. I couldn't read him, but I hadn't expected to; I'd been warned that he may not say much. The mother was very thin and petite. She looked almost as vulnerable as the children and obviously had additional educational needs. When I looked at the mother, all I could think about was how much I wanted to mother her. My urge to reach out to her and hug her was almost overpowering.

I held on to what the social worker had said to me:

'When you meet them, think about what they've done to their children.'

The mother kept a steady commentary going through the meeting.

'I like Pam, I like Pam.'

'Thank you,' I'd say.

She'd look at the social worker, and then her partner.

'I'm pleased. Pam's going to be looking after my children. I like Pam.'

'Thank you.'

'Do you live on a main road?'

'No, I don't.'

'Do you live in a cul-de-sac?'

'Yes, I do.'

'Oh, that's good. Have you got a garden?'

'Yes, I have got a garden.'

'Oh, that's good. I like Pam. I like Pam.'

She looked to her partner for reassurance, and he nodded.

After a while, she ran out of questions, and we all sat in silence. She smiled at me, and I smiled at her.

That was it, the end of our meeting. There was nothing else. No malice. Nothing more to be dealt with.

They agreed there would be a mailbox. They could write to me once or twice a year about the children. If they wrote to me, then I would reply through the social services and do my best to answer their questions. There was to be no other contact.

They did write for a few years and the children read what they had to say with some bemusement, but eventually the letters stopped, and the children forgot, and we all moved on.

When each child got to their eighteenth birthday, one last letter would arrive. A little apprehensive despite myself, I would approach the child about it.

'Look, your mother has asked to get in touch. Do you want to?'

Each of the children said 'No' with no hesitation or regret.

So, that was that. That previous life was ancient history,

long gone for each of them, and they were all the better for that.

The meeting with Rebecca's father was different. He had decided that he wanted her back. Social services told me that this couldn't happen because of his background, so, when I met him, it was without Rebecca. He was a stocky man, not tall, with a powerful air of aggression about him. He too had a refrain through the meeting, but it was different in character.

'Rebecca's mother will have told you all sorts about me and it'll be negative.'

'Well actually no,' I said. 'She hasn't mentioned you.'

That made him think and I could see I'd made him angry. I wished I had been more tactful.

'Well, I want to see her when she's eleven.'

'You can't,' said the social worker.

'What do you mean? She's my daughter. It's my right to see her when she's eleven.'

'I really don't think it is,' she said.

He leaned over the table and jabbed his finger at the social worker.

'You go and sort this out, love, OK? I've been thinking about this for a long time.'

They argued for a while until the social worker got angry. 'This is no good. We must get this checked out. I need to talk to our lawyer.'

She got up.

'But—' I said. She had told me I wouldn't be left alone with him.

'I won't be long,' she said, and then she was gone. She even shut the door behind her, which she shouldn't have done.

The man shifted in his seat. He was obviously uncomfortable. He probably didn't want to be in there with me. I eyed him. I was alone with a volatile man who clearly didn't like me. I was, in his mind, the only reason he was losing all access to his own daughter. It wasn't safe, and yet, under it all, he had such a beaten air that, for a moment, I couldn't help feeling for him.

He started in again.

'I bet her mum's been slagging me off.'

'I tell you what,' I said. 'While we're waiting. Give me something good about yourself. Something I can tell Rebecca later in her life.'

'What do you mean? I'll be seeing her soon.'

'Something she'd like to hear about you.'

'Well ... I ... What do you mean?'

'Something she can be proud of.'

He thought for a moment. He was shocked that he couldn't think of anything.

'I mean, I ...' he said, getting nowhere.

'It doesn't have to be much.'

'Yeah, alright, I know I've done nowt.'

'I didn't mean it like that. I mean, she just wants to hear something good.'

I watched him think.

'What have you been doing lately? Is there anything there she might like to hear about?'

'Not that I can think of.' His laugh was a bitter rasp. 'Typical me, isn't it?'

He fell silent.

'How's it going with work?'

'Can't stand it,' he said.

More silence.

'What about the way you feel about her?'

'I've been bad to her,' he said. 'That's why I want to see her, don't you get it?'

'That's a start.'

'It's not enough though, is it?'

'There must be something.'

'Can't think of owt. Why do you care so much, anyway?'

It went on like that for a long time. I stopped feeling vulnerable and felt more and more for him. Surely in the whole of his life there was something he thought good about himself. I tried to encourage him, but in all those twenty minutes we sat together, he couldn't think a single thing about himself that was positive.

The social worker came back in the end, having checked with the solicitor, and indeed there was no chance the man was going to contact Rebecca. It was nothing to do with me, and there was nothing I could have done to change it. That decision was based on a high-level legal process that considered this man a serious risk to his own daughter.

I reflected on this later, and many times through the coming years. How is it that parents can inflict such ill on their own children? It's so far from God's design for the family, and yet it goes on endlessly.

The meeting ended, and I was finally free to go, but it was difficult. The parents all had to leave the building before me, and I had to stay behind until we had word from the police that the parents had left the area. The danger was that someone would follow me and find out where I lived. It was the most surreal experience and left me feeling like a criminal.

Of course, it was the right thing to do. Of course, we couldn't take any chance they might follow me home. They couldn't ever know where I lived because we had to protect the children. Unwelcome approaches, even abduction, weren't unknown. But hiding away like that brought out the enormity, the severity of what I was doing. As I sat waiting in a corner of the office, all I could think about was how much my life was changing, and what an immense responsibility I was taking on.

I say 'I'. In fact, my mother was to be deeply involved. I knew I could rely on her to help, and that was amazing. Of course, there was also God, who I trusted even more. Many is the time I've been pulled up for saying 'we' when all people can see is me acting on my own. Mostly when I say 'we' I mean me and God, with me doing my best to work as God's hands and feet in whatever's going on.

Those two meetings in the social services office in Lincoln were the last times I ever saw any of the birth parents. All these years later, I realise how that was probably yet another helping hand from God. Grimsby and Cleethorpes are only really forty miles away from Lincoln, and Cleethorpes is a well-known seaside resort. It was entirely possible the parents would come over to the East Coast for a day on the beach, but, in all the years, I never worried when I was out in public. If I'm honest, I never really thought I'd see any of them. Then, if ever I was concerned, all I had to do was to focus on my dream. God had asked me to do this, so I was clear He would protect us. The children were in His hands. Where could they be safer?

The very last encounter with the children's past life came after they had been with me six weeks. The social worker wanted me to take them back to meet the foster parents again. I knew how it had been for them, but even so they had lived there for eighteen months, so I expected there would have been some attachment and they'd be pleased to go back. How wrong I was. From the moment I mentioned that we'd be going over there, the fear returned to them. It built and built over the day, and the drive over was silent. As we went into the house, they all fought to cling on to me. What was surprising, and most affecting, was the way Stephen looked at me, with a mute look of betrayal. He was two, and far too young to know what was going on, but the terror he expressed when we went into the back room of the house was unforgettable. We lasted an hour, and then we left. I drove back to Grimsby, angry with myself for having let myself be talked into it.

I called the social worker,

'Right, that's it. They're never going back there.'

We never saw Jackie again. I heard she took on two more boys, and that didn't work out. After that, she was barred from taking on any more children.

49

So, it was over to us. (Me, my mother, and God.) They came to me in the March, and we started school with the girls after the Easter. We gave ourselves to them completely in those first few weeks before they started school. We took them out every single day because I wanted to fill their minds with good new memories.

Social services told me later that I was one of the first single people in the country to adopt a sibling group of four, and that I was charting unknown waters. Whether that is true, I don't know, but we certainly had an eventful beginning as we learned just how far we could go with them. One of the first jobs was a proper haircut for them all. We took them to the hairdresser and discovered that they were all terrified. They wouldn't let her touch them. It took ages to get them used to the idea, as all they'd known so far was Jackie dragging razors through their hair.

I had to be so careful about taking them anywhere else, because these kids were so fearful, and were for a very long time. If I sat down on a chair, all four of them would be on top of me. If I had anyone else there, they would be petrified and hang on to me, clinging to me, all four of them.

In the very first week, Mum and I took them to Sargent's Ice Cream café at Hibaldstow Park. It was a new park, with slides and swings, and I thought they'd done it beautifully, so I was sure the children would enjoy the afternoon.

Not so. They were too frightened to come on the swing. Too frightened to go down the slide. All we could manage was for them to sit on my knee and me hold them. We'd swing gently, I'd hold them, and they'd scream. People must have thought I was so cruel, but I knew it was something we had to go through. All I could do was reassure them. We'd swing, gently, and I'd talk into their ear, soothing as best I could.

'It's fine. Look, it's good. It's nice. You're OK. I've got you.'

It wasn't just the swings. Sometimes it felt as though I had to do that gentle introduction with them over every single thing. I've never seen children so terrified. They were frightened of animals, frightened of people, frightened of everything. It was just a terrible time for them. And, if I'm honest, it wasn't good for me either. I was up every hour of the night with John for nearly six months. I had to constantly reassure him I was still there. I prayed over them every night. I'd wait until they got to sleep and go into their rooms and pray in the Spirit over them. I did that every single night, right through into their teens. Then, after I'd prayed for them, I would pray for myself.

One early misadventure came during an afternoon at a horse show-ground in the countryside outside Grimsby. You could get in among the horses and stroke them. Again, with gentle coaxing, and leading by example, the children learned to overcome their fears. The horses worked their calming influence, and I was so happy. Before we left, the children were stroking the animals as though they were old friends and I felt like we'd made a breakthrough. The afternoon ended. We got in the car and set off for Grimsby. By the time we were halfway home, John had begun to wriggle and scratch. By the time we got home to the house, John's hands, arms, and face were a livid red, and it seemed like his whole body was swollen. He was still covered in eczema, but none of us had known he had an allergy to horses as well. We called the doctor, and he sorted him out that day, and we worked together to understand what was causing his conditions. We changed his diet and put him on goat's milk, and all the skin trouble became manageable.

We went on trying with petting zoos, especially when Ruth decided on a horse-riding experience for her birthday. I dosed John up on antihistamines and swaddled him in a coat, gloves and balaclava. It was a success, and he made it through to the very end of the afternoon before any irritation began. We eventually found out that it was cats, and horses of a certain colour, that would trigger the allergies.

After a period of looking for less eventful places in the outside world, I listened to the voices telling me that the children really needed to find their feet at home before they would ever properly enjoy going out into the world. I installed swings and a climbing frame and other playground toys in the garden. I went on until I practically had an entire park in a house, including a roundabout. The kids loved it; it felt safe to them, but it introduced them to the idea of running around and making a noise with no criticism. It did them all the world of good because it attracted a lot of other children from school, and so they made friends.

Working on their fears was the dominant theme through those early months, and the damage they had been dealt cast a very long shadow, surfacing even when I thought it had been long beaten. (I'll never forget the effect of a giraffe poking his nose through the car window at a safari park!)

It wasn't all hard work though, and soon we were all heading in the right direction. A little while after the children had arrived with me, the social worker came to the house. As I walked her through to the kitchen, we could hear the children upstairs. They were running around and playing. She turned to me in surprise.

'Who the heck is making all that noise?'

'It's Ruth,' I said.

'No way. Ruth doesn't speak.'

'She does now.'

By then Ruth was chattering away like any other happy child. It shows how the system can condemn someone wrongly. In the minds of some of the social service workers, Ruth was going to have special educational needs. But after a month or so, probably at around the time that the children realised I meant what I said, and that I wasn't going anywhere, and they really all were welcome to stay forever, both Ruth and John came fully alive for what was possibly the first time.

Mum often said to me she believed I had all those confirmations from different people about taking the children on, because if I ever questioned what I was doing, then I'd always know that God was in it. But actually, I've never questioned this path. All the way through, I've been aware that this was something that God had asked me to do. I couldn't deny it after those dreams.

Financially, the allowance was far lower than that given for fostering, but they made sure that I was well looked after. I didn't need to worry about working. I think they knew how troubled these children were. They said they didn't want me to have the worry of looking after a vehicle, so they gave me a car until they were 18. Social Services knew what I was taking on, but they never told me it all.

I know we were all on an unusual path, because the situation was novel enough for Cambridge University to follow us until all the children were 18. They'd come every few years and interview me. Everyone thought we'd have a lot of problems and one or more of the children would leave home and end up back in care. It was interesting to see how things went on the record. We were the biggest success story they'd ever had.

50

I got the girls into school, and then we gradually got John into nursery. Stephen was at home and my mum was a big part of looking after him. She thought the world of him. She was very present throughout and was my absolute backup in my battles with the schools.

Which were getting more frequent than I wanted. After a time, when we realised Rebecca and Ruth were getting short-changed, I suspected the teachers weren't taking them seriously. The unspoken attitude was that they were just foster children, they won't be here long, so there's no need to bother.

This was a flashpoint for more than one heated interview at the school. I found myself fully able to take on anyone for the children's welfare. I'd come through so much inner healing, and I was growing in confidence. I wasn't being an overprotective parent. These kids—my kids—had gone through hell, been abandoned, suffered trauma after trauma. But that was over, and I was there for them now. They were no longer just foster children; they were my adopted children, and from now on I would make sure they got the best treatment possible, so look out world. We all settled down, and built bridges, and the school was brilliant and supportive in the end.

The church was the real breakthrough. The body of Christ welcomed my new family, in a genuine, deeply practical expression of Jesus' command to 'Let the little children come to me, and do not hinder them, for the kingdom of heaven belongs to such as these.'

However, I'd been brought up as a Pentecostal and we'd always been in the Pentecostal church. At this time, however, the Pentecostal Church wasn't keeping the children once they got to around the age of twelve, and I so much wanted the children to be grounded in God's Word. There was another complication, in that I didn't agree with how they tried hard to get children baptised and filled with the Holy Spirit. I felt some of the kids were too young to realise what they were doing. That's certainly only my opinion. In some places it might be OK, but I'm not sure about children like these four, who had suffered such damage and were still very much healing and forming their own identities. I had to be careful to act in their best interests—especially when social services were going to be involved for quite some time until the adoption was made final.

But I knew I wanted them grounded in the Word. It was important to me they had the Word inside them. Also, I knew the Baptists were excellent with the Bible, and had fantastic children's work. So, after a lifetime in Elim Church, I changed my denomination. I left the Pentecostals, and I went to the local Baptist church.

It soon became clear that the minister there at the time was a lovely guy and a real family man. I thought the world of him and his wife. They were all so good. As soon as they saw me arrive with these four children, he threw his arms wide-open. I had to smile. They were absolutely petrified, but I was sure that in the face of such warmth, no fear could last too long.

I was half right. They wouldn't go into Sunday school on their own. In fact, for a long time, they wouldn't do anything on their own. The pattern was for the church to have their service first, then the preacher would give his talk. At that point, the kids would go out to Sunday school. Not my four. They would often literally hang onto me. The pastor soon spotted this and changed his pattern. Before he got on the pulpit, he would come directly to me. He made a fuss of the kids and gave them all a hug. Then he'd go on the pulpit. After he came off the pulpit, he used to come back to me before he'd go to meet anybody at the door. He'd get hold of the two boys, one in each arm, and hold them tight. Pretty soon, they loved him. Even at the end of the service, as he was standing at the door saying goodbye to people, they would cling to him.

He did that every single Sunday for a long time. It was the best thing anybody could have done for me because trusting him got them used to church as well. One major attraction was the church puppet team. They'd stage little shows—and sometimes quite big shows. The kids got more and more involved, until they were going to puppet group every week, and another children's club. Eventually, the kids got fully involved, and the place became like a second home to them.

Slowly, they trusted people, and slowly their hearts healed. They became calmer, more confident, and their own personalities shone through, until more courage from them led us down some very unexpected paths.

51

The first drop of water on my arm surprised me.

It was a baking hot day in June, and the grass was parched. The bushes were deep green, leaves covered with a fine layer of dust. The sun was high in the clear sky, and the children were away up the garden, playing on their swings near the house. All round the neighbourhood came the voices of children, out playing in the sun. The boys at the bottom of the garden next to me were having a lot of fun, running and shouting as usual. They were a little older than my two boys, but I'd been thinking for a long time they'd all get together and play. It hadn't happened yet, but I lived in hope.

I wiped the water off and carried on weeding the border.

There was a strange pattering behind me that came and went. I ignored it. I wanted to get the border done.

'Mum. Mum!'

It was Stephen's voice, and he was scared. I turned to look, and he gesticulated up. I looked to see a spattering of spray arcing high in the air, coming from the next-door garden and tracing a path all across our grass.

The boys next door were yelling frantically now, and I could hear water spray. I stood on tiptoe and looked over the fence. Of course. They were all running around armed to the teeth with giant green, red and blue super soaker water guns. As I watched, loose shooting sent another jet of water flying up, up and over our heads and onto our grass.

Something of the young woman who planted the cardboard skeleton all those years before came back. I ran up the garden to the back of the house and the outside tap. I got hold of the hosepipe and, surrounded by puzzled children, I put my fingers on my lips.

'Shhhhh.'

I turned the tap on full. I winked at the children, pointed the jet to the floor, and headed for the fence.

'Mum—what are you doing?' asked Rebecca.

'Shhhh,' I said and pointed upwards.

Sure enough, another spray of water came over into our garden.

I grinned at them all.

'Shall we?'

'No Mum, No, you can't, you can't ...'

'Oh, I think I can,' I said.

Putting my finger over the end of the hosepipe, I directed a giant spray of water up, up into the air high above the middle of next door's garden.

There was a sudden silence that made my children quake—and then came the noise.

Screams of outrage, lots of shouting, and so much laughter.

My children looked at each other, apprehensive. What had their mum just done?

Then it came. Four different super soaker jets of water, all flying over the fence and onto us.

Stephen yelled, John yelled, Ruth yelled, and Rebecca said,

'Go on mum.'

So, I did.

I pressed my finger tight over the nozzle and sent the hosepipe jet up high and far back over the fence. I must have hit someone full on because there was an awful lot of yelling and laughing.

Before I knew what was happening, another super soaker jet had come back over and caught me full on.

Laughing fit to burst, I turned to look at my children, and I couldn't believe what was happening. John and Stephen were absolutely petrified. They charged at me and were clinging to me.

'Mummy, Mummy, are you hurt?'

'I'm not hurt.'

'They're hurting you.'

'They're not, really they're not.'

I shushed them, gently. I'd had an idea.

Some might have called it 'a reckless escalation'.

I called it 'brilliant'.

I looked at each of the children. Slowly, gravely, I asked, 'Do you think we should fill the buckets?'

'Nooooo.' 'Please Mummy.' 'Please don't.' 'I'm scared.'

They wouldn't let go, and I was thwarted. Under constant bombardment from the garden artillery next door, I had to put the hosepipe down and usher them back inside. Such it is, being a mum. I've never quite forgotten the disappointment—we could have had such a water fight. We only had one jet to next-door's four, but they had to stop to keep reloading and we had two buckets. It's only reasonable to think that we would have won hands down.

. . .

In many unpredicted ways, like a scary water fight, children grow. Most obviously, despite the way they had seemed out of their comfort zone, in the days and weeks after that afternoon, all of them seemed just a little more capable of cutting loose, all the more capable of having simple fun.

This change was most unpredictable for John. After the water fight, he developed a fascination for water. Four years old, he'd started nursery school that term. I'd pick him up from school and every day there'd be a little bag with his clothes in it. He'd be playing with the water fountain. Or he'd wet himself. Or, if there'd been a puddle, he'd gone into that. There was always something.

One day, a teacher came up to me. Her lips were thin lines, and her eyes were cold accusations. She presented me with the usual bag of his clothes.

'I can't believe this one,' she said.

'Go on?' I smiled, but she wouldn't join me.

'I can't believe—none of us can believe—what he's done this time.'

'OK?'

She hesitated, struggling for words. She looked around her to make sure no-one was close enough to hear and leaned into me. Her voice was low, urgent. It was obviously very important that I understood the gravity of the situation.

Despite myself, I leaned in. This sounded good.

'His back was all wet, so we asked him to show us what he'd done.'

Fair enough, I thought. John didn't speak at all at that time, so that was about the best way to get the information.

'So, we said, "John, how did you wet yourself this time? How did you get your back all wet?" He took us into the boys' toilets. There was a urinal and of course he was fascinated by it. So, he showed us what he'd done.'

She stopped, struggling to contain her disgust.

'John had *sat down in it*, and it had *flushed on him*.'

She was so straight faced. I just wanted to laugh.

'It nearly flushed again while he was showing us. And when it finished. He looked like he wanted it to happen again. Why, oh why, is this boy so fond of water?'

I had to get round the corner while I could keep a straight face. I took the bag of clothes, took John home, and told the children what their brother had been up to. We laughed and laughed.

The old, scared, shy me was going fast, and I was becoming a different person. Completely different. I was coming into my own. The kids were my responsibility, and I wouldn't let anybody get in the way.

John had another memorable day a little later when we went to Lincoln Crown Court to finalise the adoption. The children were so excited. It was a small thing for the English legal system, a huge thing for us. In the room were just the judge and social services, me, my mum, and the four children. There was no opposing barrister; the process was a simple rubber-stamping. It had taken three years of constant inspections and many challenges, but we were there. All the birth certificates were changed, and everything got in line. It was complete, and final, and irreversible.

After such a long road, it was quite a surreal day, most vividly represented by the Judge sitting John up on his chair and putting his wig on his head for the photographs afterwards. We celebrated well. MacDonalds (of course) after the court, then a fortnight in Florida Disney.

• • •

I had been saving so long for this one, and we had such a good time. But even there, things weren't plain sailing. The fireworks at Disney were loud, the characters in their costumes were scary. The girls were more or less OK with it all, but the boys seemed scared again. I had to work hard with the Disney characters to show them they were OK.

It wasn't until we got home that I realised a deep truth. The adoption being settled, the holiday in Florida, all was wonderful, and yet in some ways, nothing had been resolved. When we looked at the videos of the fireworks, there were shots of the children in the background, all screaming, all terrified.

These videos gave me pause for thought. Even in the middle of this happy family holiday, there was fear. I realised the path to healing was long, perhaps longer than I had ever imagined.

Overall, we were three years in, and it was going well. They all had private tuition to help bring them on, and it was all going well. Also, they had such a lovely relationship with each other. They were so very caring. John would always look after Stephen. Even if I was taking them swimming, you'd see them both holding each other's hands, walking down the side of the pool. It wasn't just for each other. If somebody fell over in the playground, those boys would stop everything they were doing and make sure that a teacher had gone to them. They were really sweet, and very caring.

Another funny moment was when the school called me and asked me whether I knew John had been giving money to other children at school. I wasn't, but it made sense. I had suspected that money was going missing from the house. I'd have cash set aside for bills, and I slowly realised there was less there than I thought there was. John eventually confessed. They had been reading 'Ali Baba and the 40 Thieves' at school and it had been given to them with a heavy moral message: it's good to steal from the rich to give to the poor. Realising that he came from a family that wasn't struggling financially, John had taken it on himself to carry this out. He enlisted Stephen, and the two of them had been acting as a secret force for good by redistributing their mother's money.

There were low moments too, of course there were. On the day we walked out of that Lincoln courtroom, and they were fully adopted, social services ended all their support. Fair enough, they had more work than they could cope with, and I was deemed strong enough and capable enough to manage on my own from then. I did manage, but there were low moments. What they didn't tell me back then—because they didn't tell anyone back then—was that the great majority of adoptions were failing at that time. *

I remember one time I was in social services just before the final decision, and I was telling them how hard I was finding it. They just looked at me in surprise, and said,

'You're doing so well! Look at how the kids are coming on.'

'So why is it taking so long? Don't you trust me?' I said.

'It's because you're one of the first single parents in England to do this. That's made all sorts of headaches as a kick-off. Then Rebecca's dad's been contesting literally everything. What's more, people don't normally get adoption allowances, so working out the financial package to free you as a single parent has been a right old battle.'

That surprised me no end. I genuinely had no idea, and

---

* I was told by an insider in later years that around 75% of adoptions failed at that time. This sounds incredible, and was certainly not common knowledge, but a friend and her husband who also adopted two children around the same time were eventually told the same thing.

their commitment to getting me through was a conversation I revisited many times in the years to come.

52

My single moment of deepest darkness in my life is when my mum died.

My dad had died when he was 60, just before my mum was 70. She was nine years older than my dad, and she survived him another five years. During those years she had come to life, realising that so much more of the world was OK than she had ever realised.

The bad news came in the first year I was fostering, just nine months after Dad died. Mum loved spending time with the children. It was all like a different world to her. She suddenly found that she depended on me a lot—her close friends had moved away, and she still had the battles about how being a pastor's wife always put a barrier in with people.

There was no clearer sign of her rebirth than the fact that she discovered she liked to go to the cinema. She would sit there with her bag of sweets like an eager child and laugh all the way through the film. So many times at the end she would turn to me in surprise and happiness.

'There's nothing wrong with this, is there?'

'No, Mum, there isn't. It's all good. We can come back every week if you like.'

And yet, in the middle of this rebirth, God was quick to frame it all. She had five years to herself, but she lived four of them in the clear shadow of death.

That first December I put on a big party for her 70th. She'd never ever had a party. And I staged it like 'This is Your Life'. It was a great big thing. She absolutely loved it. She'd had nothing like that. In fact, she'd never had anything, bless her.

Then she had been invited to go on holiday to the USA by her cousin. I was so pleased that she had said yes. It was such a sign of how free she was feeling. A trip like that would have been unthinkable while Dad was alive.

A couple of weeks after her 70th party, just before she was due to go, she found a lump in her breast. She went for all sorts of investigations and scans, and they told her it was cancer.

She had treatment, drugs of some sort. She went back after six months, and it was clear things weren't working. But they thought they could avoid surgery if they kept the drugs going for another six months. Was that a mistake? Or was God certain of what He wanted all along? Either way, after the six months, things were worse. The drugs hadn't worked, and the cancer had spread.

One of her lifelong fears was amputation. And that's exactly what she had to have in the end. They gave her a mastectomy, yet it was too little, too late. The cancer had got into her lymph nodes, got into everywhere.

She was ill, and we knew it was deadly serious, and yet things settled down. There was so much to be done every day, and that amount of distraction took her mind off her physical illness and was a great help for her.

A year into her illness, I began the process of adoption and then Rebecca, Ruth, John and Stephen came to live with me. Mum saw me going through all this roller coaster and was overwhelmed.

I knew she could be very emotional when the children were around, and assumed it was related to her illness, so it was a shock when I found out there was another reason.

After one day I found her crying, I sat her down and asked her what I could do to help. She talked for an age, and I finally understood. She was sad about her cancer, of course she was. It was an ever-present cloud of fear. But what pressed her harder was seeing how the four children clung to me like they did.

I didn't understand this, and my first reaction was to get angry. How could she be so selfish? But that's not what she was saying. We talked some more, and she expressed a deep truth that had been half hidden, even to her.

'Seeing you and those four? It's too much. I can't cope with it, Pam.'

'Why, Mum? You know I'll always be there for you. I'll never stop doing that—I'm just a bit busy at the moment.'

'It's not that.'

Her eyes filled with tears again and she struggled to speak. I watched, confused. I gave her a hug in the end.

When she'd stopped crying, the explanation finally stuttered out.

'You never had. This. Love. Not like this. Not from. Me.'

'That's OK, Mum. Times were different—'

'—It's not OK. It's not. I let you down. I can't believe

you've got so much love to give to them. How do you do it? How have you got so much?'

'Mum, they've got to have it. They need it.'

'I know. I know. It's so hard sometimes ...'

Her voice trailed away, but I knew what she was saying. She wasn't jealous. She was feeling a failure. I'd never had that kind of love from her or from anybody, and she couldn't understand, or believe, how much love I had to give my own children.

Children are pure and they knew nothing of this. They just loved her. Stephen, in particular, grew very attached to her. They had such a good, simple, loving relationship.

Slowly her heart softened, and she stopped blaming herself. She asked God to forgive her, and she opened up. She embraced the whole situation and went through a big healing as she realised it was OK to love people.

One evening towards the middle of these five years, I was at a Businessman's Christian Fellowship evening. Once a month, I'd pay one of the church elder's wives to come and babysit on Monday evening. That evening was the only time I ever had any time away from the children. I didn't know many there as people came from all over, and so I felt I could just be me. Plus, because it wasn't just a local thing, I knew I was getting something fresh.

This one night, a man came up to me at the end and started prophesying over me.

'Pam,' he said. 'I've got a word from the Lord for you. I think God is saying, "Don't be fearful. You are not to worry about the future."'

Bear in mind, he was saying this when Mum was very ill.

'God will give you a warning every time anything's wrong,'

he said. 'Just like you get a warning light in a car to say that you haven't put your seatbelt on, or you need petrol.'

The most amazing thing is that has been true. Through all these years, I'll always know in the Spirit if something's not quite right.

53

Mum lasted four years after being diagnosed. As a nurse, she was very proud. She wouldn't let me get any help in until the very end.

When she got very ill, I had the children to look after too, but I also had this lovely couple as friends who helped me so much. The lady helped to run the Mums and Tots group in the back of the Baptist church. She was absolutely outspoken and absolutely lovely. Because I had four young children, she'd come and sleep in my house for me while I stayed with Mum. I would make sure the kids were in bed and then go to Mum's. I'd be there first thing in the morning, see them off to school, and I was back to my mother's again for the rest of the morning.

It seemed for a while that Mum wouldn't accept any outside help, no matter how ill she got, but as things progressed, she did finally let me help her more.

Three weeks before she died, she ended up in bed all day. It was only then that she'd let me get anyone in. She had to have oxygen in her room. By the end, she couldn't even use a commode. It was awful.

I told Aunt Rose how bad she was, and Rose came up to be with her. I secretly hoped she might help me a little, but she had hardly been with us five minutes before she went down with bronchitis herself. That was a hard time. I put her in one bedroom, and I had my mother in another. I spent the day running up and down stairs, feeding them, nursing them, sitting with them when they needed company. It was a powerful time for them both, reunited at such a time. Every day was precious, and Rose suffered almost as much as Mum as she watched her sister slip away.

It got so I was up all night with Mum. I was exhausted, but the people in the church were fantastic. Knowing I had no time for them, they just left meals on the doorstep for us all. I had these four children as well, and I had to keep life as normal as I could for them.

Mum's breathing got worse and worse until the battle was almost more than she could bear. I had to fight the hospital to have a device put in her stomach so that we could press a button whenever she needed morphine. They weren't keen at the beginning, and it was a battle that went on, because it became more obviously needed as time went by.

Two weeks before she died, she wouldn't let go of my hand. Even before I went to the loo, I had to ask Rose (when she wasn't coughing from her own bronchitis) to put her own hand in Mum's to keep her from distress.

The device for her stomach, to let us administer the morphine, finally arrived one evening, and I realised they were changing their message to me completely. The doctor took me aside and told me,

'When you feel she needs it, just give it to her.'

That was not the most helpful thing he could have said.

'Oh, my gosh,' I thought. 'Every time I press this button, I could kill her. How am I supposed to know when she's had too much?'

'Has anybody spoken to you about what to expect?' he said.

I looked at him. He was a nice man. Gentle, and doing his best. But he was on one side of a gulf, and I was on the other. No matter how many times he had done this work, he'd never be there with me.

'She'll go peacefully,' I said, fierce in my distress. After all, she was a devout Christian, so how else could things end? The Lord would take her gently. What else could happen?

'It may be like that,' said the doctor, 'but she may be climbing the walls.'

I tried not to listen. He wasn't a man of God, so he was sure to have that wrong.

The next day she died exactly like he said. It was a gruesome death, which lives with me still. I heard afterwards that she wouldn't have been in pain, that it would have been all hallucinations, and her anguish would have been reactions to the oxygen and the drugs. Whether that's true, I don't know.

The doctor said to me she wouldn't be aware of what she was doing. All I know is I can still see her trying to get her breath. She'd gasp, and gasp, and gasp, constantly raising her herself up off the bed, pushing herself up as hard as she could go against the bedhead, constantly rising up against the wall. Time and time again, for hour after hour. It was awful. It was gruesome. I wouldn't wish that on anyone. And I couldn't understand why God made it happen like that. It was so hard to see her go through it.

Even worse, she'd always talked about what her father had gone through with his cancer. She'd sat with him when he was dying, and it had been immensely painful for her. She had feared it for the rest of her life, and now, at her life's end, it had happened to her.

One particular scripture would not leave me:

'What I feared has come upon me; what I dreaded has happened to me.' (Job 3:25 NIV)

I've read somewhere that you have fifteen seconds once a fear has come upon you to defeat it before it takes hold. This makes sense because the Apostle Paul says we must:

'...take captive every thought to make it obedient to Christ' (2 Corinthians 10:5 NIV).

Certainly, ever since seeing my lovely mum in this awful place, I've done my best to conquer all my fears by giving them to Jesus at the very moment they come upon me. I don't always manage it, and I know I can still feel fear, but I can try my very hardest not to act out of fear. In fact, sometimes I deliberately do things because I'm scared of them. I will not have my fears come upon me.

It was just at Christmas when she went. She had her 75th birthday on Sunday the 12th of December 1999. They had a visiting speaker at the church, and he came to our house to pray prayers of intercession for her. He stayed a while, but he was weeping as he came out of her room, and I never found out why.

She died two days later, on Tuesday the 14th, at twenty past four in the morning, and we buried her on Friday the 17th. It happened so quickly because I didn't want the funeral to go into Christmas. Christmas was for the kids, and I had to protect that.

The funeral really affected me. Far more than my dad's funeral.

My brother Phil came down, and many local people came.

CHAPTER 53

The two girls came with me to the church and then they went back home, and we adults went on to the cemetery. I didn't feel it was right for the boys to go; I thought they were too young.

I felt God at this time. It was amazing: people appeared from nowhere. When it was time for the wake, people rallied around and provided food for us all, and handled the entire event.

I was a wreck. I was so close to breaking. Mum was my best friend. She was everything. I felt so lost, really lost.

My friend Chris walked through it all with me as an intercessor. She and her husband were brilliant.

Then we had to face Christmas itself. Again, the people around me were wonderful. Every year I'd collect Christmas presents for the kids, and we'd store them in the boarded-out loft in my mother's house. Every year on Christmas Eve, there was a tradition that the neighbours in the cul-de-sac would get together and walk over to Mum's house. I'd already have the presents wrapped, so the neighbours would get all the Christmas presents down from the loft and, once the kids had gone to sleep, bring them over to my house. It was lovely. My mum had a big part in it all. The fact the neighbours got together to do it again without being asked nearly knocked me down—I was in awe at how good people were.

Christmas came and went, and I coped, and it was fun enough for the children even though they badly missed their grandma, but by the time we got to New Year's Day, I was struggling. I had a friend round for the afternoon, and I couldn't pretend to cope any more.

'Would you just sit with the kids for half an hour?' I asked.

I walked round to my mother's bungalow and went into the room where she had died. It was still all furnished. Everything was still there, all her clothes, all the knick-knacks on the window ledge. A pair of her shoes lay under the bed. I couldn't stand it. She was my closest friend. She was everything to me.

I felt an upwelling in my stomach, like a nausea filling my stomach, filling every part of me. I had to let it go. I began to moan, and groan, and then I began to shout, and howl, and soon I began to scream. I roared with grief. I bent double, and fell to my knees, and fell to the floor in the end. Throughout, I was screaming and screaming and screaming.

It lasted half an hour, and then I was done. It was what I needed to do.

I got rid of what was left of her things, which is something you should never have to do. All those things are too much in the end. The number of decisions you have to make as you dismantle a life is agonising. Philip lived a long way away, and so it all fell on me. I felt the weight of our family history—almost literally, as all Dad's books were still there. He'd even had an organ, which we had to work out what to do with.

The big surprise for me was how hard it was to be in church. If I'd been asked before, I'd have said that I expect it to be a comfort to be with my church family. Not in this case. I just couldn't be in there. I wondered whether the enemy was using this attack to separate me from prayer and worship, but I don't think it was that. It was simply that the open hearts and loving nature of all those people asking how I was, looking at me with compassion, seeing me as I truly was—weak, broken, in pieces—was just too affecting. It threatened to open me up too widely, and I feared losing my composure completely. It may have been pride, but I couldn't bear the thought of breaking down in public. I still took the children along, and I could just about cope well enough to get through the worship music. But as soon as the children went into the Sunday school, that was my cue to clear off to my friend's house.

I kept close to God in that time, but for six months that was how I handled church.

The children coped, each in their own way.

Rebecca cried and recovered, all very straightforward.

Over the autumn leading up to my mum dying, we'd had a lot of problems with Ruth. She had hated how ill Grandma was, and it had come out in issues at school. She was so close to Grandma that I thought I was going to have real problems with her after she died. But when she heard the news, she just said to me 'I've got to be a good girl now', and she was. All the problems went away.

John didn't seem so affected. He still wasn't talking, so he just grunted.

It was Stephen who surprised me. In the middle of all the trauma, he was as quiet as a mouse. This didn't seem too strange; he was a very quiet little boy. He had spent a lot of time with Grandma because she'd take him off on the bus and they would go off for trips together, but he seemed more or less fine. Until one day in early January when the school rang and told me he had flooded the boy's toilets.

I assumed it was an accident, but it emerged that he had asked another little boy how to do it. That boy had showed him how to block the drains, and all the toilets, with toilet roll. That showed a premeditation that shocked the school and worried me. He was clearly far more distressed than I had realised. I looked back over the last few months and realised what had gone wrong.

I saw the head teacher. She was kind, but she was

concerned. Something like this was completely out of character for him. Something had to be going on at home.

I nodded.

'I know why he's done this. It's to do with my mother's death. It's because I didn't allow him to go to the funeral. Would you let me have him off school for a week or so? So I can help him heal?'

She agreed, and he came out of school, and he and I had some deep talks together. I soon found that I was right. He hadn't seen the funeral, and so he couldn't grasp what had happened. He was having terrible ideas about the event that weren't true and were frightening him.

I realised he wanted to go through the whole thing. I began by taking him to see the funeral cars and told him how they had driven through the streets carrying Granny in a coffin. Next, he wanted to see a coffin, so I had to take him down to the crematorium. Then I took him to the grave in the cemetery and I held his hand as we looked at all the flowers.

It took a couple of days in all, and my heart hurt as I watched his earnest face trying to assimilate all that had happened. But it worked. Once he had seen it all, and we'd talked it through, and he'd understood, all was fine.

54

When all the children were safely in schools that were right for them, I had a few hours a day in which I could look around for things to do outside the home.

Things rarely happen in isolation in life. You can look through things you have done, or have been done to you, and a pattern emerges. Sometimes things begin in a very small way and take years to come to fruition. Sometimes you can see the pattern, and you can see how God has given you smaller jobs to prepare you for the big challenges many years ahead.

These days, my working life means I must negotiate deals every week. I can see the very first seeds of that in the little crochet business I began when I was twelve. But those years when the children were young were the first years that I truly realised I had a real skill at haggling.

All my life, I've loved a bargain. I get such a buzz. If I pray before I go into a shop, you can guarantee I'll always get something. Everybody used to laugh about me. My children were the best dressed kids you'd ever seen in all your life. Designer clothes, you name it; they had the lot. But it was all bought and haggled for, to the point where, if you knew what I paid for each, nobody would believe me. People at the church would always ask,

'How is it that your kids are so well kitted out, but when we go to these places, there's nothing there?'

All I could do was shrug. I love buying. I just believe in God for things, and the Lord has always been good to me like this.

The way this first came to serious fruition was like this. I'd heard about a couple in town who were working with Ukraine relief, trying to get money to build a church in Ukraine. They were brilliant and were doing fantastic work. They got funding in the end and brought over a group of Ukrainian children who had been through the horror of Chernobyl. The funding wasn't colossal, so when these kids arrived, they had nothing beyond what they stood up in.

I was in town one day and I noticed that one of the bigger shoe shops had a sale on. Everything was reduced in the sale because they were going to be refurbishing the shop. Mum was still alive then, and she was with me. We stood outside the shop, looking in the window, checking out the deals. And then I felt God speak to me.

'Go in and ask to buy the lot.'

'Where do I get the money from?'

'Just do it.'

I turned to Mum.

'I feel God wants me to go in and ask to buy the lot. He says don't worry about the money,' I said.

She raised her eyebrows.

'What, all of them? Why would He want you do to that?'

'I have no idea.'

'Are you sure it's God speaking?'

She knew too well how much I loved a deal.

'I'm sure.'

She shrugged and headed off towards the shop door without hesitating. She got halfway in, then realised I wasn't with her.

'Well, come on then.'

I loved her so much at that moment.

We got inside the shop, and, feeling slightly foolish, I delayed the moment of truth while we looked at what was in there. There were men's boots at £65 a pair, women's shoes, children's shoes, boots, trainers; so much stock left and all so expensive.

I found the manager and summoned my courage.

'How much would you let me have all your stock for? All of it.'

She frowned.

'What do you mean?'

'If I wanted to buy all your stock, how much would you charge me for it?'

The manager didn't know what to make of me. Her frown deepened to annoyance.

'It's going to charity. Ukraine relief.'

'Ukraine?'

'Don't worry, I've not gone mad.'

I explained the situation as best I could. She got no more friendly.

When she realised I wasn't having her on, she went into a back room for ten minutes.

When she came back, she was smiling.

'I've just spoken to my boss. She says, if you give me a pound a pair, you can take the lot.'

We counted the pairs, and she gave me the total, and

indeed, it was £1 per pair of shoes, no matter their condition, no matter their list price, no matter their size.

I wrote a cheque for the lot and then had the next problem. How the heck was I going to get them home?

The one thing I knew was that if we kept the shoes in their boxes, we'd have needed a couple of small vans.

'Empty them all out,' I said. 'There's no way we can do it like that.'

We got all the shoes out the boxes and stacked them in a pyramid on the shop floor. The manager got us a roll of bin liners, and pair-by-pair we bagged them up. When each bin liner was full, we tied the top and stacked it on the fast-growing pile by the door. When that was done, I went round and got the car and brought it as close to the shop as I could manage.

My mum and I began the massive job of transfer the bags and loading the car. It was still quite a walk, and some bags weren't light.

'We're going to be doing this all day,' I said to Mum.

'I need some help here,' I said to God.

Out of the blue, I saw the parents of Paul, the boy I had fostered. They smiled and waved and came over to talk.

'Now then, Pam,' they said. 'Are you OK with those bags?'

'You are just the people I need,' I said.

'What's that then?'

For the next hour, they helped me and Mum ferry all the black bags and cram them into my car. I should have known that God would have people there ready to help.

The last, most amazing part of the story was that people in the church got to hear what I did and gave me donations. It all balanced out, and I never paid for a pair in the end.

I thought that if I could do that in Grimsby, I could do it in Lincoln. I went over to another shop in the same chain that was being refurbished, and I did the same. Except that I got them at 50p per pair this time. Hundreds of pairs in all.

We ended up with enough shoes to kit out a coach load of children plus all the adults that came with them. Every single person got a brand-new pair of shoes. Probably the first brand-new pair of shoes they'd ever had. There was enough to go back to Ukraine for the families too.

All this came from me just being obedient. It satisfied me as well. I just love a bargain. And, looking back, the combination of deal-making and shoeboxes was prophetic for my next stage in life ...

55

I've always been a workaholic. So, as soon as the children started at school, I had to do something. For a while I was in social services doing contact work, which was an eye opener. I put myself on a three-year college course in textile design. Later, I volunteered at Citizen's Advice, which was fantastic training for what God had planned for me. They sent me on courses. They taught me how to read people, and generally understand people more.

And then, one year after my mother died, I got a call that changed my life.

Operation Christmas Child started as *Pack a Shoebox*, founded in Wrexham in 1990 by a guy called Dave Cook.

The original idea was to help Romanian orphans at the end of the Cold War. Dave's sister Jan came up with the idea of gifts packed in the shoebox as a way of sending a 'Christmas stocking' wrapped and packed with love. A real message of hope for children in the toughest of circumstances.

Dave put out a local radio appeal for blankets, toys, medical supplies, and transportation. The community responded generously, and they ended up sending seven lorries over to Romania. This first load included just under 3,000 shoebox gifts.

By 1993 it had grown to where Dave partnered with Franklin Graham, (Billy Graham's son), and his organisation *Samaritan's Purse* and the operation got the new name of *Operation Christmas Child*.

A lady in Grimsby started a local branch of Operation Christmas Child in 1998. I'd helped them out in late 1999, in the months before my mum died, so they all knew me.

The following year, the lady got ill and couldn't go on. Samaritan's Purse called me directly and asked me if I wanted to take it over for them as Area Coordinator. They were halfway through a campaign, and they were desperate. I took it over in the autumn of 2000, and for fourteen years I didn't stop.

I wasn't paid; I volunteered and lived on the adoption money. It suited me, because it was something I could do during the day while the kids were at school. I had to be led by the Spirit. This thing was so varied, there was no way I could have done it on my own. It changed every day. As the kids got older, and when we got to the end of each year's campaign, we'd get busier, and I'd get somebody to babysit for me.

To build Shoeboxes in the first place, I went round the local schools giving talks and got them on board. God gave me favour again and I was passionate about it. Pretty soon I was out doing talks wherever they wanted me.

The public would fill a box and send it in. Sometimes it might be half empty. Or there would be things in the box that you couldn't use. You had to top the boxes up. We wanted every child to have the same, to be blessed the same, so we used a lot of fillers and top ups and extras. That needed all sorts of resources around the year.

I loved going into schools and receiving shoeboxes from the children. It was as though we were sending a box of love from one child to another. I will never forget one little boy gave his teddy; the head told us afterwards how everyone had been so touched. Because of family difficulties, this little boy should really have had a shoebox himself.

We had many stories like that. The less privileged schools would give us amazing things.

We did a lot of work with the press. The press came to follow us, and I'd get the Grimsby Telegraph involved every year. I'd invite the editor to come and do the annual opening of the warehouse at the end of October. I did it deliberately, so we got the attention of the press, and then they'd follow me round for the whole time. The editor came year after year. I got to know her well and still do. It all grew, and we had a lot of fun along the way.

One year early on, I realised that Wilkinson's January sale would reduce all their Christmas stock down to a penny. This was a chance to get a massive head start on the next year's box fillers.

I picked up the phone.

'Right Jen, I want you to meet me at eight o'clock in the morning. I'll see you outside Wilkinson's.'

'And what would I be doing outside of Wilkinson's at eight in the morning?'

'You wait and see. You're going to be really, really busy and you've got to work hard. Be ready to run.'

'See you there.'

No more information needed, bless her. Jen was fantastic. A

genuine character and loads of fun, her business experience was always a great asset to Shoeboxes.

So, at 7.55 this (very icy) morning in January, she and I were clutching our coats close and shivering outside the locked store. I could see the staff moving inside, and I looked at my watch. There was no-one else queuing behind us yet, but it was only a matter of time.

'So, are you going to tell me what we're doing here?' she said.

'When those doors open, we go in. I want you to grab as many trollies as possible.'

'How many trollies?'

'As many as you can, and then follow me.'

The doors opened, and we went in. I looked left and right. The place was empty, but that wouldn't last for long.

'Right,' I said, as I headed towards a long line of trollies. 'We're going to make a dive for it right now.'

We separated the line of trollies and wrestled them around us. I pushed one in front and dragged two behind me, and Jen somehow had four in orbit around her as she marched.

I led her on a charge towards the Christmas stock.

'See all those rows?' I said, 'You're going to pick everything up off the shelves and put it all in the trollies.'

'I can't possibly do that.'

'Yes, you can. Trust me. It's just the two of us.'

We rounded the corner into the aisle and stopped in our tracks. Three ladies in Wilkinson staff uniforms were already clearing the shelves and dumping the contents in trollies. My heart jumped as I saw four or five trollies already piled high behind them. We were too late! I'd called the store the day before and let slip what I was after. Had the manager decided they didn't want us to have their stuff after all?

'Come on,' I said to Jen, and ran forward, the trollies clanking behind me.

The supervisor peeled off from the other ladies and I got ready to argue my case.

'Hi Pam,' she said. 'What are you after, especially?'

I looked at her, confused, and she smiled.

'We thought we'd help you before the rush starts.'

I had a massive sense of relief. They were there to help. They'd been getting everything in the trollies before any of the customers got in. They'd been piling everything in because they wanted it all to come to us.

The manager had promised me I would get each item for a penny. The only catch was we had all sorts of items and the lot had to go through a till. That was OK. We were focused and very determined!

That morning, we took trolley load after trolley load. We got it all in the van, and it filled the whole thing.

The till receipt was yards long. Jen took it home because she was fascinated with it, and she showed it to her son.

'What about this?' she said. 'Bet you've never done shopping like this before.'

He took it in disbelief and scrolled through it in silence.

'Mum, you'd better go back,' he said. 'There's been a mistake. I think it's too much. This can't be right.'

'This happens when you go shopping with Pam,' she said.

'Pam or no Pam, you need to go back. This can't be possible.'

We didn't, of course. Wilkinson's wanted to make a wonderful donation to us, and we were thrilled to accept.

In the following years Wilkinson's would ring me every January, and they filled our van every time. It was incredible generosity, and invaluable to us as a charity.

The old joke came back with a vengeance, and people

talked more about how you always got amazing deals if you went shopping with Pam. Of course, it was nothing to do with me. It was all God. I used to wait for the Holy Spirit to speak to me about the shops that were going to be closing. Once I heard, I could go into that shop, and I could ask for anything and come away with everything. But unless I thought the Holy Spirit was telling me, I couldn't do it. Believe it or not, if I didn't feel that prompting, we wouldn't get a thing.

56

It always amazed me how the schools, and the public—every type of person across Grimsby and Cleethorpes, in fact—got behind the Shoebox campaign each year. A lot of donations came from ladies who knitted all year around. They would give us stacks of shoeboxes filled with lovely gifts. Then there were folks who would go around second-hand shops and car boots, buying items like cuddly animals, dolls, little cars, and toys. They would take these abandoned treasures home, wash them and let us know they were ready for collection, ready for the campaign to start. Year after year it would go on and still does.

The numbers of people involved grew steadily. Each year, I'd have a team going into schools to give assemblies. We needed a transport team to get things to and from the warehouse. We had a fillers team, and a team to show the filler team how to fill effectively and consistently. There was a team to check the finished shoe boxes. We had a finance team. All sorts of teams. In the end, I broke it all down into teams of people to cover every area.

Every single box was supposed to be covered in Christmas

paper when it arrived with us. Some people wouldn't cover some shoe boxes, or we'd need more boxes. Some would have been damaged and needed to be repaired. We probably got through a mile of Christmas wrapping paper every year. I had an entire team of guys who spent all day every day covering boxes for me. I needed all this paper. I needed glue, I needed Sellotape, I needed everything you could think of. I'd listen to the Holy Spirit, and it would arrive.

Then, of course, I needed all the fillers, all the gifts to fill each of the boxes in an exciting, appealing way. When I was doing it as international aid, people would give school uniforms, shoes, kitchenware, so many things. It would all be shipped abroad. The amount of stuff I got was unbelievable, thrilling.

'This is crazy,' I'd think. 'This is God providing for these people.'

My kids used to hate it when I was younger, especially after Christmas. We'd be walking through the shopping precinct, and I'd get that feeling from the Holy Spirit and I'd say to them,

'Do you mind if I just go into this shop?'

'No Mom, please don't.'

'Oh no, not today, Mum.'

'Please, no!'

I'd walk in and the poor kids would follow me, and soon we'd be walking out with piles of stuff and paper, all of us coming down the street trying to get into the car. It was a standing joke, but once again, all I was doing was being obedient. I listened to the Holy Spirit and did as the Holy Spirit told me, and He blessed our little Shoeboxes initiative far beyond anyone's expectations.

• • •

He answers prayers, there's no doubt about it. One day, a company from Hull called us. They wanted to know if I could receive a donation. The centre of it was a stack of pocket calculators, ideal for the classrooms, but there were so many other items ideal for children. Some of it could be sent away as aid, but some of it was going to be ideal for the shoe boxes. It was a mountain of brand-new, fabulous goods. There was much more than we could use in that year. This was a gift that would set us up for years to come. I listened to what the company had to say in disbelief and gratitude.

'Yes, please,' I said. 'We'd love to have it. That's so kind of you.'

'No problem. We'll have it to you by five o'clock.'

'I'm sorry?'

'We've got a lorry taking it all away this afternoon, but we can get him to divert to you before he heads south. Where do you want us to drop it? You'll need to get it unloaded, of course.'

I put the phone down. I felt energised. Everyone who knows me well knows I rarely say no, but this was a problem, and I love to solve problems. I looked around the office. The place was packed. We were in the middle of the shoebox campaign, and we were incredibly busy.

'We need to pray, Jen.'

Jen looked at me, eyebrow raised.

'This lorry's coming this afternoon, full of the most amazing stuff and we've got to get it unloaded. I have to give two days' notice for a forklift. So, we haven't got a forklift. We're going to be hand loading this lot off if we're not careful and this is going to be high-up work.'

'Oh, my goodness. That's dangerous, and we don't have the right team in.'

'The lorry can't stay for more than an hour, either. We either get a forklift, or we lose it all.'

'You're right. We need to pray,' she said.

'We do,' I said. 'God can do it.'

Shoeboxes team was mostly made up of non-Christians, but we had a core of Christians from different churches, and we weren't shy about involving our faith. We always started in prayer in the morning, for example. But this was different, and we needed everyone on board.

I called together every single person in the office that day and told them about the delivery. Everyone got excited.

'There's one slight problem.' I said. 'All the items are on pallets. We need a forklift to remove them from the lorry. We have to give two days' notice to get a forklift, and the lorry will be here this afternoon. Can I suggest we pray?'

'What, all of us?' asked one of our staff.

'Not if you don't want to, but if you do fancy it, then that's great.'

Not a single person turned that down. So, gathered in a big circle in the warehouse, we all prayed, believers and non-believers, side-by-side, all speaking to the Lord, thanking Him for his generosity and asking for help.

Time passed, and nothing happened.

I thought about calling round different companies to see if I could borrow a forklift. Maybe God wanted me to take the first steps. I resisted. This time, I wanted to be strong in faith.

Lunchtime came and went, and the phone didn't ring. People got nervous around me. I could tell they wanted more action. I could have got anxious, but a strange sense of calm fell over me. We had given it to God, and His will would be done. Deep down I had that familiar sense in my bones. I knew God was in it and He wouldn't let us down.

Later that afternoon, as time really was getting tight. I was standing by the window in the warehouse. I looked down the street, and I could see an articulated lorry heading our way. I strained and could read the name of the company in Hull on the side. This was the lorry from our donor, and this was the moment of truth. But where was the forklift?

Then something behind the lorry caught my eye. I peered, confused, and then the lorry veered a little and I saw what was following it. I smiled and called Jen over.

'Look.'

I pointed out of the window. Praise God, you'd never believe what was coming. There was my lorry, and just behind my lorry was a forklift truck. Both were heading our way.

Jen just looked at me.

'This must be one of those God-incidences,' she said.

'No doubt about it. He is good,' I said.

We went down to speak to the drivers, and the forklift driver was amused by how excited we were.

'I saw the lorry as it passed along the trading estate,' he said. 'I thought, I bet that lorry is going to Pam. And I bet Pam could really do with the forklift.'

We couldn't quite believe it.

'I just felt I had to follow the lorry,' he said. 'Not sure why.'

He shrugged.

'We'd better get cracking.'

So, we got it all offloaded in plenty of time, and our warehouse was stacked with gifts that would supply us for seasons to come.

We had no end of times like that.

57

People have asked me how Shoeboxes grew so big. The obvious answer was that it was a great idea. Easy to grasp, easy to contribute, and overall, it just made sense. But there are plenty of initiatives that have all that and never get off the ground.

Finding an army of volunteers is difficult, and many charities have foundered because they couldn't raise a team—and couldn't keep it once they had it. I made a huge effort to keep our volunteers from year to year, and so I did my best to treat every single volunteer with respect. I always sent every volunteer a card for Christmas, and I'd write something personal in each one. I used to have to spend hours doing that, but it made all the difference. I would go visit them too, and often went round to their houses to pick stuff up. That made a big difference on both sides. I loved to meet the people who gave so much time to help us, and it showed how much I appreciated them.

Another thing we did for the volunteers was simple ministry. Some of our volunteers were very lonely, and some of them had special emotional needs. Being in a great big gang who were all focused on doing good in the world is an incredibly energising and connecting experience. There was a lot of fun, too. One year someone put some long johns in one of the shoe boxes. One woman put them on and paraded around the workshop to great celebration. There was always something happening, and so many random times when people were laughing. Some things you used to get in the boxes you wouldn't believe. (Conversely, some things you wouldn't want to know. But that's another story. Not everyone had the right idea, shall we say?) It was all about praying for the right things and believing God would provide. He always did. The times we would think, 'Oh, we're running out of fillers. How are we going to get fillers?' And they would just arrive.

However it happened, the same volunteers came back to help, year after year, and things continued to grow. Eventually, I was given all-year-round access to a disused factory on the Humber Bank. We needed this kind of massive place because of the scale of the packing operation. In the end, we had perhaps 140 onsite volunteers who would come in regularly to help pack, but there was a much wider network.

Soon I had about 100 ladies knitting for us, making all the hats, scarves, and gloves. We had people buying dolls in, washing them all, re-dressing them and fitting them out. Some people would go around town collecting soaps and other things like that. It was all sorts of things, all so good. We'd have a team re-bagging sweets. Collecting material from old blinds which we turned into pencil cases and headbands. There were hundreds of people involved, all doing different things. It was incredible, and I ran with it, and I absolutely loved it.

We learned that anything could happen, and all we had to do was be ready. With us beginning to do more general aid we needed more storage. Years before a local Christian businessman had converted a huge commercial property called the

Ice House into a Christian centre. He kindly agreed to let us use part of his premises to store all the aid ready for going abroad.

I'd get phone calls from schools when they were refitting. The number of times I got all the old desks and chairs, all the old educational material, the lot. One company gave me paper and pens. We got everything. I don't know how many lorries went to Crimea. I think we had one go to Kurdistan and one went to Kenya. It all went to start schools. I can remember counting all these chairs on to the lorry, late at night. All the other lorries were going out as we worked. We filled one with accessible park equipment and that went out to Romania.

A local hospital was refitting the children's ward, and they offered all the old equipment to us, on condition we never made a fuss in our publicity about it. Once again, there was another unworkable time constraint, in that I only had a day to take everything we wanted out of the building.

'Lord, what am I going to do with this?' I thought. 'It all needs to go out as aid.'

I got in touch with Samaritan's Purse. They had a lorry they could send us, but it would take a week before it arrived.'

'No,' I said, 'I've got to get this out tomorrow.'

I rang a local company; I knew the owners were Christians.

'I don't suppose you can help me,' I said. 'I need a lorry or a container of some description so that I can get all this hospital furniture and equipment from the hospital. I need it all out so it can go as aid. It's got to be hush hush.'

They came up trumps. They even spoke to New Tribes mission society. New Tribes send missionaries out all over the world, so sending us some help was simple for them. Some of them came down to help us. The lorry drivers brought some more guys as well and some of our volunteers came.

The hospital was amazing. They had told me initially that

the hospital was very short of drip stands, and yet they gave us all the drip stands they could. We also got all the beds, the incubators, all the curtains, bedding, lockers. You name it, we were given the lot. Even medical equipment. In the end, we sent enough out to Crimea to start a small hospital.

There was such excitement at the end of each year's campaign as we waited to see how many boxes we had done. We had the number posted up, and everyone was excited to see if we could beat last year's number. We always did.

I was always pushing them for a bit of fun.

'Right. Come on. No, I can't finish on an odd number. Come on. We've got do another one. Can I have another one?'

If somebody came in with, 'We've got another two here.'

I would say, 'No, I can't have an odd one. Where's the next one?'

It was all about encouraging people and helping people get on board with it. Everything was such fun. The room would be six feet deep with boxes. The lorries would go out, or the vans would come in with the boxes from the schools. They'd get emptied, and the boxes stacked up against the walls. There'd be a wall of boxes all down one corridor, then up along another. You'd see thousands of boxes all lined up to be processed. Every single one had to be checked. We had to make sure there was no glass and no liquid in there. That everything was in date. That the box was filled up. All the rest of it.

One year, I won a Princess Diana Award for all this work, and they put on a special reception for me at the football ground. My name is still up in the Town Hall.

Of course, my name got out there quite a bit because of that. The advantage was that, at Shoebox time, we had a guarantee that every week, sometimes every day, we would be in the paper. That got a lot of attention and opened many doors.

We did Shoebox conferences most years. We'd have a meal on Saturday evening and then we'd have some sort of Christian entertainment. One year we took a puppet show down from Grimsby Baptist church, all the kids, everything. There were about forty of us. We put on *Joseph and the Technicolor Dream Coat*. We had a great show there. They'd been used to performing it, so it was very polished, very powerful. Absolutely brilliant, in fact. People said it was better than the real thing. Every time we put it on, we used to get a standing ovation. Every single time. Again, all the credit goes to God. He blessed the performance.

One highlight came when I took a group of our team over to Romania to give the shoeboxes out. I'd never done it before, and I wanted us to see how they all lived.

The editor of Grimsby Telegraph said to me, 'How about us sending a reporter with you? Getting them to report back every day on what you do, and to follow you for the whole week?' We did that. They followed us everywhere.

I took John with me, and we stayed with a couple who were missionaries. Bob had been a pastor in the north of England. His children had volunteered in their local shoeboxes appeal, and that had resulted in one of his sons having a pen friend. The family was from Romania and one day the son had received a letter saying that they had to leave their home as they couldn't afford to pay the rent. The church investigated, found out it was true, and helped this family.

As a result, this pastor and his wife moved to Romania and worked with the people in the villages. They were very passionate about what they were doing, and they were having an enormous impact. He had bought a plot of land, built a house, and built a community centre. We stayed in that house and saw what he was doing. Shoeboxes still send out boxes to him today. They go out into all the villages and the surrounding area.

Visiting Romania made a huge impression on us all. The first thing we noticed had to be the poverty. We'd seen nothing like it. And the cold. It was minus 27! Our team had taken lots of brand-new aid as well as shoeboxes. We were privileged to go into some of their homes, schools, and also into the Roma camps, taking shoeboxes, sweets, and aid goods. Seeing the children's faces as they opened their boxes was worth all the hard work back at home. The way they shared their sweets broke your heart. One little boy had a tennis ball in his box, and when he found it all the boys disappeared into the hallway to play football. The excitement was electric.

They would sing for us, and even wanted to share their precious sweets with us. What a difference to the children back home. Even a tube of toothpaste was like a million dollars to them.

We gave out as many new clothes and blankets as we had, as well as other aid goods, but we couldn't believe the conditions people were living in. Often there'd be no running water, no sanitation, with six people living in a room no bigger than ten by eight feet. They would cook, sleep, and live in this one room, and they literally had nothing. You saw no toys. The children would play with a piece of wood, or, if they were lucky, an old tyre. But what came over time and time again is how happy they were. We came back and many of us meditated deeply on how God blesses people, and whether we had our priorities right, here, in the affluent West.

58

Once again, nothing lasts forever. The world turns and you hear God's voice as He calls you into new territories. Even at the peak of activity with Shoeboxes, He always had other plans for me, and my time with Shoeboxes was always going to be finite.

The very first seed of this new direction came in 2006. This is the year that I realised there was a real darkness in the world, and that I had responsibilities to my children beyond what I had planned for. It was the first step in a train of events that led to me coming out of Shoeboxes in the end, on to an even greater responsibility.

I guess any organisation can make enemies, and, somehow, I still don't really know how, by 2006 that had happened.

It was my daughter Ruth's prom night. Rebecca had left home by then, but a friend came to stay and she, I and John and Stephen celebrated with Ruth and saw her off in her prom dress.

She'd just gone when my friend said to me,

'I'll take the boys back to my house. You and your friend can have an evening out.'

My other friend came round, left her car at my house, and I drove us both into town for a meal.

We got back late. As we drove up to the house, I could see a dark shadow over my friend's car. There was something wrong with it. Something dark and twisted about it. My friend followed my gaze and gasped.

'Oh, my goodness, what's happened to my car?' she said.

'I don't know,' I said. 'Let's get the boys to bed so they can't see this.'

As we got out of the car, the neighbours from over the street came over. They were very agitated, but they had to wait. I got the boys to bed and went back downstairs. The car was a burned-out wreck, twisted metal scorched and charred black, and drenched in water. The neighbours told us how they had seen the car on fire and called the fire brigade. They said the car had been close to exploding by the time they got there. They had had to evacuate the street.

No one was hurt, and the insurance company paid out, but that was the start of a mini campaign of intimidation against us that went on for a good few months. In consultation with the police, I ended up installing advanced CCTV and other security measures in my house. We still don't know the full details of who was behind it all, but it left me with a shapeless sense of dread as I realised how vulnerable the children could be, and how much I still needed to look after them.

59

John was coming up to sixteen. By then he was in a special school for children with learning difficulties. I had no idea how complex his needs were when I adopted him. He's such a lovely boy and, like so many of our friends with learning difficulties, has so much to give. We can all learn so much from them.

As parents we are the ones who struggle with the fact that our children are different. Coming to terms with it is hard. If I'm honest, I'd been in denial about John's capabilities for a while. The first time the issue had been raised was when John was eleven and leaving primary school. I was told he wouldn't make it at Secondary School and that a special school would be better for him. I did already know he had difficulties but hearing him discussed by other people was when the reality hit home.

It was while he was at this special school that I really worried about what was going to happen to him when he finished his education.

Day after day, my thoughts ran round and round like this.

'So, he leaves school. Then what? Do he and I stay at home

all day? Clearly not. That won't help him. It wouldn't help any of us. But what else is there? Can he get a job? What can I do?'

It was still 'us'. Rebecca had left home by then, but Stephen and Ruth were still there, and they too needed thinking of. In many ways, John was a typical young man, with hormones everywhere. If he was at home all day, bored, restless, I knew we would all fall out. If I committed to staying at home to look after him for the rest of my life, what kind of life would he or I ever have? And his whole life would make him totally dependent on me. What would then happen to him after I had gone?

I looked around for help, and there wasn't very much out there. I thought harder. Could I start up a small business? Did I know anyone who would give him a small job, even if it was just sweeping up? Then again, what employer would take on the responsibility?

It was Summer 2007, and less than a year before John would leave school. That was no time at all. What was I going to do?

The answer was birthed in prayer. Every Friday night at that time, I met with a group of friends. We were all actively seeking God; we all wanted Him to speak into our lives and find out how He wanted to use us. It turned out that these meetings would bring revolutionary breakthroughs to many of those who came along, including me.

One lady there wanted a baby, but she was in her mid-forties and her husband was quite a lot older. We met, and prayed for them, and soon afterwards she fell pregnant with a baby girl.

Another couple prayed for a new direction and ended up starting a children's ministry in Kenya.

Another couple did the same, and moved into publishing ministry material and good, godly teaching material.

Shortly after the sessions, God spoke clearly and loudly to me about too, about how I could help John.

I actually talked about this in the opening pages of this book. If you remember, it was a September day in 2007 and I was on my way home from Dunholme with a carload of shoeboxes, and I was agonising over how I would look after John in the future. God spoke to me, and His peace fell on me as I drove into Grimsby. To pick up that story now, I'll tell you what happened next.

After coming over Caistor top, and driving along the smooth, empty, dual carriageway, I drove across town. I was filled with excitement about the encounter with God. I took the boxes back to the warehouse, where we would store them until the Shoebox campaign proper started in November. Some volunteers had assembled there to help us offload. One of these was a particular young man who had come along with his wife. They had kindly given up their afternoon to come and help us. It turned out that he would be key to this next stage.

I was distracted as we were working, because my head was spinning with what had happened to me, and the gigantic implications of what I was considering. It therefore took me longer than it ought to have done to remember that the young man was a solicitor.

'OK, I'm going to try this new idea out on him,' I thought.

So, after we'd unloaded, I invited them back to my house for a coffee and I told them what had happened earlier in the day. The couple were Christians and went to a local Baptist church, but I don't know if they were used to the idea of hearing directly from God in the way it had just happened to me. I was on fire with possibility, past caring what people thought, so I told them the whole story of what had happened on the road, about how God had let me know He was with me, and that how I had been given confirmation that I should start much-needed day facilities and care provision for people with additional educational needs. I expected him to change the subject, or tell me I was crazy, and that I had lost the plot. Instead, his response was fast and direct.

'I think this is brilliant, and I definitely want to help. Can I begin by setting up your charity status? I won't charge you, of course.'

They left my house an hour later, all of us buzzing with the energy of the conversation. I waved them off and closed the door, shaken. I couldn't believe it. God was already in this and bringing people alongside to help.

God unleashed a flood of ideas in me. I couldn't believe how abundant it all felt. It was as though my subconscious had been working on the problem for ages. Or perhaps it all just came directly from God.

The ideas came in a torrent. It was overwhelming at first, and over the next few weeks I wrestled to sort out the tide of creativity and possibility.

It all finally began to crystallise when I and my friend Chris came up with the name. I thought of 'Rock' and Chris added 'Foundation'. There were two reasons this was a good name. One simple, and one more complex.

Obviously, if you build something on a rock, it's a good foundation, and I wanted to be that rock for many disadvantaged people.

Alongside that, there is the time in the Bible when Simon Peter declares Jesus was the Messiah, the Son of the living God.

Jesus hears this and says, *'On this rock I will build my church.'* (Matthew 16:18 NIV)

It has always seemed to me that Jesus wasn't directly saying Peter would be the rock, more that Peter's faith would be the rock.

I wanted very much for this new initiative of mine to be based fully on faith in Jesus. The name 'Rock Foundation' itself would act as witness and declaration of this faith, while describing exactly what we hoped to achieve for people with additional educational needs. It was perfect.

There was a lot to do in getting Rock running, and for some years I worked hard on both Shoeboxes and Rock, running them both side by side. Some of my friends thought I was crazy when I told them what I was planning. I just smiled. I could see they were thinking 'She'll never do it.'

In one meeting around that time, I was speaking to the editor of the Grimsby Evening Telegraph. I mentioned I was thinking of starting this new charity called Rock. She was polite enough, and encouraging, but a couple of years later, she said to me she really thought I'd lost it. She'd seen what I'd done with the Shoeboxes program, how I had built all that up, and it was incredible. She'd seen how the trip to Romania had been incredible, mainly because every night they'd run a double page reporting back on what had happened. But when I first worked on Rock, she really thought I'd finally gone mad. There's no way she could see me having the time or energy to start a separate charity. But I was fine. I knew that, with God on your side, all things are possible.

Rock took up more and more of my time and my imagination, but God had it in hand. I realised He had helped me build a fantastic team at Shoeboxes that had every area covered, so I could be sure that, every time I had to pull away a little more, they would do more and more, and I could keep moving away into this new calling.

I was very sad to give it up, but I knew I couldn't do both that and Rock justice. I also knew that Shoeboxes could run on their own. And they did, most wonderfully.*

* I ended my time with Shoeboxes in 2014, when we were just about to move into Heneage Road with Rock. By then we were running all year round. We'd had an incredible time, a fantastic time, and I had loved every minute. Thanks to God's graceful provision, we never lacked a thing. When I started, our Grimsby branch was doing nearly 4,000 shoeboxes a year. I grew it to 27,000, as well overseeing the international aid for the area. By the time I left, we were one of the biggest warehouses in the whole of Operation Christmas Child. We had great fun. I loved doing it—and we saw such miracles.

60

What was conceived in 2007, what was prepared for in 2008, was given birth in 2009.

Once I had had the word from God about how He wanted me to begin Rock, and once I'd got over the surprise, I spoke to Him directly.

'Lord, I hear what You are calling me to. I will do it on one condition and one condition only: You will be the boss. You take the responsibility. Because it's too big. It's huge. I can't do that, so You must put people alongside me to help me.'

He's never let me down on this ever since. If I ever get in a hole (and there have been many holes over the years) I go back to God and say,

'Come on, you're the boss. This is what I need.'

If we don't get it, I know we don't need it. It's easy.

So much of 2008 was spent in preparing the way. The first practical step was to find out what was already available in the area for people with learning disabilities. I fast realised there was not a lot.

I went to look around various places. My friend Jen often

accompanied me to meetings. I think she just liked my buzz, how excited I was.

We met with Grimsby Council, and the people who dealt with resources for people with additional educational needs. They told me we needed nothing in Grimsby. They told me it was all catered for and that they didn't need my services. I started naming different people with learning disabilities and they didn't know any of them at all. I realised in the end that the only people they really knew of were those who were severely disabled, who probably needed feeding, and who they were already funding. There was nothing else there at all.

I could have come away disillusioned, but that never happened because God had spoken to me. I knew there was a need, so I had to do it. That carried me on with the research, and pretty soon we realised it was the same story everywhere, all across the county: a great lack of facilities.

Around this time, God organised it so that I was asked to advise on a board in town. The board was bang on target, specifically aimed at discussing people with learning disabilities coming out of school and going into adult provision. There were about twenty people in the room. Doctors, head teachers, many professionals, all sorts of people. I'd been invited on as one of the parents, but I was very quiet at the beginning, as I felt very inferior. It was my first time on this kind of thing, and I was petrified. Even after all the healing I'd been through, I always looked down at myself. I still had very little confidence in myself, so going onto this board terrified me. All these qualified people—and me! I was just normal secondary school, Jane Average basically, with none of the qualifications they all had.

As the meeting progressed, I sat there thinking, 'Why am I doing this?'

Yet, as I listened to the things they were saying, I got more and more frustrated. Some comments coming across the table were so misguided I got angry.

'Hang on,' I thought to myself. 'They can't possibly do this. If they do this, this will happen, this will happen, this will happen. They can't be serious. This is ridiculous.'

I found myself on my feet and going for it. In a very nice way, of course, but I found myself telling them exactly why they couldn't do this, why doing that would be a disaster. I couldn't believe what was coming out of my mouth. I felt myself speaking strange, educated words I didn't know I knew, and even more miraculously, pronouncing them perfectly. Even as I was talking, I was thinking, 'Where is all this coming from?'

I must have gone on for a good ten or fifteen minutes, and then I sat down. Nobody was more surprised than me, and whatever I said never went ahead. But the respect I got afterwards was unbelievable. Even today, I have respect from those people, all because of that meeting.

Afterwards, I went back to my car. I sat there, shaken.

'God, what just happened?' I said.

God merely reminded me of the scripture *'Open wide your mouth and I will fill it'. (Psalm 81:10 NIV).*

I think God was teaching me a precious lesson that day. All He wants is people who will be obedient and make themselves available. If You believe in God and ask large things of Him, He will do the rest.

I began to put my own board together and we set up a charity bank account. Business plans got underway. I had meetings with advisors like E-Factor. Things were moving.

Soon I was incurring overheads, and I realised I needed to fund this properly. I looked at various ideas, and I thought of having a Fun Day. I could see something like that raising a few hundred pounds at least.

A man at the Baptist Church wanted to help. He loved classic cars and owned several himself. He said he'd bring some of them down. There were connections at a factory out on the Humber Bank, and he convinced them to let us have their sports field.

We advertised it in the local press and with flyers around town, and it was all going OK. There seemed to be interest, and people were talking about it, and I had high hopes that we could begin well.

The day came, we went out, got to the field—and it bucketed down. God sent heavy rain all day. The field was a swamp, and the event was a washout. I turned back to God, feeling both angry and forlorn.

'So, what was that?' I said. 'What was the point? Didn't I hear You, Lord?'

I had been humbled and was very hard on myself. Where had I gone wrong? Had I been too proud? I resolved to listen more closely to God in future.

That wasn't the end. A couple of days later, I received a phone call from BBC Radio.

'Pam, we heard about your fun day. We're sorry it didn't work out. But are you trying to start a new charity?'

'I am, yes. Why?'

'We're interested in finding out more. Could you please come in to see us tomorrow morning? We'll do a live interview.'

I'd never done live radio in my life, and this was a startling idea. I got in touch with the people on my board. I was excited, and I thought they would be too.

'Come on the radio with me,' I said. At which there was a lot of throat-clearing and much changing of the subject.

Rather mysteriously, no-one was available. It seemed not many people were keen on doing radio.

I was undaunted. This had to be from God. He calls us and tells us to 'fear not'. What choice do we have in the end?

So, I went along to the studio alone. They interviewed me live, and I told them all about what I wanted to do.

The following day, the BBC called again.

'A solicitor wants to get in touch with you. Is it all right if we pass your number onto him?'

I spoke to this solicitor, who said,

'I heard you on the radio yesterday and I thought, this is the sort of thing my client would like. I spoke to my client, and they said yes, they liked it very much. So much so that they'd like to meet you.'

I went to meet the client in the solicitor's office. It was an older, local lady. Her husband had been a successful skipper in the Grimsby trawler fleet and had made a small fortune. When he died, this woman had inherited a lot of money. The condition on the money was that a certain proportion had been left to charity, and that would be given out to different good causes, but by invitation only.

So, from that meeting, from that washed-out fun day, came Rock's first five thousand pounds. And that was only the beginning. This person has been very generous over the years since. In fact, I've been told now that anytime I need funding I'm to go back and to ask them and they will do what they can to help.

Next, we needed premises. And to start doing something. We needed to actually get going in some way or other.

61

God laid it on my heart to speak to a man called Eric Carter. He was an ex-minister who was the manager of the Ice House, a local Christian centre. He attended the same church as I did but went to the earlier service.

I knew the Ice House well because we used their underground garages as storage for aid. They were very good to us that way, so I knew what the Ice House did in general, and I knew there was renovation work going on in there but I knew nothing else.

I kept on putting it off.

'Why do I need to speak to him?' I'd think. 'What do I need to say?'

God kept nudging me to find him at the earlier service. This tussle went on for weeks, maybe even months. God must have got impatient, because one Sunday morning I went to church, and Eric was coming down the aisle towards me. He had changed services.

'OK Lord, I'll speak to him,' I thought.

I shared what God had laid on my heart. He listened for a time and surprised me.

'God is in this. It's incredible,' he said. 'What can I do for you?'

'I would like to run your café,' I said.

The words came out of my mouth without my help. I thought to myself, 'What's happening? What café?'

He says, 'How do you know we're building a café?'

'I don't.'

He looked at me, suddenly serious.

'Pam, this is God doing this. We're struggling and we can't afford to employ anyone.'

'What about your cleaning?' I said. 'Give me the franchise of the coffee shop and I will do the cleaning of the building for you.'

'How do you know we've got a problem with our cleaning?'

I shrugged. I knew nothing about his problems. But God did. And Eric agreed.

'This is definitely God,' he said. 'Leave it with me. I'll talk to the board and come back to you.'

His board called me in, and they agreed it sounded good. They made me a proposal. They would give us an unused area in the Ice House to develop Rock, plus the franchise of the café (also in the Ice House) and in return we* would undertake to do the cleaning of the Ice House. We settled that Rock would start at the Ice House Christian Centre on the 12th of January 2009.

---

* I had literally no team in place at that point. 'We' was very definitely God and me this time!

62

I was very keen to get the café going as soon as possible, because I wanted to bring in regular income. I needed a business up and running in the background to get the money in to do the bigger plans.

God supplied all our needs. A housing corporation gave me a grant for the kitchen appliances. The council and two other organisations also gave us grants. A lady volunteered to start as a cleaner for me and another lady came and worked in the kitchen.

God showed up in the tiniest details. One I'll never forget. It seems small, but it's a true marker of how it felt clear that God was in the project. My main cleaner had booked a fortnight's holiday about a month after we had begun, so I was concerned about how we were going to fulfil our cleaning commitment. I had been praying throughout, and God had already promised me He would help us but only when we needed it.

It was getting close to the day, and I realised we surely

needed help at this point. I said to God (as I have done so many times) 'You're the Captain of the ship, so please help!'

A little later an elderly lady walked in, wanting to see me.

'Pam,' she said. 'I was praying this afternoon. God told me you had a need, and that I was to meet the need. Now, what can I do for you?'

I wanted to hug her. In fact, I think I did!

She came and covered the cleaning for that fortnight. She brought her granddaughter to help. Nothing would stop her. And nothing would stop us.

This has always been a policy of mine. In hiring, I never tried too hard. I felt God saying, 'People will be drawn to Rock. Don't look for people. Many will come from the most amazing places because I am going to do enormous things with you.'

We hit the date, moved in, and really got going. God was teaching me so much, and I had a lot of learning to do. He blessed us in so many ways. Another lady gave us a brand-new computer for the office. We prayed for a kitchen and thirty minutes later, an entire set of kitchen units arrived, donated by a local well-wisher. Desks and filing cabinets were all given to us. The council offered us all our staff training for free, and another lady volunteered to give us some days every week to help us with our admin. A Christian businessman came to see me and said God had told him to come every week and give me free coaching. This was invaluable, especially as all this was new to me and I was very much on my own.

We had our first student, a Down's Syndrome girl, on the fifteenth of April 2009, and our first funded placement of another student on the 11th of May. Rock had well and truly been birthed.

Talking to the council I could see the need for larger meeting spaces, so I asked the Ice House if I could book it out for conferences and so on. The Ice House took the rental income for the space but we did the catering and were paid for that. Again, I say 'we'—again, I mean me and God. There were volunteers, and the students would help out in the café, but more often than not I was working on my own, so it was nothing for me to do a buffet for 150 people—I thrived on all that.

Later that spring, another gentleman walked in and gave us his gardening business, including all the tools and equipment, so I took on someone to run that entire business, and slowly an income emerged. I took on one part-timer to do my cleaning for me. I got the kitchen going. I got the café going.

That first year, I brought in £92,000. It was an incredible time.

63

God continued to guide me in the strangest of ways. I'd employed a man to do some kitchen work. He wasn't up to par, and he wasn't doing his job properly, so I asked him to come and see me.

As he walked into my office, I felt God speak to me.

'Ask him about his debt.'

We sat down, and I looked at the man. He was in his late forties, and he'd lived at home all his life with his mum. She'd died a few months previously, and he'd found life hard since then.

'Mike, how much debt are you in?'

He looked at me, absolutely gobsmacked.

'How did you know?' he said.

'I didn't sweetheart, God's just told me.'

'No, really, how did you know?

'I didn't.'

He told me a figure, and I knew it was off.

'No,' I said. 'It's not that figure.'

I'd worked at Citizen's Advice, so I knew there was always more.

'That's not right, sweetheart. There's a heck of a lot more than that. You'd better tell me all of it. It won't go any further.'

He told me a figure. Again, I knew there'd be more.

'Tell me the lot.'

He told me, and it was a huge amount. He could have been put into prison because he was behind on his rates as well. His mother had died, and he was about a week away from losing his house.

'Does your pastor know?' I asked.

'Yes.'

'Have they done anything about it for you?'

'No.'

'Would you like me to help you?'

'Yes, please.'

This was the early days of Rock, and I could still get myself some time. I went to his bank, I went to his building society, and to his mortgage company. I did the lot for him, and I got everything reduced.

The last job was to sort his benefits out. I knew he could probably get a benefit called DLA because he wasn't a well man. I worked on that, and we got everything due. We saved Mike's house for him, and we got him protected from any more damage. He stayed in his house until he died a few years ago, secure with no financial problems.

64

In the first year we witnessed God's blessing, but in other ways it was very hard. I ended up working long hours into the early hours of the morning just to keep on top of things, and there was the whiff of opposition from those around us.

One thing I have noticed over the years, especially in the church, is the number of ministers who start a ministry and in the first year find Satan coming against them. It's no surprise that this happens; Satan knows exactly where your weaknesses are, and he'll come against you to try them. It was no different for me. I had opposition from four surprising directions in the first year. It sounds melodramatic, and individually they may all have been fine, but all combined, these four problems threatened to take me under.

The very first time I noticed we had a problem was when a local group approached us. They wanted to fund me and what was happening at Rock. I couldn't accept and turned it down with thanks. It shouldn't have been controversial; we were a

Christian organisation, and they had very different beliefs to us. However, they wouldn't take no for an answer, and kept on trying to give to us. Over that first period, they got past me twice and put money into Rock through the back door. I discovered what had happened, and both times I took the matter to the Lord. I and the team prayed over the gift. We prayed God would use this money for good works, and we asked for the gift to be covered with the Blood of Christ to purify it.*

The second problem came from an employee. I always tried to hire Christians, but that was no firm guarantee of integrity. As the year went on, I hired the young cousin of a good Christian I knew. The young woman was training to be an accountant and so I let her do our accounts for us. I really liked her, and I wanted to give her an opportunity.

It wasn't long before I thought,

'Hang on, a minute. Some money was in here, but it's not gone through the bank.'

I'm very conscious of money. I'm always on it. Even today I know exactly what's going in that bank. I've always kept my own separate accounts as well for any cash. Any cash, I know exactly. I know exactly where I am in the shops. I know exactly where I am with the business, and I've always kept that.

I spoke to one of my board members.

'Look. I've got a very awkward thing. One of the elders in that church, his cousin is in charge of the money, and we've got over £1,000 missing.'

---

* I've since developed a policy around this over the years since then. If I do a get a gift from a source which I'm not sure about, I try to use it more for the community around Rock rather than the actual buildings. The money goes for food or similar.

The young woman's job was to do our accounts and handle all the cash. It had clearly presented her with more temptation than she could handle. We decided not to get the police involved, but just to talk to her. The board member handled that, and he was very good.

The young woman stopped working for us, and she paid us back, eventually. We never got the police involved. It was a thing she needed to learn, and it's probably stood her in good stead for the rest of her life. We could have prosecuted. She could have had a record. But she didn't.

We've always tried to help people that way, and so we've had all sorts come through.

65

The third level of opposition, or interference, came from a surprising quarter: from the very people I had picked to help guide the fledgling organisation. The local group with the opposing beliefs and the pastor were mild situations compared to the battles that raged inside Rock.

One of the biggest problems was that when I'd set up the board, I'd tried to do things sensibly and strategically. I had tried to pick people who could represent every strategic sector of expertise I thought I'd need. I tried to find a board member who was a solicitor. I tried to find an accountant. I looked for a local businessman and somebody from social services on the board. I felt Rock would be far stronger with all these experienced people with special skills.

I didn't know that building up a board like that was very wrong and would work out to my peril. Whoever I wanted, whatever support I needed, it wasn't this. Pretty soon, they all started trying to put me into a box, to make me work like they would work in their secular jobs. It may sound reasonable given that's why I asked them to join, but the problem is Rock wasn't really a secular organisation. Their way wasn't the way I worked, and it wasn't the way God works.

Trouble really came to a head when they tried to manage my time. Whenever anyone new walked in through the doors, I made it a habit to welcome them in and find out about them. My board saw that as me being distracted and tried to stop me. It was an absolute nightmare. I'd learned that if God told me to have a conversation with that person, then it usually meant something, or led to something positive. I lost count of the times God had told me to drop what I was doing and talk to this person, and it turned out they had been just the person I needed for something. If I hadn't just stopped what I'd was doing and gone over, or if I'd told them to come back and make an appointment to see me, I'd probably never have seen them again, and Rock would have missed out on so many of the blessings God had in store for us.

Of course, single-minded focus, and rules and boundaries are probably what should happen in regular business. But I couldn't communicate to my board that Rock was different. We weren't doing regular business; we were doing God's business. I worked by listening for God's voice and stepping out in His will. If God told me to do something, I would go for it. So, something would come up, I was willing to go for it and the board would try to stop me.

'We haven't got the finances, we haven't got this, we haven't got that, but we need this, we need that, we need the other.'

'Well, forget it. I'll just go in faith.'

I wanted to take a step of faith. They wanted to see the money there first. They wanted to see everything in black and white. God doesn't work that way and so the whole thing just wasn't working.

The disagreements escalated into clashes, and the clashes turned into battles. Things got serious. I walked into one meeting and found a big whiteboard up in there already. Written across the whiteboard were my instructions. I'm sure they were well-intentioned, yet they read to me like abrupt, nonsensical, binding commands:

'Do this like this.' 'Do that like that.' 'This is how it will work.' 'This is how you will manage your time.'

I left that meeting distraught. There was such pressure on me to change my ways, and it was coming from my supposed allies, the skilled professionals I had invited in to help me. I struggled to make sense of what I was feeling. I knew they were acting out of the goodness of their hearts and trying their best to help me. So, was I just being silly? Inexperienced? Stubborn? Rebellious?

All I could think was 'No, this isn't what God wants me to do. This isn't right.'

This fight ran on, slowly building over the weeks until it reached a crisis in a meeting at my house.

We were all sitting around a table, and I felt the criticism had been relentless. Whatever I suggested got shot down, and we were at complete loggerheads. The phone rang, and I excused myself to take the call. We spoke for a few minutes, and the call ended, but I didn't go back into the room. Instead, I sat on the stairs and cried, until I was sobbing.

'God, I can't do this,' I thought. 'I started this, but I can't do it like this. I'll have to give it up. I'm so sorry.'

Expecting more struggle, more pain from God, I was surprised when a strange sense of peace fell on me. I realised the decision brought me calm, and I realised it was right: I had got Rock going, but now I'd give it up and let the professionals take it onwards. So be it.

I walked back into the room and stood in front of them.

'I resign.

Silence. I was surprised. I thought they'd be pleased.

'This isn't right. It's not for me. It's better you all take it on. You know what you're doing.'

They could see I meant it, and their faces fell.

'You can't do that,' one of them finally said.

'Well, I can't do this,' I said.

'Pam, you can't walk out.'

'Why not?'

'We need you. Rock is yours.'

'Not any more. It feels like Rock is nothing to do with me anymore.'

There was consternation in the room, but they couldn't dislodge the sense of peace I had. I knew God was with me and that was all I needed.

'Have a think,' I said. 'Put your heads together and let me know what you need from me to hand over, and I'll give it to you. You'll do a much better job than me, I'm sure.'

'Hang on a minute. Just a minute, please. Just have a seat.'

I looked at the speaker, and then at the faces of the rest of them. All I could see was consternation—and worry.

Slowly, slowly, I took a seat.

We talked for ages, but my position was simple: either they let me resign and they take over, or they let me manage the way I felt God was telling me. In the end, they agreed to keep me, on my terms, and Rock had passed a major crossroads.

The experience taught me a lot. Although these men were Christians, most of them were from a church tradition that didn't accept there was such a thing as baptism in the Spirit. When people in that tradition get baptised, they believe they receive the gift of the Spirit, but they don't get the infilling, that direct experience that usually leads to speaking in tongues, and which can be so overwhelming and give you so much confidence. I realised with regret that we weren't suited to be building Rock together.

Over the next few months and years, one-by-one I lost these board members and one-by-one I replaced them with men and women with real, active and lived faith, who would stand firm on God.

My position has always been that I want board members to see God at work. If you're bringing your tithe into the storehouse, God will bless it and you'll keep the devourer away. I've learned that myself through the years and God has blessed us that way. I've always found you cannot out-give God. Sometimes I've had to stand up, and I've just taken a step of faith and done it. It's never easy, but I've done it in Rock time and time again. God has met our need and far more. Whenever I come to a position when I'm thinking 'What is happening here?', or I come to a crossroads and I'm thinking, 'Come on God, what are You doing?', I always go back to God and say, 'OK, God, what am I doing wrong? Is there something I haven't heard? Am I not listening or is there something I should be doing?' Sometimes God speaks again, and I hear it more clearly. Sometimes it's going back to the last thing that God said to me and realising that I haven't done it. Whatever the cause, giving problems to God never fails. He always brings the solution.

66

As this first year came towards its close, the fourth, and greatest, interference came from inside Rock, from another of the people around me, another of the people I'd chosen to help. This was a member of staff who was causing a lot of problems for me personally. I can't go into these, but, combined with the battles with the board, and the pressure of work, it all made me very low. If truth be told, I was close to breaking.

First, my children were still young. I'd finish at the Ice House at three or four o'clock, come home from work and be with the kids until nine o'clock at night when they started going to bed. Once they were in bed, I'd start work for Rock again, and go until two in the morning. The next morning I'd be up at 6.45 am to make school clothes ready, prepare breakfast, and drive them to school before coming home and tidying the kitchen. Housework, shopping, washing, all got handled in the gaps.

All that year, I'd been getting everything in place for the business; all the policies and procedures, all the other documents. My life was basically being on my own and getting all that admin done. That meant that I wasn't paying attention around me. I was just busy working. So, I never saw what was going on, and how this member of staff was going off the rails.

It was in October. I was at peak capacity. I was starting up Rock in the office space downstairs in the Ice House and starting up the new Shoeboxes campaign in the upstairs rooms there.

One day I came into my office and found a sign that made me realise I would have a problem with this person. This all escalated quickly and brought me down very fast. In the run up to Christmas, various people around Shoeboxes and the Ice House wrote to my board and told them how bad it was. The board and I were still at loggerheads, and even after that had passed, there were still issues. On a personnel issue like this, they took no notice of me. They simply wouldn't believe me.

67

By the time it came to Christmas, I was on the edge of a breakdown. I just couldn't see how to resolve the problem. It was truly horrible, and I could see no way to make it less so.

I went home on Christmas Eve, not wanting to carry on. Thank God I'm not a quitter. I saw to the children, and I got a Christmas ready for them. We did a Christmas morning, and they were playing until Christmas afternoon while I was in my bedroom crying and crying. I was so, so low.

I knew I had an appointment with God on Boxing Day. I had let a member of staff control me, put me down, and challenge me in various difficult ways. It had been horrendous, and I felt so inadequate.

On Boxing Day, while the kids were busy playing with their toys, I went into my bedroom on my own and I sat praying before the Lord.

'Father,' I said. 'I can't cope with all this.'

God spoke to me.

'You may not be qualified on Earth as far as conventional

education goes. But in my eyes, you have been through the tests you need, and you're qualified for the job I have given you.'

I listened, comforted a little, but in need of so much more.

'Go to your father's promise box,' he said. 'I'll speak to you through that.'

The promise box was an old wooden box full of one hundred little paper scrolls. On each scroll was written a different Bible verse. Each verse was a promise, based on and around words given by God in the Bible. I don't know where my father had got this box, but it had been a part of my life for as long as I could remember and was one of the few things of his I had left. Strangely, I'd never really touched it. When he had died, I had taken it home, put it up on a shelf and forgotten about it. I'd never really even opened it. I'd certainly never consulted it in this way.

But that day I went straight to it. I opened the little metal clasp and picked a scroll at random. I opened out the scroll and read the words of the promise:

'God will speak to you within the hour as to what you are to do.'

I came downstairs and put on the TV while I got myself together.

It was tuned to a channel called God TV, with a minister speaking about people being controlled by the enemy. How they can do you wrong. How they can try to try destroy you.

Typical stuff, and not so interesting, but I was still trying to master my emotions before facing the children, so I sat and listened. I found myself filled with a slowly growing sense of disbelief. I couldn't believe what I was hearing: in the details of what he was saying, he was literally talking about my whole situation.

'You can deal with it yourself,' the preacher said, 'Or you can let God deal with it. If you let God in, then He will raise you up in front of your foes, and vindicate you, and He will deal with them.'

Filled with hope, I vowed to let God handle it all. Once again, that wonderful sense of peace fell upon me, and my anxiety and my fear and my misery left me. God is good, and He is in charge. It's our job to remember that. I went back through to the children, and the rest of Christmas was wonderful.

The holiday season ended, and I went back to the Ice House and carried on with work. Nothing happened about this person directly, but then one day, a couple of weeks into January, a board member walked into my office. He just looked at me.

'The person you have a problem with? They'll be gone within half an hour.'

'OK,' I said, in surprise.

'Lies have been told. We believe you were right.'

There was no apology, no more details, just that brief statement. But he was right, and the employee left. I never asked why, and I know no more about what had happened between them, but that departure cleared a massive weight and anxiety from me.

God then went on to speak to me about forgiving those who want to hurt you. That process helped me find final and complete peace over the situation. The promise had been kept.

68

Spring of our second year was much steadier. The trouble was past, and Rock grew. I desperately needed a manager to work alongside me. We couldn't afford to pay anyone. But God knows what we need, and He promised me He would always bring someone alongside to help me. Soon enough, He did.

Ken Smith was someone I'd known many years before through church. He and his family were lovely people. I hadn't seen him for quite a few years. He'd been a sailor, even served in the Marines at one point. He'd taken early retirement when he was 60 and got himself a boat. He had been given permission from his wife and family to sail around the Greek islands. He was in the middle of all that, island-hopping, swimming, and sitting in the sun in the Aegean Sea, when God surprised him by telling him to sell his boat and to get back to Grimsby.

An obedient servant of God, he sold the boat, came back to Grimsby, and came back to his family. He did not know what God wanted him to do, but he wasn't the type to sit still, so he wandered into the Ice House one day and we renewed our acquaintance. Before either of us knew what was happening, he was coming to work at Rock as my manager.

What a blessing he was to us! God knew exactly the person we would need, and he had him all prepared for us, with the right skills and everything he needed to contribute fully. Most importantly, Ken had a godly heart. In among managing just how I needed him to, he found time to give much more. He had a wonderful pastoral heart and blessed the place by smoothing things over. Some afternoons he'd even bring his guitar in and sit with our students, playing music, leading them in praise and worship.

He was fantastic, and, for the first time, I had someone on board who truly watched my back. He was there for me a hundred percent. He knew how I worked, and he knew my heart. He knew how I prayed about things. He knew everything, and we had a lot of fun working together. Given how down I was on men before, I think God did me the world of good through working side-by-side with Ken.

Meanwhile, God was at work in other directions. The Ice House had more rooms upstairs that needed renovation and they said we could have them for Rock if we did the work to make them habitable. We agreed to that, so long as they provided the materials. In return, we could have the premises rent free.

The government at the time ran funding schemes aimed at getting people ready for work. This was very beneficial for us, and we did a lot more building work under that umbrella. We took on 22 people and a foreman for six months, and the government paid for it all. These were people on the dole, and we were teaching them skills. We literally converted everything upstairs and soon we were making progress on creating workshops for the students: woodwork, needlework, sewing, crafts, and a kitchen.

In another initiative, the Probation service came to me and asked me to think of some way that we could help guys leaving prison. They were looking for something that would get them engaged with society and help them move on with their lives and find work.

I came up with a fabulous scheme. I knew a guy who had an old shop, and he wanted it converted into flats. It was just the project. He would pay for all the materials and we and these guys would be the labour. The Prison Service paid for a foreman, and we got it set up. They began at nine o'clock and they had to work a full day, five days a week.

It turned out to be the biggest success. The Probation service was thrilled about it. So happy, in fact that, the following year, they got the funding, took it all away from us, and ran it themselves. Only to find it collapse. For some reason, God's blessing was no longer on the scheme.

Rock continued to grow, and more and more students with learning disabilities joined our workshops as more people realised what I was trying to do. Around then, God blessed us with another grant of £5,000. A local business also gave us all the left-over Christmas stock, twenty brand-new leather chairs, plus tables, and brand-new children's clothes. A local club took us on as their charity of the year and agreed to help us out with basic woodwork tools because now we were running woodwork classes as well. A local shop gave us a cash donation. This all happened within one week. Praise God.

Next, we were asked to go in for a contract with the local

community housing to clean up all the alleyways and do some gardening. Amazingly, God blessed us with the contract for 18 months. We were asked if we would like to take over an allotment, and then we were given everything on it—all the sheds and the tools.

We were being so blessed by people's generosity, but I really felt the Lord speaking to me so clearly. He was telling me not to depend on grants, partnerships, or the council, but to be reliant on Him. We had a carpenter on board, and we were to concentrate now in that area. The old verse from Proverbs was very close to my heart and it was a delight to find we had a God we could trust so much.

'Trust in the Lord with all your heart and lean not on your own understanding; in all your ways submit to Him, and He will make your paths straight.' (Proverbs 3)

Yet, amidst all this forward motion, I had a surprise. My friend Chris rang me and said God had given her something for me.

Chris had moved away to be near her daughter a few years before. She was too far away from Grimsby to be involved in our daily work at Rock, but had always included us in her prayers, so perhaps this distance gave her a clarity about the spiritual plane too.

When she called, she was concerned. God had given her a picture of me on my knees praying with a battle going on around me. She said I was to ask God how He wanted me to pray.

There must have been something going on in the spiritual plane around us that was causing disturbances. Within an hour or two, another long-standing missionary friend called Shirley also got back in touch with me after many years of us not seeing each other. She wanted to know if there was any prayer request. I talked her through what was happening, and she said,

'Pam, there's a battle going on around you. You're not in this battle, it's not about you or Rock, but it's going on around you, and so you need not to be caught in the fallout. You must pray to release armies of angels to protect you and Rock.'

We prayed for powerful prayer armies of angels together that day, and soon afterwards, Shirley agreed to be Rock's Prayer Warrior. Praying for angels is something we continue to this day. I've noticed frequently, even in this year as I write this book, that when I let this prayer lapse, we slowly get more and more problems. That's never a surprise. God has shown me how letting the prayer go creates a hole in our spiritual barricades, and the enemy takes ground. Today I won't walk out of the house without praying for armies of angels around me.

69

It may have been fallout from the spiritual battle around me, or it may have been because I was actively seeking God, but I had sensed an unease around me. Something somewhere was off.

I asked the Lord whether I was doing the right thing. It wasn't long before He spoke to me.

'You are doing the right thing,' He said. 'But you're doing it in the wrong place. Expect big things. I am going to open doors for you. Expect the best.'

Reassured, I kept my eyes peeled for the doors opening. During that time, I had a couple come to me about their son, Matthew, who was at university. This lad was an A star student at Caistor Grammar School, but he had found university wasn't for him, and he was looking for something else to do. His grandfather had given me my first job all those years before at Ross Foods, and so they asked me if I could help. I think there's a lot in honouring people who have helped you, so I took Matthew on. He had little work experience, but I had the idea of asking him to write some grant applications. It was a slow beginning, but it wasn't long before he was getting some success.

I felt I should approach the council about an old school which had been standing empty. It was called Lindsey School, and it was huge. I had the sense that it was supposed to be for us. The council said it could work out. They had hired a local property management firm to deal with those premises on their behalf, and they put me in touch. They hinted they would look favourably on us taking the building, but the problem was that they wanted to meet at a point when Ken was away on holiday and couldn't attend. None of my board was free either. This was scary because I suspected God was up to something and I wanted some backup from my team in the room.

So, the meeting with the property company came along and I felt God telling me to take Matthew with me. He had only been at Rock a short time, and though a healing had begun in him, he still wasn't in a great place. Before we left for the meeting, I asked everyone in the Rock office to gather around and pray that God would go before us. I didn't know what I was going into, and I didn't know what was expected of me. I could have been going into the lions' den for all I knew. But off we went.

Once again, I sat outside the office, waiting. I was in a state of deep self-doubt. All the usual questions were running around my head.

'God, I haven't got a clue what I'm going into. I haven't got a clue what I'm going to say. I haven't got a clue what I should have with me. I don't know what I'm doing here. God, I've taken this step of faith; please go before me.'

There was a lady and a gentleman there to ask the questions. It could have been intimidating, but I had stopped worrying the moment I stepped in the room.

'We understand you want this building?' they said.

'Yes,' I said.

'So how much are you prepared to pay?'

'I'm not.'

'Ok so how much rent are you prepared to pay?'

'I'm not.'

'Are you expecting us to give you a building for nothing?'

'Yes.'

'You mean you expect us to give you this building which is so many acres and belongs to the taxpayer, for nothing?'

'I do.'

I was acting coy and cheeky, but by then I was thinking, 'Come on God, turn up, turn up, I can't keep this going.'

'And how would you do all the repairs?'

'How do you think we've done the building work up at the Ice House?'

I saw them pause and consider that. They didn't know the government was providing all the money, and I had a complete team in—and I didn't feel the need to tell them.

'And why should we give you —'

'Why shouldn't you? Look at the work I'm doing in the community.'

Again, inside I'm thinking,

'I've only just started. I haven't even done two years. Come on. "Look what I'm doing for this community?" Unbelievable. Who do I think I am?'

I kept on being this cheeky for fifteen minutes or more. I was just about holding it together, but I didn't know how long I could keep it going and I was getting desperate for the Lord to show up when the gentleman interviewing me held up his hand.

'Pam, stop!'

I thought he was going to tell me to get out. Tell me I was

crazy. Tell me he had seen straight through me, and I was wasting their time, and it was all over.

He looked from me to Matthew, who was doing anything he could to avoid meeting anyone's eye, and back to me.

In fact, he said, 'I don't know what's going on here, but you're making me very emotional and I'm not an emotional person. I don't know why, but I feel I've got to do everything I can to help you.'

I don't know who was more surprised. I caught the moment, leaned forward, and looked him in the eye.

'I'm so glad,' I said.

The meeting lasted one hour and fifty minutes. Finally, we all shook hands and Matthew and I left. I realised Matthew was white as a sheet. I hoped he was OK.

We got outside, out in the fresh air, and he finally looked up. His eyes were wide,

'That was incredible,' he said. 'What happened?'

'God turned up.'

'I'll never forget that meeting.'

To be fair, neither of us ever did.

In fact, this meeting was a turning point for us as a charity. Since then, I've realised that every time I've had to move forward, every time I've gone to start a new venture, every time I've had to do anything, I've always had to be the one doing it. I can't send anybody else in my place; God never allows it. Every time I've tried, there's no-one else there; God has always put me in the position that it's me and me alone who can lead these things. I now feel this is God showing us how this is nothing to do with us; it is Him, God, doing it.

70

This was to be the start of a fantastic relationship. That property management company got right behind us. There was a long way to go, but it was clear they would do everything they could to help us get into the building.

There was a lot of work to be done our end, so we started talks with a small Christian company. They were lovely, godly guys who had gone into business on their own. They were architects, designers and builders, and they were helping a lot of churches with their building projects. They began work for us. Soon they were making great progress on the designs, as well as all the background work on finding grants.

The only downside was every time they did a sizeable piece of work, we never saw too much change from £10k. That was a huge amount of money for us, so I was taking a big step of faith, and even I still needed to cultivate that attitude.

That was a fantastic time, in that taking those leaps of faith every time we needed to commission another piece of work showed me how God would help me in ways that were unbelievable. When I can look back, I can see that, ever since I started Rock, I've never wanted for anything. Never from the day I started, even from somebody bringing in a brand-new computer for my desk, or as simple as paper and pens, we've never wanted for a thing. God has always said to me He would give me things just as I need them, never before.

This applied to the people, too. In those days, every time I took on a team member, especially if they were a manager, it was a step of faith. On the face of it, we never had the money to pay them. But every time I took a step of faith, God met my faith every single time. He never failed us. Not once. Money would come from grants. It would come from donations; it would come from anywhere. If I needed anything. I used to say to the guys, 'Tell me what you need. Give me a wish list. Let's see what God does.'

It worked the other way, too. God would say to me, 'Tell me what you need. Give me a wish list.' Then I'd pray, and we'd wait to see what God provided. The times God just brought it in! We never wanted for anything.

71

So, we went on, working on our plans for Lindsey School. There were other pressures too. I was still running Shoeboxes alongside Rock, but they had recently lost their warehousing facility out on the Humber bank. The owners had needed the factory back after all these years. I'd moved Shoeboxes into the Ice House but it was obvious the Ice House was nowhere near big enough. I was going to need somewhere else for the campaign.

By late summer of that year, we had reached a roadblock. We needed an air-flow system in the Ice House, and the owners weren't prepared to pay out any more money on the premises. They also wanted us to pay rent on the property at so much per sq. foot. If we couldn't pay, we would have to leave. We were already running out of space so there was no way we could afford this. But to leave wasn't a straightforward decision. We had the franchise at the coffee shop which was bringing in revenue, and they had told us we could have the space upstairs providing I got the building work done for them. But then they said they also wanted us to pay for utilities and it became clearly unsustainable.

Ken was very unhappy, and we went to them and appealed this new direction, pointing out the work we'd already done and the money we'd saved them, but they wouldn't shift their position.

Complicating it further, God had already told us about looking elsewhere.

In the end, we thought all these difficulties were God's way of telling us to move out.

To make a long story short, we decided we still had to finish the building work. We felt we must honour our word and complete the work and then God would honour us, so we carried on with that for a while.

But the situation with the rent wasn't going away, and I still needed warehouse space to run that year's Shoeboxes campaign.

I was meeting the council every month about our plans to develop Lindsey School. They were now talking about giving the school to us on a scheme called a 'Community Asset Transfer'. This is a scheme set up to transfer the ownership of publicly owned buildings into the stewardship of suitably responsible community organisations. The relevant headlines for us were that we would take ownership of the school for at least twenty years, and take responsibility for keeping the buildings in good repair once we'd moved in. The attractive aspect to all this was that it was a tremendous vote of confidence in Rock, and, more tangibly, we wouldn't have to pay to buy the building.

At one of the meetings I said,

'Look, can I be cheeky?'

They weren't surprised at this. They'd already said that I

was the only person in Grimsby who could be cheeky with them.

'What is it this time, Pam?'

'I need a building for the Shoeboxes this year. Have you got anything going? I just need it for six weeks.'

'Leave it with us. We'll see what we can do.'

At the end of the next meeting, they said,

'We think we've got somewhere for you. There's Holme Hill school round the corner. Let's meet on Wednesday. We'll take you around and we can see if it would be suitable.

I arranged to meet them there the following day. In the meantime, I went for a drive by. It wasn't far at all from where we were. I must have driven past hundreds of times, yet I'd never noticed it was there. It looked good.

I came back to the Ice House, and I said to Ken, 'I'm going to be even more cheeky tomorrow. I'm going to ask for that building for Rock.'

The following day, two people from the council's property management company, a manager and his assistant, took Ken and me around Holme Hill. It was an old Victorian building but was ideal for us as a charity. The company were looking at letting us have a couple of rooms as they had plans to let parts of it out to several organisations. I had bigger ideas. I had seen that they had a big hall standing empty. That would do so well for the Shoeboxes packing. So, halfway round our tour, I made my move.

'Can I be really cheeky?'

'Pam, it wouldn't be you if you weren't. What do you want?'

'Look. Shoeboxes is huge. Did you know we've lost our warehouse?'

The manager nodded, puzzled. Yes, he had heard that.

'How does that affect things?' he said.

'I need that big hall for it. And I could also do with that other big room. And all that cottage there. I need all that lot just for the Shoeboxes.'

'Oh wow,' he said.

'But tell me something. Could I be really, really cheeky? Is there any chance you'd let me have the whole of this building now for Rock and Shoeboxes? While we're waiting for Lindsey School to come along? I really need to be in the same building because everybody needs me, and it would save so much travel.

Almost without hesitating, the assistant said, 'That sounds like an incredible idea.'

'We'll have to run it past the council, though,' said the manager.

After that, it simply made sense for them to extend our tour round the entire building. We opened doors, went along endless corridors, up and down staircases, opening up more and more locked doors, wandering in and out of more and more rooms. I was more and more excited: the place was massive, and it would work so well for us.

And I could tell something was going on in their minds as they got used to the idea. It came out in questions like:

'Pam, could you do with this for Rock? What about that? Would you like this? Would you like the other?'

Then they even started writing stickers with Rock's name and putting them on piece of equipment. They stickered everything in the kitchen, all the big industrial cookers, all the fridges and freezers, lots, and lots of equipment.

By then, all I could think was,

'Wow! God must be in this!'

Then they said, 'Right, we're going to take you somewhere else. This will never ever happen to anybody else.'

It was happening again. Though this manager was leading the whole thing, his face was white. He could not believe what was happening. I was so excited, thinking 'OK, God? Come on. Bring it on.'

With that, they took us out of the building entirely, and along the road to a big disused Victorian church. It stood in its own grounds, on a busy crossroads, and had been boarded up a long time.

We paused before the door, and the manager looked at us. His face was bright, light, and happy. He couldn't believe what he was doing, but he loved it.

'We want you to go around it. Anything at all you want is yours. This will never happen to anybody else in this town.'

He turned back to the big old wooden doors, took out the key, and slowly the doors opened before us. We stepped in and looked up and around in amazement. It was massive inside, and it was being used as a council store.

We spent another hour looking around in there, all of us aware that something significant was happening. I never actually took anything from the church; God's favour was incredible, and He had already given us everything we needed by giving us Holme Hill. That simple fact of sufficiency is always a sign, and that it had happened again made me feel secure that God was in it.

72

There was no doubt, no hesitation, or last-minute haggling. The council said we could have Holme Hill for two years. A process that would normally have taken eighteen months was done in six weeks, and then we were leaving the Ice House, on our way to our new, maybe temporary, building.

Even with such a clear move of God, there was opposition, and the enemy did his best to hamstring us. I can remember one Christian brother stopping me as we were packing up in the Ice House, saying,

'Pam, look at all the building work you've done here. Give up now—how can you possibly carry on?'

'Give up? No chance,' I said. 'You ought to see what God is taking us to.'

'But Pam, you've put everything into this place. You can't possibly do it again. Don't you think you've done enough? People are worried about you. They think you're taking on too much …'

I stared at him as he talked on. How could he possibly be saying this? Was it even him speaking?

Gently, I reassured him.

'The Ice House has been a good training ground and it won't be wasted. God knows what He is doing. Besides, how do I know what God has in store for me? There's probably a bigger building project coming up and now I've had the experience.'

The very last struggle to get out of the Ice House was to do with all the white goods in the kitchen. They'd either been given to us, or we'd got them through applying for grants, so technically they belonged to us. However, the Ice House wanted us to leave them. Neither side was happy, and Ken was upset enough that he wanted to fight for the goods. Unusually, I disagreed with him.

'Don't worry. Let them have them all,' I said.

'But we got these from that grant and paid a lot of money out for them. We can't afford to give them away.'

'Let them have them. Let's walk away. God is no man's debtor.'

Next day I went into the office, and I said to Ken,

'Guess what? I've just got an email.'

'Go on?'

'It's someone from Scotland who used to live in Grimsby. They saw our charity and they work for a catering company. They've got all this ex-display industrial catering equipment that's ten times better than what we had. It's all brand-new and they want to know if I'd like it.'

He looked at me, unusually speechless. I shrugged.

'There you go. Give it to God. God will give it back.'

That gift didn't change anything; we needed to treat people as we expected God to treat us, and so we finished all the building work before we left, as we had promised.

There was one final blessing. Just a week before we moved into Holme Hill, a charity called Giving World contacted me. They picked up excess production stock from factories and distributed it to charity. They had a lot of stock from a big factory in Wales. It was a whole range of organic cleaning products, and the quality was fantastic, the best of the best. The offer was that we could keep 10% of it for ourselves and give 90% away to families in need or other organisations.

I said two pallets would be perfect, mainly because we only had room for two.

A few days later, it arrived. Ken and I went out to look at the lorry and did a double take. We both had the same thought. There was no way that was just two pallets!

In fact, there were twenty-two pallets. The driver and his friend offloaded them and left us to it. This was not good. The Ice House is built with great flights of concrete stairs, and the lift was low-capacity and very slow. There were a lot of steps to the top floor where these boxes needed to be stored. I got all our volunteers mobilised, and we got going. The boxes were incredibly heavy because it was mainly different liquids, but we all got stuck in.

Four hours later we were done, and my name was mud.

We kept the 10% back and got in contact with every charity and church group we knew to distribute the products. In the end, 3,000 families benefitted from this one delivery.

73

So, on October 20th, 2011, we entered our new home at Holme Hill. God had been good, and this was another new chapter in the life of Rock. We were all exhausted, most especially Ken. The move had taken us a long week and none of us were getting any younger. We had twenty regular students with us, and we went straight into the Shoebox campaign as we were desperately trying to unpack. It was crazy, but we got through.

Holme Hill was a very old building. Parts were subsiding, and there were cracks everywhere, but we were grateful for a home. As ever, we gave thanks for how we were looked after. The building badly needed decorating, and a paint shop blessed us with a van full of paint and painting equipment. We needed wood for a counter we were building, and soon a church blessed us with a lot of very expensive wood. There was nothing we needed that God didn't provide.

God blessed us, but we learnt a lot of lessons. It was a bad moment when the training provider organisation who had been working alongside us went off with all our ideas. There is a famous verse in the Bible that points out Christians shouldn't be unequally yoked with non-Christians, and I've seen that play out enough times that we have now got a strict policy that we will work with the right people, but we won't partner with anyone but Christian organisations, and even then, only after scrutiny.

Soon after moving into Holme Hill, we came under spiritual attack from an anti-Christian movement in the town. Word reached me. They were spiritualists of some sort and were opposed to our faith and the way we were growing. On one occasion, we got into work and found the outside of the school had been wrapped about with wide magnetic tape. There was so much of it, tangled round the gates and tied in many circuits round parts of the building. I don't know what they'd recorded on the tape, but I'm sure it was nothing godly. We pulled all the tape off, and went praying round the building, coming against any curses.

Other times we had strange objects placed in our building, such as voodoo dolls and dark occult and spiritualist books placed among our own books on our bookshelves in many of the rooms. We even found one or two of the spiritualists walking around the inside of Holme Hill, praying against us. One in particular, a lady in her 60s or 70s, was very distinctive. A friend and I would follow them in their footsteps, praying as we went to undo their work, and we took the occasional communion in the school. One day, Shirley came in with a friend. They brought little stones with a word of God embedded in them. We put them round, above all the doorposts, in the corners of each room, above window frames, so the word of God was everywhere. That seemed to quieten things down.

74

Rock was growing. Our twenty students had become sixty. We were running many different workshops, including needlework, woodwork and a craft room. We even had a whole room laid out with a huge model railway network. Some train enthusiasts came in and did it all for us. I was very chuffed—when I was a little girl my brother had a model railway, and I wasn't allowed to play with it! We also had a second-hand shop in the building, an IT training room. Then there were other rooms which I rented out for business courses so I could bring an income in. There was a big hall, and we had parties in there.

One great thing was that I'd started a Victorian tea-room, complete with grand piano. I had all the girls dressed in costumes with old-fashioned mop hats, long aprons and white blouses. I had all the boys in bow ties and tuxedos. The kids loved it because they loved playing out the roles. We had an old Victorian sweet shop too, and a smaller kitchen to train the students in cooking and food preparation. It all went very well, and people used to come in just for the experience. I loved it, and I'd often have meetings in the café with members of my team.

One day however, enjoying the sense of long-gone days was far from my mind. I was sitting at a table in the corner, a cup of tea going cold in front of me, a sense of doom taking hold. I was listening to Ken as he talked into the phone. It was going badly. He was on the phone to our water supplier, who wanted to know why we hadn't paid their bill for £12,000. Ken wanted to know why the water company weren't admitting their mistake in over-charging us so dramatically. It was a tense conversation, and neither side were backing down.

He finally ended the call, his face red.

'They're not budging.'

'They've got to. How can they not see their mistake?'

'It's sheer obstinacy, that's all. It makes me furious. How dare they?'

'Are they sending people round to inspect properly this time?'

'Not likely. They say they've done that to their satisfaction. They're talking about instructing their lawyers.'

'Oh, great. So, what?'

'We've been round all the pipes everywhere. It has to be a mistake.'

We stared at each other.

I looked down at the bill, creased from being passed around. Nothing had miraculously changed. The Water Board still claimed we owed them the money.

'Even if we pay it, which we can't because that would scupper us, what's stopping them doing it again this next quarter?'

We stared at each other, out of ideas. It had to be a mistake. We'd only been in there a few months, and we'd scrupulously checked the meter readings when we moved in. But how could we prove it?

I finally found the loose end as I was leaving the building later that afternoon. I was on my way to my car, across a big carpark. The weather had been good that spring, and it had been a very hot week. The carpark was pale grey in the sunlight—except for one tiny patch, far out in the middle of the dry tarmac. I'd seen it before and never paid it much attention, but all week birds had been pecking at it, and today was no different, as a sparrow was out there pecking away.

Finally curious, I walked over. The bird flew off as I approached, and I looked to see what it was doing.

The patch was ragged, about the size of my hand, and far darker than the surrounding tarmac.

I knelt down to touch it and realised why. It was wet. Wet through, in fact. On this hot sunny day, this patch of tarmac, yards away from anywhere, was soaking with water. The birds had been pecking at it all week because they were thirsty.

I struggled to understand. Had someone emptied a coffee cup before getting into their car? But I'd seen the patch before on sunny days, always in the same place. Was someone spilling coffee every day? I touched the liquid and raised my fingers to my nose. Nothing. It was clearly just water.

Water. That always came back, with no tap anywhere close by …

Ken and I got busy. We studied plans and discovered something interesting. We got the water board in, and they listened. Back in the Victorian café, Ken took another call. He nodded and gave me a thumbs up. He came off the phone and told me they had agreed: one of the main feeder pipes into the building ran directly under the patch in the carpark. Much of the place was built on sand, and things must have shifted over the years. There was a joint there. It had to have sprung a leak. There must be a small pool of water under the carpark.

I could only laugh at this. With the amount they wanted to charge us, it would have to be a lake rather than a pool.

Ken went back to the water company and had another long conversation.

Good news: after inspection, and a mini-survey, and due consideration, they agreed with us. There was a leak down there, and it was the reason for our high bill. (High? I thought. Extortionate more like.)

Bad news: none of the council, the landowner, or the water company would take any responsibility for the water lost. They would fix the leak, relaying all the pipes, but we would have to pay for the water. We were back to the £12,000 they already wanted from us. Back to lawyers and prayer.

What made it worse was that there was one last piece of planning work to be commissioned regarding Lindsey School before the plan for the renovations and the conversions went through to be financed. That planning work was going to cost us £10,000, and had to be finished by a certain date, after which they would make their ruling. It was a genuine dilemma. All the signs were that the council would decide in our favour. The problem was that, at the time we only had £25,000 in our bank account, so the costs for the renovations plus the water bill would just about wipe us out—let alone the fact that our accountant wanted us to have a reserve of at least three months expenses.

We had a board meeting, and I explained the situation. We agreed everyone would go away to pray about it, before coming back to meet and give our answer.

75

Waiting for this decision was an agonising fortnight. The board meeting came round fast enough, and all the board members voted. It was a serious occasion, as the decision would have serious implications, and no-one knew what the other was thinking. Also, Ken and I had agreed that if we were to go on with the last piece of planning work for Lindsey, it had to be a unanimous decision.

The vote came in and it turned out that we were all in favour of paying both bills and going on with the work we needed to do for the Lindsey application. The feeling many people on the board articulated was that of course we go on—God is testing our faith, and we have no choice but to honour Him.

That single moment of decision made such a mark on me, and it's one reason I feel it's so important to have a board that is 100% made up of people of faith. From that day, God turned things around and we started to build up our reserves. Out of the blue, the water board ended up giving us a reduction, so we only had to pay them £7,000. Then more and more money came in, and I was delighted that, even though we paid the £10,000 for the extra planning work, our bank account never went below the £25,000. How could we ever doubt God was in this?

Well, not so fast. Holme Hill was sorted out, in the final meeting over Lindsey School, we were side-swiped and sent reeling. At the very last minute, the council accepted a new cash offer for the school from another party. We had spent £48,000 in proving our case, and it had all come to nothing.

The whole board was stunned. It hit them all really hard. Ken was devastated.

They all expected me to flop, but all I could say was,

'Fair enough.'

'What do you mean?'

No-one could believe my attitude. I was surprised, but I wasn't defeated, not by a long way. I knew God was in all this, and He would never let us down. That simple truth gave me phenomenal strength. He had a plan and all we could do was pray for His will to be done.

I comforted the people who were most tormented by the result, and I did my best to explain why we were OK.

'I'm not bothered about this. Why worry? God's no man's debtor and I know He's got something else better for us. Let's just wait and see what it is.'

76

Life in Rock is never predictable. So often, just as we're flying high, something will come out of nowhere against us and give us a terrible blow. On the other hand, things that seem like disasters can, just a few days later, be turned round by God into something amazing.

This was a similar time. Even though we had lost Lindsey School and all that money, Rock was having a positive impact in the town; not least when I was invited to represent Rock at a local awards evening. I was reluctant, as that sort of gala event really wasn't my style. I would have preferred not to go along. I was still battling my need to stay out of the spotlight my feelings of lack of self-worth. My problem was that Rock had been nominated for an award, it was a big thing in the town, it was all over the press, so I had little choice in the end.

I prayed for strength, and courage, and freedom, and went along with Matthew. When I got there, the press came straight up to talk to me. They took me to one side, took some photographs of me, and were generally all over me.

'What on earth is going on?' I said to Matt. 'They're not looking at anyone else. Why are they picking on me?'

The evening was for work that people had done in the community. All the charities in town were eligible, plus people could nominate ambulance drivers, doctors, anyone in the whole of Grimsby and North East Lincolnshire. The place was heaving. There were people from churches, doctors' surgeries, carers, everybody from every walk of life across the whole town.

Rock ended up winning in our category and I was really pleased. What an amazing thing—I couldn't wait to let the team know!

We got to the end of the evening, and I was getting ready to go, when they announced the overall winner.

It was me. I had won the whole thing. I couldn't believe it.

What amazed me was that there were so many people in the audience who had come against Rock over the years. People who had told me they didn't need Rock in this town, or who had opposed us. They were all there, and I had won in their category.

It was then that I remembered that word spoken over my life years before, that God would raise me above them all. For one evening, after all the problems I'd had, the personal, with my board, with the council, just for an evening, God raised me up above them all.

In true Rock roller-coaster style, soon afterwards we had an experience at the opposite end of life. It began on a day that my older daughter Rebecca had brought her three children into Rock. I showed them round, made a fuss of them all, and we'd had a lovely afternoon.

I hadn't noticed that one of our students had been paying

us attention all that day. He was a young man aged 26. I'll call him Robert. It's not his real name. He had physical and learning disabilities, but his real problem was that he'd come from a rough family life. The poor man had gone through a lot. Violence and abuse of all sorts, until he ended up with us at Rock. He had mental health problems as well. At the end of one day, he was going around the building with a big kitchen knife, and we didn't know what he was going to do. He was quite capable of using the knife. That day we called the police in, and they sorted him out.

The second time, a few days later, was much worse. He took a knife again and made threats, and shouted, and hid himself away in a room down a corridor. Everybody was petrified.

I got put centre stage because he said he had put the knife down, and that he wouldn't do anything at all until I got there. He said that the only person he would speak to was me. The police agreed I could try to talk to him. In fact, that unless he would speak to me, there was no guarantee of a peaceful resolution.

I remember every step of going down that corridor.

A few prayers later, I tapped on the door of the room and called his name. Not too loud. Everything quiet and respectful.

I waited. Nothing.

Maybe he'd gone to sleep. I knocked again. A little louder. There was a scuffling sound in the room, then nothing.

'It's Pam. Can I come in?'

A long, long, wait. Then he spoke.

'If you like.'

I looked round behind me. There was a police officer at the far end of the corridor, and she nodded to me.

'OK. I'm going to come in now.'

I stepped through, warily, ready to turn and run, and I scanned the room fast.

The young man was sitting under a table in the far corner of the room, and he'd obviously been crying.

'Pam!' he said.

'Hello,' I said. 'What's been going on?'

I looked harder at him. His face was vulnerable, full of pain, and yet there was some hope there, too. I also looked at the knife laid across his lap.

'What have you been doing, then?'

'Not much. Oh, Pam, I'm so sorry.'

'What's that knife then, Robert? I thought you'd said you'd put that down.'

He looked down at the knife and seemed surprised to see it. He picked it up again and looked at the blade. I saw his knuckles were red and bleeding. I looked round for signs of damage to the walls but couldn't see anything. Distracted, he weighed the knife in his hands and looked at me.

'Can you do me a favour, Robert?'

He shrugged.

'Can you?'

'Maybe,' he said, finally.

'That knife does look a bit dangerous, if I'm honest.'

'It's OK.'

'I don't know if it is, to be fair. It looks very sharp.'

He considered the blade and pulled a face. Maybe.

'Can you put it down properly? Maybe even throw it over there for me? Then we can have a proper chat.'

He weighed it all up for a moment or two, then shook his head.

'Not at the moment.'

He rubbed his fist into his eye.

'I've got a headache.'

'I bet you have.'

'It hurts, Pam.'

'I'm sorry about that. We can get the doctors to have a look at you in a minute.'

'Can we have a proper chat now, Pam?'

'Of course we can, Robert. What's been happening then?'

'I saw you with that lady.'

'Which lady was that?'

'The lady with the babies. You were being nice to her. She had blonde hair.'

'Do you mean Rebecca? She's my daughter, Robert.'

'She kept calling you "Mum". And when you held those babies, you were like a mum.'

'They were my grandchildren.'

'You looked like their mum.'

'Well, I love them, Robert —'

'— Can you be my mum too?'

'I, er.'

'Will you be my mum too?'

I looked at him, at his red-rimmed eyes, at his dirty jumper. At the way he hadn't shaved for a few days, at his tatty jeans and his battered shoes. At the way he was curled up like a child. At the knife on his lap that he had completely forgotten about. My heart broke for him.

'I can't be your mum, Robert. I'm so, so sorry. But I can be your auntie.'

He looked at me, wide-eyed.

'Honest?'

'Honest. Just when we're in Rock, not outside.'

'You mean it?

'I do mean it.'

He stood up, and the knife clattered to the floor, and he stepped over it and came to me. He wanted to hug me, and I hugged him back. We hugged for a long time.

'Sorry Pam. I'm sorry.'

'It's OK, Robert, it's OK. Shall we go out and see the others now?'

'Yes, OK.'

I took his hand and led him out.

I went to see him once at the hospital. Once he came out, he dropped by Rock a lot. Then he would disappear for a while and then he'd come back in. This went on for quite a few years.

Once he said, 'I can come here. No-one mocks me. Nobody makes fun of me. But everybody accepts me. Accepts me the way I am.'

That, more than anything, thrilled me.

77

Rock was founded with the specific remit of caring for people with additional educational needs, but almost from the moment we went into Holme Hill, God had been opening my eyes to the wider need around us. Almost every day, people were knocking on our door asking if we could help them, and I felt God was speaking to us loudly and clearly about feeding the poor.

I talked to the Rock board about it, and we decided God was leading us to start up a food bank. We pledged that, when it was God's timing to do so, it was something we would explore.

Almost like clockwork, while I was away visiting Ruth in Watford, I had a phone call from a gentleman called Richard at a charity called His Church, based in a village just outside Grimsby.

'Pam, you don't know us, but your name's been passed on to us. Would you like some fruit and veg?'

Obviously, I said I would. The timing was phenomenal. I

knew of the pressing need for food in our community, so I just thought, 'Wow, OK! Thank You, God!'

It was just before Christmas, so I said I wouldn't be back in Grimsby until Boxing Day.

'Don't worry Pam, we'll be over to you then.'

Stephen and I duly arrived at Holme Hill on Boxing Day. The building was standing empty because everyone was off for Christmas. I looked down the road and saw a great big van heading our way. I looked at Stephen, and he looked at me, and we were both thinking, please don't tell us all this is for Rock.

It was, of course, and it was the best of the best. It was all from the top supermarkets, and nothing was going off. It was all exotic fruit and veg, and the nicest you could imagine, every kind you could think of. It was incredible and there was so much of it. Which gave me my next problem. What was I going to do with it? There was way too much to take to all the churches.

I decided it would also go straight out to people in need. I got a couple of staff to come in, and we spent all Boxing Day making up all these beautiful hampers. We blessed over fifty families, and then we were able to bless our staff at Rock with a hamper each, too.

One lady had her family coming up the following day. She wanted to give them a meal, but she only had meat left over from Christmas, no veg, and no money to buy any. To make matters worse, her daughter-in-law was a vegetarian. She had prayed 'God, will you meet my need?' and soon after, she got our phone call, offering her fruit and veg. The excitement and praise to God was wonderful!

Eventually I had just one hamper left; Stephen asked me

who I was going to give it to. I said I don't know and said, 'God will tell me'. The name of a couple kept going through my mind, but I argued back with God, telling Him they didn't need it. In the end I went to drop the hamper off with them. They opened the doors and their faces dropped in disbelief. The husband had been told he was going to be made redundant, and they had just been praying as a family, asking God to meet their need.

We went into January, and I simply couldn't avoid God anymore. I told the Rock board about the food.

'This has to be God saying this is the time to start a food bank!'

They agreed, and we started planning.

I always believed that we've got to be transparent and that we don't override anybody else or tread on anyone's toes by doing the same thing, so I began by going to another organisation in town which was already running a food bank.

'Look,' I said. 'I really believe God is telling us to start this food bank. Can we learn from you? Can we come under you and be a pilot scheme for you?'

The woman who was running it at the time looked unimpressed. I had taken Matthew with me to give him some experience, and she turned to him and said,

'And what are your qualifications?'

What right had she to ask him this?

It was a bad start, and things only got worse. It was a bad meeting. We left with nothing decided at all. We got a letter from them in the end saying they didn't want to be associated with us.

'OK,' I thought. 'That's fine, we'll just do it ourselves.'

We contacted His Church, who said they would supply us on a regular basis. God also funded us through our local council. We set up some tables in our own building, opened the doors, and got going. The word soon spread. Soon the Rock food bank could play its part in feeding a great number of families in need in the local area. Not only were we and His Church blessed, but so were many other desperate people.

78

That spring I knew that we only had six months left in Holme Hill, and we needed a permanent home. Early one morning in March I was on my way into work and for some reason I went a different way. I drove down Heneage Road and saw a For Sale sign. I didn't think about it and drove on.

Later that afternoon we had an email back from the council to say they would be happy for us to stay in Holme Hill, but they would like us to take on the outside maintenance as well as the interior maintenance.

None of us as a board was happy about that. Holme Hill was a listed building in great need of repair, and it was more than we as a charity could take on.

I mentioned I had noticed this other building for sale on Heneage Road, but I felt it would be too small for us. Someone else pointed out it was deceptively big inside, and the following day I and another board member went for a look around the property.

The vandals had got in and taken all the copper piping. There were holes in the roof, smashed up windows and sanitary bowls. The kitchen had been destroyed, and the whole place needed repairing and decorating top to bottom. But I went round it and saw potential.

It was on for sale for just under £200,000 and Ken agreed that it could work. We didn't know at the time that all the drains had collapsed underneath the building.

'OK,' we said. 'Let's go for it.'

Despite everything, I was struggling with the idea. I kept thinking of the building with the two pillars on it in the dream I'd had so long ago. I was sure that dream was fully prophetic, and I realised that in the deepest chambers of my heart, I had been expecting our next move to have been into that building, wherever it was.

However, I'm a big believer in dealing with what's on the table in front of me, and what was on the table was clearly provision from God. We needed £60,000 for the deposit, and that simply came into our bank account, with more besides.

Ken was a great comfort.

'Pam,' he said. 'I know Heneage Road isn't what God showed you in your dream but look at it this way. God's taking you on, so it's a stepping stone.'

That stuck with me. He was right. Who was to say this was God's last word on our buildings?

Surveys were done, a mortgage was agreed, and work started, from the collapsed drains right up to the roof.

We worked all hours, engaging whoever we could find to help.

Again, God was amazing. We found we had exactly the right amount of money for the deposit, legal fees, and survey fees and for all the major repairs. God was so faithful. One company came and did all the cladding work on our walls in the kitchen. They donated their time and materials, which would have cost us thousands. We received kitchen equipment on a grant, some for next to nothing. A carpet shop came in and supplied us with new vinyl flooring for all our toilets and fitted a long hallway carpet. We received all the paint we needed at a ridiculous price. Everything we needed, God supplied, and before too long we were in our new old building.

At which point, God pulled back the curtain on one of the deepest rivers in my entire emotional landscape. In the most surprising way, He revealed a jigsaw piece that had been missing from the very centre of my life for so long that I had almost forgotten it wasn't there.

79

It was a shocking revelation that came in a vision. It turned my whole life upside down, while making so much sense of so much of my past.

One of my friends was a social worker and had done a lot of therapy for children who have been very damaged. She dealt with bad cases and got amazing results. She was doing a doctorate in a new therapeutic technique called EMDR. She asked me if she could use me for her dissertation.

'Well, you can,' I said, 'But I've dealt with everything over the years. I don't think I've got much left.'

'Do you mind if we just try it?

'Is it safe?'

'I believe so.'

'Then, why not?'

We got together, and we had an hour together to try out this new thing. It was a strange process. First, we spent some time pinning down a picture of a place of safety. For me, it was a stream, in a field, in dappled sunlight under trees. After that, it was a matter of answering questions while following my friend's finger as she moved it from left to right and back again in front of my eyes. Apparently, that movement causes a pattern of very specific brain activity, which is very helpful for bringing old trauma to the surface.

I felt uncomfortable but nothing came to mind, so I went away thinking that was it. However, the session had obviously unlocked something in me, because that night I took all the old family photographs out. I don't dwell on the past, and so that was something I never normally did. That evening, I spent a long time laying the pictures out around me. It was very moving to see Mum, Dad, and Phil from so long ago.

It soon became clear someone was missing.

I realised that, up to the age of seven, there were lots of photos of all of us. When I was very young, there were lots of photos of my dad holding my hand. Then, when I got to seven, that all seemed to stop. There were hardly any photos of me, and certainly none of Dad holding my hand. I looked at all the school photographs and found the same thing: many photos of Phil, none of me.

I sat and looked. My mind worked.

I plunged back through time. Fragments of childhood poured out on me. Memories rose in a cascade.

I dropped into a vivid scene. A vision around me.

It was a memory of a trip to Liverpool we took when I was seven or eight. We had gone over to see my dad's side of the family. In the memory, I was in my grandfather's house. I was standing in the long hallway. I could see again the coats hanging, the telephone table against the wall, the tatty pile of phone directories, the scruffy doormat and the thin carpet. The smells were there again: old dust, Vim, the coal fire. A strange scent of gas, a hint of damp in the air.

The house felt dark, cold, still, quiet. So different to our own noisy house.

I walked down the hall towards the kitchen, then … nothing. The vision faded.

The next day, I told my therapist friend what I'd seen, and that I couldn't remember what happened next. She shrugged. I racked my brains, but there was nothing else there. All I had was that single moment.

She didn't comment, but she said we could probably go deeper. Did I want a second session?

I did.

That second session was different. I entered the vision again, but I went further. Very much further.

Once again, things were very alive, very vivid. But this time, when I walked down the hall, I heard a voice. My grandfather. He wanted to see me. He had a present for me.

I turned into the front room. I saw myself in there, alone with my grandfather, as he sat in his armchair and looked up at me. I was alone with him, and it was just the two of us in there, and he was smiling at me, and his ancient eyes were watery, and his teeth were long and yellow and old, and his smile was awful and he lifted his arms to me and I felt terror and I was slipping down, down and—

'— stop!' I yelled. 'I can't do this!'

I think my father knew his own father had abused me, and I think that's why he turned against me. After that, I could never be his little princess again. I was spoiled goods: to look at me was to be reminded of a great evil.

I could finally explain why my dad had treated me as badly as he did. He had failed to protect me. Every time he saw me, he felt guilty. Felt powerless. Felt like a failure. Perhaps, just perhaps, the same thing had happened to him.

None of that excused him, but it helped me so much.

I believe that guilt fed into the arguments between my mum and my dad. I believe she knew what had happened, and I believe that's why she never went to Liverpool as I was growing up. I believe that guilt ate away at them, and turned them against each other, and I believe that afternoon in Liverpool is even why, just a couple of years later, I was sitting in the car watching my dad try to kill my mum.

Most strange of all was how I twice went through all the training with foster care and adoption, yet I never once saw the signs of abuse in myself. Why did God wait so long to reveal it? I'll never know. But those two therapy sessions made sense of so much in my life that I'll always be thankful I let my friend experiment on me.

80

God continued to speak. In February 2014, a minister called Duane White came over from the Church of Christ in Oklahoma to speak at our church. God has really anointed this man and he's a fantastic evangelist with a prophetic gifting. Stephen loved him and would follow his preaching online.

I went along to the meeting with Stephen. My first thought was how busy the place was. It was packed out, and many of the ministers in the town were there.

As Duane finished his sermon, he said,

'I've got a word from the Lord.'

I was shocked when he walked straight over to me in front of everybody else. Even more shocked when he pointed at me and spoke.

'There is a supernatural provision for the vision God placed on your heart. The provision will not come from natural circumstances or man, but from Heaven through people. He is going to give you creative ideas, and He's going to fund what He has put in your heart.'

I was left reeling.

My first reaction in these situations is always to ask how could I possibly doubt after such a strong word?

The next stage is for common sense to come in. The Bible tells us many false prophets have gone out into the world, so we should test every spirit to see if it is from God. I have learned to do exactly that. If someone speaks into my life in this way, I pray into it and write it down, so I can revisit it later. I'll leave the word in my notebooks, and I'll wait and watch.

Waiting is important. So many people doubt when they get a word like this, because it isn't fulfilled straight away. I've always had a long timeframe on this. I believe that if God promises something, He will deliver it, even if it takes years. I choose to believe what God promises and I have to stand on my faith and stand on that promise.

An example is the time God gave me the word through Tony, when He told me there'd be a river running silver and gold and it would run in, and run out, in an endless cycle. It's always happened like that, in both my personal life, and for Rock. Every time funds look like they're getting low, I must think:

'No, God gave me that promise all those years ago. I still stand on that, and I'll stand on that for the rest of my life. God promised me, and either God is a god of his word, or He isn't. There are no halfway houses on that road.'

That same week, I had an email from our local shopping centre asking whether Rock would like a shop in the main shopping precinct in Grimsby.

'Yes, please!' I wrote back. The rent on places like that was anything up to £100,000 per year, and they were giving it to us for free. The only downside was that we would have to move shops every seven weeks. That was nothing. We were so grateful. It would be a fantastic outlet for us to sell all the garden furniture we were now making in our workshop at Rock, and it would be a great blessing to us. That week, we were also given some fabulous office furniture and a cheque for £250. God was good.

I looked back on the word from Duane White, and thought, once again, 'How can you doubt God?'

81

A month or two later, God spoke to me again.

The context was that, as Rock grew, I still had a problem about being the boss. I fought it, but I just couldn't cope with the idea that I was the responsible one, and it was my duty to lead all those people. Some people call this 'imposter syndrome' and say it's particularly common in women. I don't know about that, but I saw a lot in that title. Despite everything I had achieved, I felt like a fraud. I just couldn't believe that every day all these people looked at me and I led them forward. All the time, at the back of my mind, I was waiting to be unmasked as the useless little girl I still somehow felt myself to be. It was getting harder as Rock grew, because I'm a natural introvert, but as Rock grew, I was invited to different meetings and social events. I'd even have MPs invite me to go to their home at Christmas for drinks and networking. Honestly, in those days, I hated it. Even now, if I'm honest, it still makes me uneasy.

One evening, a friend and I took my son Stephen over the river to Hull to see another American preacher, Nathan Morris, from Shake the Nations ministry. Nathan goes all over the world on his crusades, and he's a phenomenal man. I had seen him many times and had grown to think a lot of him. As did many people: every time he came, the service would be packed, with hundreds of people at every event. I had heard many stories of how God had used him mightily, in healings and all sorts of ministry. The curious thing was that every time I had been to see him, he had picked me out from the crowd to pray over me; and every time this had happened, I had felt the anointing of God come over me. He didn't know me from Adam, he still doesn't, but of all the hundreds of people in the service, he would pick me out every time.

So, as we were sitting in this meeting, right up in the balcony somewhere, half behind a pillar, I was wary, yet hidden.

'You'll never get me now, Mr. Morris.' I thought and sat back, feeling secure and far out of reach.

I'd had a difficult week, so while we waited, I was praying about my feelings of insufficiency.

'Dear Father, I know I have a problem with being the boss. Please help me.'

'Pam,' God said. 'You need to deal with this. Listen, you may not have the qualifications, and in the world's eyes, you may not be qualified, but in my eyes, you're more than qualified. I've qualified you.'

I heard that with reluctance, but then the meeting began, and Nathan came on stage, and I focused on him. Only to hear Nathan talk about something I recognised.

'Somebody here tonight in this meeting has a problem,' he said. 'God has anointed them, but they have a problem about taking up their responsibility as a boss.'

He ended up making an altar call for those people, and for other issues, and hundreds of people went down for prayer.

I turned to my friend and said,

'I really think you need to go down for prayer.'

That sounds funny now, but it shows the truth: I felt inadequate, and I was struggling to believe that God could have called me over other people.

We both went down in the end, and I hid behind another big pillar. Once again, I thought Nathan couldn't get me there. I stood with my eyes closed, praying away, but the next thing I felt was a hand on my head. It was Nathan, praying for me. He had found me among hundreds of people.

God really did something with me there. He told me clearly and firmly that I had to take this responsibility on, that He was expecting me. He told in no uncertain terms to 'Rely on Me only.'

I didn't want to, but after that I had to, and I found comfort and help in that. It certainly helps when it's God doing it and not me alone. Almost instantly, we saw sparks of new creativity rewarded when we applied to be on a national TV show.

Before I talk about that, I want to say what happened to my son Stephen that night. He also heard God speak into his life in the most vivid way. Here he is in his own words.

82

STEPHEN'S WORDS

From a young child until I was eighteen, I had a recurring nightmare in which a large, grey-haired woman would chase me around the upstairs of a house. I guess this is from my very early years: I can't remember very much about being young but know I and my siblings suffered terrible abuse while we were being fostered until Mum adopted us when I was two.

All the way through my education, I always knew I was different; I was adopted. Mom always made it clear. In each stage of life, childhood, growing up into adolescence, she would always say,

'I want you to know that you're not my biological children, but that God gave you to me, and that is priceless. If you ever want to see your parents or connect with them, you are more than free to do so, and I will never stop you.'

However, from a young age, I decided that was not for me. I was so happy with my new mum that I had no interest in meeting the biological parents who abandoned me.

School was difficult. I never knew how to connect with other children. I didn't know how to communicate. I had horrendous struggles both socially and academically, and I was bullied from childhood all the way through senior school, even being beaten up in one of the science classes. I had no confidence, to where my communication was almost non-existent.

I think I always knew that there was a God, that He was there with me, was real, was someone that I believed in. But it wasn't until I was about maybe 12 years old that I officially committed my life to Jesus.

In my teens, that relationship deepened. Everything that I was going through made me aware of who I was in God. In my identity of who I am, as the person who God has created me to be.

I finished high school and went to college to study cookery. The first year, I was bullied again by the students around me. But my timetable worked out so that I'd have three hours on a Friday morning before I had to walk to college.

For a whole year, I used that time to pray.

'God, I believe that you've called me.' I would say. 'I believe that You have a plan for my life. I don't know what that is, but I'm pretty sure that cooking is not what You have for me. But I'm just willing to do whatever it is You want me to do, to go wherever it is You want me to go and just say whatever You want me to say. I give myself to You and I make myself available to You.'

I prayed intensely for my family.

Coming up to a year into that process, when I was 17, I felt the Lord say, 'I need you to get a notebook.'

The closest thing I had to a notebook was a diary. And in the back of that diary, there were pages for notes. So, I wrote, and I wrote. Always the same sort of thing:

'Lord, I'm not academic and I don't really know why You want me to get a notebook out and write something, because I'm not very good at writing. I don't know what You want me to do, but Lord, I pray, Holy Spirit come.'

As soon as I did that, everything changed. Over the weeks, God downloaded to me the plan and purpose He has for my life. He would talk to me, and I'd listen carefully and digest it, then write it down, on and on for ages.

I didn't really read it back properly until after I'd filled all the pages. I finally read it through, and I sat back, shocked at what I'd written.

'Lord,' I said, 'I don't know how you're going to do this in my life. I can't do this. I don't believe I'm this person. But, God, if that's what You say, I'll say "Yes" to whatever it is You want me to do.'

Underpinning all the notes I made was the idea that I was called to full-time ministry, and I would have five specific jobs. I would preach the gospel, I would see lives healed, transformed, forgiven, and delivered. God also told me I'd be married and that I'd have biological children of my own.

God told me I would step into all these things, but at the same time I would see my siblings step into places that the Lord has for them, even though that seemed unlikely: John had additional educational needs, and my sisters seemed in a different place.

'I don't know how any of that works, God,' I said. 'I don't know what that looks like. But if that's what You want, I just say yes to You.'

I still had intense fear. The nightmare I'd always had was coming again and again. I said nothing to anyone and tried to deal with it myself. Then, one evening, just as I had turned 18, around the time I got baptised, Mum called me downstairs and had a chat with me. She had noticed I was unhappy, and said,

'What's going on? What's happening?'

I would explain how, as long as I could remember, I'd been having this intense, dark, fearful dream. She listened to me for a time.

'Why don't we pray?' she said.

She laid her hands on me. She started praying out loud in English for a while. And then she turned to pray in the Spirit in tongues. She stopped after a little while.

I said, 'Wow'.

'I can't do anything,' she said.

'I feel the Holy Spirit so strongly,' I said.

I was sitting on the sofa in the lounge, and it had been very gentle until that point. But then there was a shock within me which I had never experi-

enced before. It felt like a jolt of electricity, or a bolt of lightning. I jumped off the sofa onto the floor, and I forget what happened then.

Mum told me afterwards that I began to sing and pray out in the Spirit. I was speaking in tongues for the first time in my life.

That was when I was filled with the Holy Spirit.

From that moment, I saw things completely differently. Fear left. Everything that I had gone through in the past, all the pain, everything, it all left. How I was bullied left me. How I saw my siblings, what they went through and what I went through, it all left me. God healed everything. God washed away anything that was hindering me in becoming the man that He called me to be.

A short time afterwards, I went to a big gospel meeting with Mum, over in Hull. We wanted to see an evangelist we had heard about called Nathan Morris. We didn't really know what to expect, but we knew God was moving in his life and that we wanted to be part of it, to see what God was doing, and to be in that presence.

Throughout the worship time, I had my arms open wide. Not really speaking, not really praying anything specific. Just resting in His presence. And as I stood with my hands out, I was taken from where I was in Hull to somewhere abroad. I saw a vast multitude. I was outside with a vast multitude of Asian people.

They had their arms outstretched wide, with tears streaming down their face. Almost raining tears, tears that were pounding the floor, their arms stretched out to heaven. And the sound of their wailing, the sound of their heart cry! Their hearts were open to the Lord. I heard it, and I was there. The people looked Filipino, so it's possible I was in southeast Asia. They were in multitudes. Not hundreds, more like thousands. Maybe tens of thousands. Maybe more than that. The landscape was a little sandy, more green fields. I didn't really see trees, but I saw the ground and the masses would go on for a long, long way. And I saw it.

God was doing something in that meeting. The very second that I opened my eyes, Nathan Morris jumped up on stage, even though it was not his slot. He got up there and took hold of the microphone and said words I'll never forget.

'Right now, there's someone being called to Asia…'

I did move into ministry, and I have trained as a minister, and I'm dedicated to stepping into God's calling for me. Though I have had a trip over to Asia, and explored a little, I haven't yet experienced that picture for real. However, even though I don't fully know what that looks like yet, I know it's in God's plan and purpose for me.

83

In September 2014 we finished our move into the new premises on Heneage Road. It had come as a tremendous blow to me nearly a year before, when Ken told me he was moving to the other end of the country to be near his family. God knows who the right people are, and Ken was such a blessing. We wouldn't be where we are today without him. The news he was leaving caused me a genuine crisis as I realised how much I had been leaning on him. He would remain on the board and have an involvement with Rock because the work was very close to his heart, but nevertheless, he would be gone from regular operations. I seriously questioned how I could run Rock on my own.

Ken left permanently just as we moved into Heneage Road, so once again, God's timing was incredible, and one season ended as a new season began. The months after he had gone were indeed hard, but God proved Himself to me more and more. I realised how, with God, I can do all things. I realised how much I needed the Lord. How grateful I have been over the years that God is in control and not me. God taught me a lot that next year while He helped Rock achieve so much.

19th September was the dedication service. It was extra special. Not only were we thanking God for all his provision, but I had been called over to Sheffield that same day. Earlier in the year, we'd had an idea of how we could receive and build on the word about creativity from Duane White. We had decided to apply to go on People's Millions, a television show that funds certain charitable projects. At which point, Matthew really came into his own.

I set him to work on writing the applications for the TV show. God really blessed him. We got through phase after phase, and we got ever more excited. We knew we were getting very close when they booked me onto TV training in September.

On the morning I set off for the training, I was shattered before I began. We'd been working hard to get the building done. We'd been down there in the evenings, repairing, filling, sanding, painting, doing everything ourselves, and we'd worked all hours.

I got to the training venue in Sheffield and there were nine or ten charities there. As soon as the session began, the trainers told us how they were going to make us so uncomfortable that we would hate them.

'Thank you,' I thought.

We did some warm-up exercises, then they broke the bad news.

'So far, so good. Now we're going to put you on TV to see how you come over. We're going to interview you under the same conditions as when we do the actual show, and then we're going to slate you. We're going to slate the way you're dressed. We're going to slate the way you speak. We're going to slate what you say. We're going to tear you to pieces.'

Absolutely all I needed.

I was number nine out of ten. I watched all the rest and

realised everybody else had already been on television. A lot of them were bigger charities with CEOs and fantastic budgets, and they were used to being interviewed on camera.

Everybody did a bit, and I thought they were all great. Then it came to me.

I dried up. I lost the words I needed, and I froze. All I could think of was poor Matthew, who'd put in all the work on writing the applications. I knew I'd let him down.

I finally spoke. I said 'I'm sorry, guys. I've lost my thread.'

'Don't worry about it. Just keep on.'

I knew I'd blown it, but, hating every minute, really just for Matthew's sake, I carried on and finished it.

Then they started in on everyone.

They reviewed all our performances. They were cruel. They were hateful. It was awful. They never once asked us what we thought. The team were all massively experienced in broadcast TV, and they ripped everyone to shreds. I sat there, more and more alarmed.

It got to me, and they played my screen test. I was relieved to see they'd missed out the bit where I stumbled, but then I realised they weren't even going to comment on my performance. All they did was to turn it round on everybody else. They had nothing to say, and they simply asked,

'So, what do you all think of this?'

All I could think was, 'Oh, my goodness, it's that bad they can't even be bothered.'

No-one spoke. They all sat in silence, bruised themselves, and maybe aware of how deflated I was. I'm sure some of them pitied me for what was about to come. Then one of the ITV guys spoke.

'What you've just seen? It's exactly what we expect from a good interviewee. She's got it. She's done it. She's perfect. That's exactly what we want.'

I sat there, frozen, shocked to my core. I thought it had to be God because I was so, so tired. Exhausted.

It wasn't over. We had lunch, then the afternoon came and then we had to present to the entire group about our charity. It was an identical game. They criticised everyone and were as cruel as could be. Then they came to me, and I did my talk. Once again, they turned round to ask what people thought, and once again all they said was, 'She's cracked it. We don't need more than that. She's done it.'

Not entirely true. Maybe my passion for Rock helped, but whatever it was, whatever they saw in me, it came from God.

I came back to Heneage Road, shattered from the day, and went straight into the Dedication Service for the new building. It was powerful, it was moving, and hearing Stephen preach for the first time totally bowled me over.* I really lost it. It was just an incredible service, and the presence of God was phenomenal.

Within eight weeks, our student numbers increased by 20%. It was a very busy time, and that was to continue. A few weeks after the Dedication Service, we heard from The People's Millions. They wanted to send their cameras to Heneage Road. They had chosen six charities out of the ten they had taken for training, and we were one of them.

I remember them in my office, and how the whole place felt

---

* Stephen's words:

I do remember broadly what that first preach at Heneage Road was about. The main part was sharing my testimony of what God had done in me. It was encouragement, recognising that all that we are is because of Jesus. All that we have, all that He's doing in us, everything is because of Him. We just have to make sure that we align ourselves continually in the Word and continue to develop our relationship with Him. From that place, God will begin to do more of what He's wanting to do through us. When we remain faithful to Him and remain faithful to His word, faithful in prayer, faithful in relationship, and faithful in our faith to Him, God will use us for His glory.

crammed with television people. Once again, I froze as soon as they filmed me.

I'd made a big mistake: I'd tried to plan what I was going to say. On that day, I learned the simple truth that if I don't plan my words, and just leave it to the Holy Spirit to guide me, I'm fine.

In the end, they got everybody out in the office and just had two or three people, at which point things were fine and I could do it again.

After they'd spoken to me, they went round the whole place, interviewed the kids, did a big piece on the whole thing. It was just amazing.

It screened, all the votes went in, and everybody voted for us. That was incredible. Praise God, we got more votes than anybody else in the country. It was a fantastic buzz for the whole charity.

They awarded us the main grant, so the Lord gave us £50,000. I felt that was Him returning the £48,000 that we'd lost on trying to move to Lindsey School. Out of that money we bought a laser cutter machine, an embroidery machine, six design computers and more. This would open up a completely new world for our students.

84

At the end of this year, I took on a new manager. Sabi. I knew her from church, and her husband had died suddenly. She had got involved with Rock as a general helper and helping to decorate, and then I took her on to do some admin. I felt she had a bigger part to play, and she soon took the role of operations manager. She was about my age, and I got on very well with her socially. She was full of energy, like me, and I liked that. I thought of her as a very good friend. It turned out that she was to play an enormous part in Rock in the years to come, and she was one reason that I closed 2014 on an immense wave of positivity.

Things had been muted on the spiritualist front. Every time in the past we went to move forward we found them very active, but since we had moved to Heneage Road, there had been nothing.

That period of peace didn't last long.

One day I had to go to Lincoln to see about selling some of

our products from the laser machine. I got back late in the day, and Stephen came up to the office.

'Mum, it's been awful this afternoon.'

'Why?'

'Can you remember, when we were in the other building, an old lady would come around?'

'Not the spiritualists? Have they been back?'

'Yes, Mum.'

'Whereabouts in the building did they go?'

'The tea-room and the dining room.'

I enlisted Matthew, who had shown himself to be spiritually alert, and we went down to investigate. We weren't expecting what we found. I walked through the door. I felt a spirit straight away, and it came straight for me. I felt a grip across my neck. We just rebuked it, and it came away from my neck, but it kept on trying to come for me. It was way stronger than anything we had experienced in the past.

Matthew kept on saying, 'It's coming after you.'

'I know it is,' I said.

'Pam, it's really after you.'

'I know, I said.

It followed us around in the room and kept trying to grab my throat.

We weren't scared because we serve a powerful God. We simply opened all the windows and doors and prayed and demanded the thing to go. But this one was stubborn, and not like we had had in the past.

We kept on praying and praying. We'd get away from it and rebuke it. But I just couldn't budge it out the room.

We were in there for an hour.

'That's enough Matt,' I said. 'Let's put some worship music on. We'll leave that on all night and come back in the morning. It'll go.'

We put on a Christian praise and worship CD and left it on repeat.

We walked down the corridor on our way to leave the building. To our amazement, we got to the front door, and we could hear the thing screaming in the dining room. A loud, human voice, screaming. We closed the door, locked up, and left it to it while we headed home.

The following morning, Matthew and I went back into the room. I opened all the windows, opened all the doors, told it to go, and it went. We'd weakened it by then and it was pleased to leave.

We'd won that time, but then the spiritualists did the same to us in our shop in Freshney Place. One lady in her 60s or 70s would walk past regularly, in a posture that looked like some kind of prayer. I recognised her from the odd occurrences we'd had in Holme Hill school, and we soon noticed how, after she or her friends had been praying outside our shop, trade would dry up. You could see people walking past the front as if there was no shop there. I learned she had an altar inside her house. My guess was that this wasn't an altar to God.

My colleague and I kept going into the shop and praying, releasing God's army of angels around the inside and outside. We put small crosses and the word of God in the window. Praise God, it all stopped and normal business came back.

85

Once we'd settled the spiritual attacks, we found we entered a season of replenishment. The first half of 2015 became all about God's provision for us.

We receive a lot of food to our food bank, but one week we could see we had a real shortage of vegetables and pasta. We had prayed on the Sunday evening for this, and I came into work on the Monday morning, eager to see what God would bring us. My ears pricked up as I was showing two visitors around when I heard Reception speak to a gentleman who had just walked in.

'Pam's in a meeting at the moment. I can get her to ring you, or you can call back. What would you like to do?'

At that point, I felt the Lord speak to me:

'You need to talk to that gentleman.'

I made a very polite exit from my visitors and spoke to this gentleman. He had a surprise for me.

'Many years ago, my father started a charitable trust. There's not a lot of money in it, but I can give you some. What do you need for your food bank?'

Very quickly I told him, and within an hour he was back with everything we needed. His parting words were:

'I'll email you every month. Just give me your shopping list and I'll bring in the items for you. Praise God!'

It was just another time that we could see how the more we give, the more God gives us. God is great and He was helping the Food Bank go from strength to strength.*

Later in the Spring I was approached by a building society to see if I would be interested in putting in for a grant with them. They said we would probably receive around £1,000. When we looked at the application, we realised we could put in for more. I completed the forms and sent them off. A week or two later, I was in my office and an email appeared to say we hadn't got the grant. That news took me out of what I was doing, so I went downstairs to check everything was well around the building.

I talked to the Lord as I went.

'I can't understand this, Lord. I didn't go after this grant; this grant came to us. Why have You taken it away?'

I considered what I'd said, rebuked my attitude, and finished that thought.

'I'm sorry, Lord. I'm sure You know what You are doing!'

Thirty minutes later I'd been round everyone, cheered a couple of people up, and sorted out a couple of problems, and I'd got back to my office. As I sat down at my desk, I remembered what had sent me out in the first place, and I talked to God again.

* National Bakery gives to the food bank daily now, His Church has blessed us time and time again, and a national supermarket is also giving to us twice weekly. Not mentioning all the pies, pastries and soups we are getting from many local providers.

'Lord, You know I could really do with a lift today. I really am feeling low. Please encourage me.'

With that, a second message popped up from the building society.

'Please ignore the previous email from us. We would like to inform you that you have been successful, and we'll be giving you £2,000.'

What the world said no to, God said yes.

On another occasion, we didn't get the money we'd applied for from a local foundation but the following day we heard we'd been given a £29,640 grant from a national trust, plus a £395 donation from a local firm of funeral directors!

In August that year, we took a stall to the One Event on the Lincoln Showground. This is a four-day annual celebration for those who are part of church life. We took a load of things we'd created on our new laser machine. We were new to it all, but we'd made a series of plaques with scripture on. We'd also created a range of funny Babygros with different sayings. One of our staff came up with a plaque with Bible Emergency numbers on it. So, if you were feeling anxious, for example, it would give you a verse to read. Nobody else was doing all this, so it was all fresh and everybody loved it.

A gentleman came over to our stall and said how much he loved our stuff. He asked if he could buy some wholesale. I had no problem with that, so I met him in Nottingham later in the month. We struck up a deal, and he took a lot of what we could make. Soon, through him, Rock was supplying Christian book-shops in England and in Northern Ireland, plus a lot of the cathedrals. It brought in proper revenue, and for a while it became our bread-and-butter money, while the revenue we could bring in from local shops then became extra.

All that kept us going for five years, all the way through to the outbreak of the COVID-19 pandemic. It was just incredible, and I'd often look back at the words I'd had; from my friend Tony, about rivers of gold and silver running in, and from Duane White, about God giving us creative ideas and funding us. They all showed me two things. God is no man's debtor. He'd given us back what we'd lost; and what we were making was being used to glorify God.

The plaque with Bible emergency numbers was our best seller, along with a plaque saying 'Shalom', which is Hebrew for peace, and a plaque showing one of the covenant prayers from the Old Testament. Those three have been our best three sellers, and they go on selling constantly, even in the months when nothing else does.

86

I considered the work we were taking on and how it looked to grow in the future. If we stayed on track, we would run out of space in a few years. For a while I considered the property across Heneage Road from us, even though the council wouldn't let us have it on a transfer of assets and we would have to pay market value.

Eventually I felt the Lord say to me,

'Why do you want an old property with all the maintenance it would need?'

'I don't, I admitted. 'It's really not suitable.'

'But you need more space. So why not put on an extension? You have room at the side of the building.'

I considered that for a week or two, then I contacted the board with it. Everyone agreed, so we contacted architects and surveyors, and a gentleman set about looking at grants for us. We got plans drawn up, but, including a new roof, the budget came in at over £1 million. That was a quite a challenge, and it didn't feel like the right time for us, so we never went ahead.

I still knew that we needed more room, and I was feeling increasingly unsettled.

In September 2016 I came back to the office after a meeting and Sabi, my manager, noticed I was thoughtful.

'Everything all right?'

'Not really. The meeting was fine. But with all the plans we have, we really do need more room.'

'God will provide.'

'Maybe. But when? I'm not getting any younger and I know what God showed me.'

'You don't sound too happy.'

'It's not about the work we're doing right now. That's fantastic, of course it is, but God has so much more He wants me to do, and I'm frustrated.'

She thought for a moment.

'Have you seen that building up at Caistor?'

'No. Why?'

'It was up at a million and they just knocked loads off it. Maybe it's worth a look?'

I didn't need a second hint. Something about this spoke to me, and my mind was instantly flooded with pictures from my dream from when I was sixteen.

A house. A doorway framed with two pillars. People gathered in and around the house, and I was looking after them. I was in charge, and I was ministering to them.

'OK,' I said. 'I'll drive past it tonight.'

Caistor is about twelve miles out of town, and quite a detour from my usual journey home, but I went out there with high hopes. The building sits at a high crossroads just before the long valley into the town. I parked up and looked at the outside. The gates were closed, and I didn't go in. I was disappointed. The building did nothing for me. It looked small and unimpressive. It certainly wasn't the building in my dreams.

And yet I felt a call to get in contact with the vendors.

OK God. If you say so.

The next day, I called the estate agent and asked for the price. Not good news. Sabi had got it right; it had started on the market at £980k and come down to £780k. I heard that with little surprise. Frankly, if it had been £20k, it would have been too much. All my own money had gone into Rock and at that time Rock didn't have anything like the resources to buy this. The Heneage Road building had cost us £185,000. We had spent another £60,000 on it, and we still had a mortgage for £120,000 outstanding.

So, it was a building I didn't like the look of, that I had no idea what to do with, that would need a lot of expensive renovation, that we couldn't remotely afford? What to do?

'Ask for an appointment to look round it, of course.'

'OK God. If you say so.'

I took a parent of one of the students to the viewing. My first reaction was amazement. The building was huge, with so many parts to it. What you could see from the roadside gave no sign at all of what was inside.

The second reaction was that we had walked into a place like a ghost ship. It was as though people had all downed what they were doing simultaneously and simply walked out. Teacups left, with tea still in them, the milk still on the table. Paperwork scattered around. So many small signs of life, all left standing.

And the land! The building came with ten acres. There were fields at the top, running down a small valley that bent away out of view. We looked round, then we sat outside, looking at the view that stretched away twenty miles, across fields and woods, up to the river Humber and beyond into the East Riding of Yorkshire.

Finally, the parent turned to me, and said what I was thinking.

'This would be perfect for our children.'

Word of this visit got out straight away; the jungle news is wonderful. A gentleman from the local Springs Church contacted me that very evening and said they'd heard I'd been looking round it. They asked whether, if I were to buy it, I would rent them some space. I asked why.

'We've been praying and praying for something like this for many years, but we've never been able to get a building in Caistor. Every time we try, the council block us. We believe Caistor is spiritually very dark and there's been a big witchcraft movement around there. We've been given words of knowledge and prophecies in the past that we're going to be a light on a hill. Would you really, really pray into it for us?'

I agreed that if we ever took the building, we would rent them space. That wasn't a problem at all. I always wanted to help local churches, but this time it was a two-way thing. A small rental income would be a help, but more importantly, having a good, sound church actually in our building would give us a fantastically strong spiritual covering. I was more than pleased to pray for them.

87

I got in contact with our bank. The manager had a running joke with me about how I had to have another project every two years.

'Did you realise it's been two years?' I said.

'You've got another project?' he said.

'Of course I do.'

'Of course you do.'

'There's a building. Will you come and look at it with me?'

'Obviously, yes.'

I didn't know why I was asking him out there. However much I wanted the place, and however much he liked what Rock did, the money simply wasn't there.

He came to view, and we went round the buildings and walked some of the land.

This is phenomenal,' he said. 'It's got Rock's name all over. You've got to have it, and I'm going to help you all I can.'

This was wonderful to hear. I already had a plan.

'I've been thinking. If I could get our Heneage Road building paid for, would you use it as collateral here?'

'As long as it values up, it'd be OK.'

That was great news, with just one problem: if we were going to use Heneage Road as collateral then we needed to pay off our entire debt there. We'd only had it a couple of years, and we'd made little impact on the mortgage, so we still needed £120,000 to clear it.

I went back and opened it up to the guys in the office. They all committed to pray into the situation. Other people at my church and old friends all joined in. In the end we had tens of people praying for the building to come to Rock.

It's unmistakable. Prayer changes things. Almost immediately, money started coming in again, just like it came in for Heneage Road. I couldn't believe it. It was another reminder of how God provides if we are faithful.

88

Despite myself, I found myself getting nervous. The mortgage was going to put great pressure on Rock, and therefore ultimately me. It was such a huge plan, I needed to know from God that this really was His plan. I was praying to Him about it, but I seemed to get nothing back.

Perhaps it was the enemy whispering in my ear, perhaps it was my lack of faith, but I got more and more anxious. I really needed to know that this was from God.

In October I went to Wolverhampton to see Nathan Morris from the *Shake The Nations* ministry again. Stephen was at Bible College at the time, and one of the other students wanted to go, so I offered to take us all, and Stephen drove us over.

I was suffering with my bad leg, so I said,

'Look, you guys want to go around town. Go and have a wander, I'll do a bit of window shopping, we'll meet up for a meal, then we'll go to the service.'

They went off, and I went for a browse in Next. A lady followed me in. She approached me and said she had seen me outside the shop and that God had spoken to her. He had told her to come in and tell me that if I opened my Bible anywhere, then God would speak to me. I questioned her to make sure she was legitimate, and she surprised me by giving me the scriptures I'd been given when I went to start Rock: Isaiah 60 and 61, 'bind up the brokenhearted' and so on.

'My goodness,' I thought.

'Where are you from? What church?'

She didn't answer, just talked about Charles Wesley. She left me, but I followed her, curious to know more about her. I followed close behind her, right into Marks and Spencer's, but when I got inside, she had disappeared.

I opened my Bible and I found myself in Ecclesiastes, where I read the words:

'Be generous: Invest in acts of charity. Charity yields high returns.' (Ecclesiastes 11:1, MSG)

God then pointed me back to the book of Isaiah.

'If you get rid of unfair practices, quit blaming victims, quit gossiping about other people's sins, if you are generous with the hungry and start giving yourselves to the down-and-out, your lives will begin to glow in the darkness, your shadowed lives will be bathed in sunlight. I will always show you where to go. I'll give you a full life in the emptiest of places—firm muscles, strong bones. You'll be like a well-watered garden, a gurgling spring that never runs dry. You'll use the old rubble of past lives to build anew, rebuild the foundations from out of your past. You'll be known as those who can fix anything, restore old ruins, rebuild and renovate, make the community liveable again.' (Isaiah 58: 9-12, MSG)

This spoke to me so clearly about making sure that we were doing everything right before God.

God had already told me to invest in Rock, but I would do as I was told and invest in wider acts of charity. I relaxed about the move to Caistor and looked outwards. I put some money into a charity called Green Pastures and set aside what I could spare from my own life to invest back into Rock. This followed the pattern I've always done: for any new initiative, I feel it's important that I am the first investor, the first person to put any money in, and the first person therefore to take any risk. I tithe into Rock to this day. If I don't believe in it, how can I expect God to?

One week later, God spoke again about Isaiah, and told us at Rock to read the whole of chapter 58. At that time a lot of our staff were Christians and I asked them to pray into it. I asked them to guard their own hearts, and make sure we were all doing the right things before God. Going through the text we were challenged both as a charity and as individuals. One way we felt we'd been going wrong was by opening to trade on Sundays. We stopped doing that straight away. We stepped back, looked at ourselves and made sure everything we did was whiter than white. It was a powerful time.

Over the next few months, we had a constant stream of gifts, that turned into a small river. We received five, ten, twenty thousand pounds and made larger debt repayments. We got the mortgage down to £80k, £50k, £30k. The flow of money seemed unstoppable.

It was at that point a crisis I'd been facing in the background came fully out in the open. I faced personal disaster—and then witnessed what I believe to be an obvious miracle.

89

Some Christians don't believe that God still heals. They think that the gift of healing was given to the disciples in the early years to demonstrate the glory of God in the difficult first years of spreading the Gospel. These Christians believe all the miracles ended in the Book of Acts, in the years after Jesus ascended to Heaven, and that any such stories are fake.

With apologies to those Christians, I beg to differ. It's clear to me that God still performs miracles, and God still heals people. I certainly can't see anything that would prevent God from healing one person today through the ministry of another person.*

I've seen hundreds of healings in my life and in the lives of those around me, but during this period I had an amazing, powerful healing which can only be explained by God's power. I know very little about the theology of miracles except that things seem to get very complicated, very quickly. All I have is

* Of course, the power to heal is never from the gifted person; the power to heal comes from God and God alone.

my story, and, woven through the story of trying to raise funds to buy the Caistor building, here it is.

I'd had an operation on a knee a couple of years before, and all through the autumn, my other leg had been going into pain and spasm. I couldn't understand why, but guessed it was something to do with my body rebalancing.

I went to see a sports therapist and asked her to take a look. She worked on me, but soon stopped.

'I'm not touching this,' she said. 'I'm seeing a spasm going off *here*, but as soon as I release something here it sets off *there*. I've seen nothing like this. You need to get to your doctor.'

I went to the doctor, and he referred me on to someone else, who then said,

'No, it's not your knee. You need to see a hip specialist.'

I saw a hip specialist, and he said to me,

'I want you in straight away. Your hip is about to go.'

'No way. It's September. I haven't got time.'

'I want you in hospital.'

'Not a chance,' I said. 'I've got too much to do.'

'I'll take no responsibility if this hip goes. You'll have to take all the responsibility for that.'

'OK'

'I still need a date out of you.'

'I'll come in on the 30th of November, not before.'

I thought that would give me a chance to get over it before Christmas, which meant I could get Christmas sorted out before I went in, and everything would work out fine.

I got Christmas in place for all the staff and sat back to wait for the operation. I was an NHS patient, but they were sending me to a private hospital.

November 30th came, and I went in for the procedure. I'd heard of a surgeon who was very good, so I'd asked the hospital for him. He came into the ward and told me what would be happening. He explained the procedure and said that while he was fixing my hip, he would take the chance to alter my leg length fractionally to compensate for the difference in tendons I'd had all my life.

The anaesthetist came to see me and told me I'd be awake all the way through because he'd be giving me an epidural. I didn't like that at all, so he agreed to give me some sedation as well to take me under just a little. He turned back as he left, and said,

'And we won't say anything about the headaches.'

'What headaches?' I said, but he'd gone.

We met again in the operating theatre. He was chatting with a nurse as he worked on me, and he was ignoring me completely, like they do.

'My daughter was in trouble this week at school.'

'What for?' the nurse said.

'She'd had a go at the vicar's daughter.'

My ears pricked up; I'm a vicar's daughter.

'This vicar had been in to school to complain, all the rest of it. I had to see the headmistress. We had a bit of a laugh, and we talked it through. She was fine. We all know what these Christians are like.'

The nurse rolled her eyes, and they both laughed at the Christians. Out of the blue, he turned to me and said, in a voice that seemed suddenly very low and menacing:

'And I know exactly what I'm going to do to you.'

'Oh, what?' I thought, horrified, but before I could speak, I was under.

90

I came back to consciousness after the operation, and everyone was happy about how it had worked out. Stephen came to see me when I got back to the ward. We chatted, but I was feeling strange. I didn't want Stephen to see me being ill. He was upset and anxious to begin with because he'd never ever seen me in hospital. As I felt more unwell, I could see he was getting very frightened. He was with his friend from the Bible college, so I said,

'I'm all right, love. You two go now and have your tea. I'll be fine.'

They left, and I lay back on the pillows. I was feeling terrible, and it quickly got worse.

I couldn't do anything. I was in a mess. I was so annoyed because there was a 95-year-old in there who had had a hip operation and was virtually dancing around the ward two hours after. I wasn't allowed out of bed, because every time I tried to get out of bed, I ended up on the floor. My blood pressure collapsed to 65 over 35 and I was in a terrible state.

I was the youngest person to have the operation in the

ward, and I had by far the worst outcome. You're supposed to walk straight away after a hip operation, but I couldn't do anything, and they wouldn't allow me to do anything. They kept me in bed all the time; if I had to go to the bathroom I had to go in the chair. They came in every half an hour to take my blood pressure. I couldn't stand any lights, so I had to have all the curtains and blinds closed. I also had horrendous headaches, headaches like I'd never experienced.

I was determined. After four days I thought, 'I'm not staying here.'

I asked them if I could do the test stairs. If I made it, I could leave. No matter how I felt, I was adamant that I wasn't staying in hospital anymore.

On the fifth day they wheeled me to the stairs. I climbed the three stairs to the top, and they caught me just as I was about to black out. They got me back into the chair and put me back into bed straight away. I was so frustrated.

The following day, the doctor came to see me. A new sister had come on the ward. She'd been off for so many days and she wasn't happy with what was happening to me. Everybody had justified their bit of the operation and what they had done, but she was pushing them to look at the overall picture and to take a high-level view of what was going on.

They asked another anaesthetist, and got some ideas, and then another doctor from the operating team came to see me. He looked at my records and apologised to me.

'You've got a spinal leak. That's what's been causing all the problems. The epidural damaged your spine and spinal fluid is leaking out, and that's not good at all. In fact, we've had you on the critical list for the last four days.'

I heard that with some shock.

'I want you to go home and drink as much coffee as possible. The coffee should mend it together. If that doesn't work, then we'll have to have you back and do another operation.'

I was so glad I could finally go home. A friend of mine was a qualified nurse, and so she took me home and got me into bed. I couldn't do anything for myself, but John sat with me all the time. He watched me like a hawk to make sure I was OK and made me endless cups of real coffee. The doctors in Sheffield rang every day to check how I was.

At the end of the week, the leak in my spine was mended. I found later that the coffee treatment was rather fringe, and a bit of an experiment, but in my case, it worked very well.

I was still weak. I had tried to walk outside. I did it one lamppost at a time. I'd walk to a lamppost, and then the target was the next lamppost. It was difficult way beyond what I ever imagined, and my legs wobbled and my whole pelvis twisted and lurched like I was on a ship.

I had the shock of my life when I finally worked out why I was struggling so much: the operation had left my right leg four inches longer than the left.

We thought originally that the surgeon had corrected in the wrong direction, but that wasn't so. The operation was in the correct direction, but it had just been a disaster. Four inches is a huge amount. I couldn't balance, I couldn't do anything, and I needed people to hold on to me on both sides.

They booked me in for physiotherapy, but the physio took one look before saying there was nothing they could do and that I needed to go back to Sheffield for more surgery. This was terrible news. Even worse, I had to wait until after the New Year.

91

Just before Christmas, while I was still in shock from this news, the bank sent a surveyor to value both our current premises at Heneage Road and the new building out at Caistor. I could get around a little, and I was determined not to miss this, so I dosed up on painkillers and went out with him.

We began with Heneage Road. We had paid over £185,000 for that building and spent another £60,000 more, so I wanted to know if it would have enough value to act as collateral. That would mean we wouldn't have to come up with a deposit, so this was essential.

'Of course it will be worth that much,' he said. 'Just look at the land you've got here. Look at the work you've done in the building. You've put a new roof on the back. You've done all this, and you've done everything else. Look at the money you've poured into it, you've renewed everything.'

'OK,' I said.

Then I took him over to Caistor, and I told him the price history there. He knew a little of the story. He told me it was a repossession and had been on the market for two or three years.

I hadn't known it had been up for sale for so long, but it made sense. I believe that if God wants you to have something, He will keep it for you.

We went inside, and he looked round, and he sat down with me. I waited for him to begin, but he just looked at me.

'So,' I said. 'Have you got any idea what this is worth?'

He seemed lost in thought. Then he finally spoke.

'Just look around here,' he said. 'Look at the fittings. Look at the windows, look around. Look at the finishing touches on everything. Look at the floor space, look at the land. Just think about what this is worth.'

I shrugged. I didn't really know. That was his job.

'This is worth way more than a million. This is worth a phenomenal amount.'

And that's all he would say. Try as I might, he wouldn't be drawn further.

I drove him back to Heneage Road, and he left saying he'd be in touch in the New Year. For once I didn't mind the delay. It was time for a Christmas interlude. It was a time to relax with our families, away from all the pressure. Or so it should have been.

92

Before I'd gone in for surgery, I'd got everything ready for the staff at Rock. I always give big hampers and other gifts and arrange a Christmas meal. I'd got all that in place before I went into hospital.

It was only when I woke up on Christmas Day that I realised I had done everything for Rock, but I'd completely taken my eye off our family Christmas. Everybody had presents, but I hadn't thought about any food for us. The cupboards were almost empty. We didn't have a chocolate in the house. And of course, the shops were closed.

There was stuff in the freezer, so we'd have to make do. The boys were fine with that, bless them, but I felt so guilty and dispirited. Until the phone rang.

It was His Church.

'We've got two big hampers going. Can you think of any family that needs them?'

'Let me think about it. I'll give them a ring and see if they're in. I'll come back to you.'

I had a list of families who I knew would appreciate this generosity, so I rang round. Busy with their Christmas, not one of them answered their phones.

I went back to His.

'I'm so sorry,' I said, 'I can't get hold of these families.'

'Don't worry, we've placed one of them. We'll pray about the next one.'

I heard what happened later. One of the pastors had asked their team in their church to pray for guidance on what to do. After they had prayed, two teenagers got up from opposite sides of the room and went separately to the pastor. Both said the same thing.

'God has told us who we are to give it to. We're to give it to Pam.'

Richard, the leader of the church, called me.

'Will you be at home this afternoon?'

'I'm going nowhere.'

They brought this enormous hamper round to our house, brought it in and, because I could barely move, opened it for the first time in front of me and the boys.

I was amazed. It was beautifully done, and carefully presented, but it was what was in it that really affected us. There was a turkey, all the trimmings, and everything needed for a great meal. What's more—and we couldn't believe it—there was every single one of our favourite chocolates, the kids' favourite sweets, every favourite cake, our favourite everything. It was like God had handpicked them Himself. I don't know who was more bowled over, Richard or me.

When he told the His people what had happened, they were bowled over as well because they just felt that they'd been obedient.

That's the first time I'd been given anything in this way. I've lost track of the times I've been told by God to buy things and give them to people. I've been obedient and done that, over and over. To have it happen to me at a time of such difficulty was a truly wonderful experience.

93

The New Year came and went, and we were into 2018, and Rock needed me back. We had a lot to do as part of our usual operations, plus we needed to prepare for buying the new Caistor buildings in March.

I found I could get around with a combination of wheelchair, crutches, and struggling upstairs on my bottom, and I was off and away. I wouldn't let anyone help. I was determined, and I got back to work full time.

I took stock of the money we were raising for the Heneage Road building and found both good and bad news. We had got to the stage where we had £20k left to pay off and yet everything seemed to come to a standstill. It was as though the tap had been turned off for all the big givers.

I felt God challenge us about our tithing as a charity. Rock had always given, but when we looked at our tithing, we were short by quite a lot. Our everyday money was coming in and going out just as quick. We weren't progressing forward.

So, as a management team, we made a contract between

ourselves and God. We came before God in repentance and then we all signed the contract and gave wherever we could. We wanted to be known as givers.

Straight away, and completely unexpectedly, we had good volunteers coming on board to help. Some more gifts came in towards our building project. Also, we discovered we shouldn't have been paying rates and we would be due a rebate of £6,000-£7,000.

It's important to say that this was no "prosperity gospel". We never give to receive; we give only to bless other people. It just seems that God sees these gifts and very often blesses us in return. You really can't out-give God.

Finally, God said to me, 'Ask people to lend Rock £1,000 each. Undertake to repay it interest free, over five years.'

OK God. If you say so.

Some people went along with that plan, and we committed to pay them back. Others gave us £1,000 outright. So, the thousands kept coming and soon we were close to the mortgage being paid back completely. It became clear that soon we would have all the money.

At which point, things took another twist.

In February, I went over to see the specialists in Sheffield. They took more X-rays of my hip, which revealed it all. It was clear I needed the operation redone. I went back home and sat with the Lord. A deep fear took hold of me.

What if they couldn't fix it? What if too much damage had already been done? What if I was going to be like it for the rest of my life?

I prayed.

'God, I'm going to have to take Caistor in a few months. What do I do? I can believe you do miracles. You've done miracles in the past. You've healed my back. You've healed me of glandular fever. You've done many things in the past. But I'm struggling to believe you can do a miracle like this. Can you really reduce my leg by four inches?'

God didn't speak as such, but He gave me a vision. It was a simple room, and it was familiar. I struggled to remember how I knew the room—and then I knew. It was the empty room I'd been shown on that amazing weekend back in the early 1990s, at the end of the years of healing, when I laid out my fleece and when I felt God telling me to adopt my children.

This time, the room wasn't entirely empty. This time there was a gift there, a fully wrapped present with a bow on top.

I heard the Lord say said, 'Take it or leave it.'

I took the present, lifted it up in my arms. It was light, and I could hear the paper rustle. I wondered about unwrapping it, but then the vision faded. I couldn't work out what that meant, but I felt a strange sense of peace. I knew God was in this somehow.

A couple of days later, I realised I was walking better. I had a treadmill at home, and I'd been waiting until I healed before I tried on it. This was the morning. I got gingerly on and stepped out, fully expecting the usual pain, but it never came. I realised I was walking well.

I walked for ten minutes and felt no pain.

Nervous it would somehow fade, or that I'd falsely claim a healing, I didn't mention this to anyone. A couple of days later, they took me back to Sheffield. I walked in and the surgeon met me at the reception. He noticed immediately I was walking better and sent me for another CAT scan.

The results came in an hour later, and he showed them to me. He couldn't believe what he was looking at. He kept telling me to look at the scan, jabbing with his finger. I couldn't comprehend it, but he pointed it out to me. The four inches I had gained in one leg were gone.

I don't know who was more shocked, him or me.

It was true; the leg was back to normal, and it stayed like that. The surgeon looked at it, and at me, for a long time. He poked my leg, pondered it, and eventually marvelled at it. He finally let me go. It was clear I could walk, and my leg was restored.

How the extra four inches vanished was God and God alone. These days, if I hear of anybody going in for a hip operation, I don't tell them what happened to me till afterwards, because it's not fair. That's a problem though, as I cannot *not* tell. If I don't tell people what happened to me, then I feel I'm insulting God. It turns out that everybody gets to know what happened in the end!

I can still walk well today, and since that day I've felt no more discomfort. I still have the inch and a half difference caused by my tendons—but even there has been a healing. I still limp, but the pain has gone. Previously, if I walked up a steep hill, I would often end up having to walk backwards because of the terrible pain. Just recently I was on holiday in France, and I had a great big hill to walk up. Let me tell you, I just flew up that hill!

Happy, and feeling free to be back at work without trauma, I walked into the office, and got a shock. Everybody was gloomy. I asked what had happened.

'We've not got it Pam.'

'Not got what?'

'Caistor. We haven't got it.'

'What do you mean?' I said.

'That surveyor must think the market has shifted. He's down-valued Heneage Road. He said it's not worth what we wanted for the collateral. We're way off what we need for the mortgage company.'

94

I listened, careful, and calm. When God tells me something, I don't doubt. That building was ours. God had given us it and that's it.

'OK.' I said. 'And what about Caistor? Where did he rate that?'

'He's down-valued that, too. He's devalued both properties.'

'To what?'

They told me.

'But that's fantastic!'

'It is?' they asked.

By my own haggling, I'd already got the price down on Caistor from £780k to £680k, but the surveyor had valued it even lower. I called the estate agent.

'I've got a problem,' I said.

'What's that, Pam?'

'The property's been devalued. To £505k. I'll offer you £505k and not a penny more.'

'Not a chance,' he said. 'There's no way.'

He thought for a moment.

'I'll tell you what,' he said, 'we'll take all the land away. And the contents. If it's just the buildings for £505k, then you'll stand a chance the owner might accept.'

I wasn't having that. I had fallen in love with the land. Plus, the contents were the best of the best. The previous owners had been a private school, and there was so much in there that we could use for our students. Tables, chairs, book units. Masses of wooden furniture. Top-notch nursery equipment. Ball pools, slides, desks, computers, kitchen equipment. So much more. All the top end of everything. The previous owners had left it all standing in the building for three years, so it was clear to me they had no use for it. I had factored in being able to sell some of it to fund the first essential work on the building.

'No, I said. That offer is for everything in the building, and all the land. I want it as it is or there's no deal at all.'

Everybody around me in the office was looking at me, thinking, 'How dare you do this?'

'They'll never go for it,' said the estate agent.

'Look, will you do me a favour?' I said, 'Just go back to your client. Please? It's going to be ours. Don't worry.'

He said he'd go back to his client, and we ended our call, and that was that.

We heard nothing for weeks.

I went on with the mortgage application, regardless. I had faith!

95

To get the mortgage deal, we had to pay off the Heneage Road mortgage by a certain Friday. My secretary sent the final cheque through to the bank in time, but she sent it to the wrong department, and so the people who needed to see it never received it. We found out what had happened, and she was mortified. The deadline was approaching, and the whole deal could have been damaged, but I knew this was God getting involved again.

'It's not your fault,' I said to her. 'God has done this for a reason. He's putting this last thing on my shoulders now to make a point. He wants me to take that step of faith, not any of you. I've got to go to the bank and do this personally.'

We were running out of time, so I prepared to go to the bank to pay it off via direct transfer. Just before I went, I said to the guys in the office,

'We're going to get a phone call when I come back. And I know what it's going to be.'

'No way.'

'As soon as this building's paid off, you wait and see what

happens. And that's when the faith journey begins, because there's no way we can handle a mortgage like this without God.'

I went to the bank, made the last payment, and came back into the office. Within hours, the phone rang. They put the call through to me and it was the estate agent.

'We've got some good news. The owners of the Caistor buildings have been in contact. We can agree £505,000.'

'Including the land and the contents?'

'Including all the land and all the contents.'

I stayed calm. 'That's very good news. Thank you. Thank you very much. And please thank your client for me.'

I put the phone down as the office went wild around me.

It was a huge thing for us to take on. With Heneage Road as collateral, if we defaulted on the mortgage for Caistor, then we would lose both buildings. To some people, that would have seemed like I was taking a wild chance. But, you see, I don't take chances; I stand on my faith in God. God had said that building would belong to Rock, and therefore I knew it would be so. When the surveyor said it was worth over a million, how was it that he gave an official valuation of half that? Was he being kind? Much as I long for people to be kind, I doubt that explanation very much; I believe he was an experienced professional doing his job. I believe God told him how to value it. If he wasn't a Christian, then he wouldn't have realised it was God giving him that figure, but whether he was a Christian or not, when God speaks, people listen.

96

The building was ours, my hip had been healed, and so I settled back into usual business at Rock. Our work at Heneage Road for our students with additional educational needs was blooming, and the food bank was providing a valuable service.

God continued to provide for us. A grant came in for £9,300. A week afterwards, another sum of money came to take all our students on a day trip to a zoo. Another £3,000 was given towards a wage to employ a member of staff. The manager of a local supermarket did a collection for us and gave us retail training for our food bank.

The food bank had grown so fast it was starting to attract the occasional problem user, and I worried it wasn't wise to be running it in the same building as a lot of vulnerable adults. I went back to the council. I had a favour to ask.

'Is there any chance I could have part of Holme Hill school back? A couple of rooms just to run a food bank?'

The council agreed quickly to this. When we got back in, we were surprised to see that none of our advertisements for

Rock had been taken down. We took the big back kitchen, and a big back dining room, and we were away.

We saw numbers increase dramatically, but we always saw God's provision increase to match it. As was our need, so God provided. We never struggled. At one point, we needed a van. Soon we were given a grant, which meant we could afford to buy one. Then we needed the driver's wage. God sent us the driver's wage and now we fund it ourselves. Anytime I needed anything, I just prayed about it, and God sent provision. The regular supplies of food came from everywhere and anywhere. It was quite random.

For example, early on we'd get supplies from a local fish factory. They stopped because of a bad economic climate, and the person we were dealing with left.

'I need fish, Lord.'

It was a simple prayer, but the Lord heard it. Soon after, I had a lady from another fish company call me.

'We've got this supply of fish spare. Would you like it?'

'Yes, please,' I said. I got talking to her. Before I knew it, they had committed to supply us regularly with fresh fish.*

This was so typical, and we saw God provide in endless small ways. Another example was when I was worried about cleaning a building. The very next day I had a phone call, completely out of the blue, from a company willing to send their staff in to do charity work for a day.

* Nearly ten years later, at the time of writing, they still always try to do their best to help us.

97

Doing the actual deal for the Caistor buildings was a difficult process, and the bank made us jump many hurdles over the next few months. It wasn't like buying a house. This was a big commercial property. And even if it was agreed, we realised we would have much building work to do. Before I could even open the door, we would need £12,000 worth of checks and repairs. Everything must be checked in a public building. All the electrics, all the safety certificates, everything. I'd done nothing like that in my life, so the whole thing was one huge learning curve.

A surprising worry came in that summer. A local farmer came to look at the surrounding land. He wasn't impressed, and he went away leaving us with the impression that the land was basically useless. I wasn't worried: I knew God wouldn't give us land that was no good.

One day I'd been praying and talking to God about it, and then I went out for a drive into the country with Stephen. We went out south of Grimsby, heading out towards the coast around Skegness. We were driving and talking things through when I saw a hill in the distance. I had a sudden sense something was going to happen.

'God is about to show us what to do with the land,' I said.

We got closer and saw the hill was covered with a forest of young Christmas trees. I turned to Stephen, overjoyed.

'That's what we'll plant. God is showing us.'

I spoke to the local farmer again, and he agreed with me it could work.*

By August 2017, we had jumped every hurdle, dotted every 'i' and crossed every 't'. We got the purchase completed, and the Caistor building and the ten acres of land finally came to Rock. It hadn't been plain sailing, and there had been more than one crisis along the way, but now we had legal title. We were given the keys on August 7th, 2017. Truly, the next phase was beginning.

We had a dedication service in September, and my son Stephen preached again, this time on Faith. Something that was to become more and more necessary as the year progressed!

Springs Church were very generous with their time. They came round and helped us pray for the building. One of the

* Of course, God stepped in and soon we had a donation of 400 Christmas trees from a local farmer. She came down to help us plant them and she also got her team to put up a rabbit fence for us. A few months later, we had another donation of 850 trees, and volunteers from another company came and planted them. Praise Him! The one thing is that, at the time of writing, some six years later, very few of these trees have grown significantly. Perhaps the farmer was right, and I was wrong. Or perhaps God has a longer time frame for this than I know about!

elders, Mr. Robinson, led our staff team at Caistor, the directors of Rock, plus members of Springs Church, in prayer-walking and anointing the Caistor building. We put salt all the way around the perimeters of the land and anointed the entire land with oil. We walked the fields and the footpaths together, praying as we went.

After that, they anointed me, and there were words of knowledge given to me:

'See, I will make you into a threshing sledge, new and sharp, with many teeth. You will thresh the mountains and crush them and reduce the hills to chaff.' (Isaiah 41:15 NIV)

'Every place on which the sole of your foot treads shall be yours.' (Deuteronomy 11:24 NKJV)

God was saying there was much more to come, that I could go as far as I wanted. Someone said they sensed God would give me supernatural hearing. As those words were said, my left ear immediately seemed to open up. There was nothing wrong with my ear, but it somehow felt like I'd been given extra hearing.

These were glorious moments, and they came as a great gift from God. At that point, I truly felt free. I felt that I, and Rock, could fly.*

* *Those people who gave us the £1,000 loans? We paid all of them back within three years.*

98

We slowly began to use the buildings, while dealing with the raft of new issues that brought. I was all too aware of the fact that we had a huge mortgage that needed paying, as well as a vast amount of building work still to do. I knew Rock's income very well, and it was clearly not going to be enough.

The first thing was to get a tea-room up and running. I could have repeated the Victorian tea shop idea, but God had moved us on into a new season. We developed a new café idea that was more conventional but had the chance to develop in new ways.

That was followed by a sweet shop full of old-fashioned jars of sweets, rock, fudge and all sorts—but even there I had opposition. People thought I was taking too much on. We didn't have the staff, they pointed out. We barely had the premises. We certainly didn't have the footfall.

I didn't listen. We were going ahead, out into wide new territory, and God was with us. These two enterprises were but tiny teaspoons of water in the wonderful ocean in front of us.

'If we're going to do it, we'll do it big.'

I got the tearoom and the sweetshop going, and they took off immediately. Over the years they've been worth their weight in gold.

I've always been the same. If I'm going for it, I'll go for it. I don't believe in doing small. For one thing, people don't realise how I question myself all the time; and I question God because I'm frightened of getting it wrong.* As soon as we had things together enough, and we had some residents in the house, I called Springs Church again. They were delighted when I told them we were ready. They began café church on Sundays, and some of our residents went. It was a blessing for us to begin like this, and we certainly needed their help. Problems came up, of course, and when they did, they could have an unusual twist.

* In fact, some prophets prophesied over me just before I began this book, and they said they believed God was saying I shouldn't be so frightened of getting things wrong.

99

I took one lady on in the tearoom. She wasn't up to standard and wasn't doing things right throughout. Then, two months in, I discovered that she'd been dabbling with witchcraft and the occult.

I had to get rid of her, and it was quite a nasty moment. She was nasty to the staff, and that wasn't appropriate at all. As she went, she said something to me about witchcraft, and how I'd regret falling out with her.

A week later, I bought a brand-new ice cream freezer and had it filled with ice cream. It was all completely new stock. I came in one morning and I looked at the ice cream. It was running like water. I couldn't believe it. Everything around it in the freezer was still frozen. Then one of the team called me and showed me round the toilets. We found that every toilet in the building was filled with horse manure.

We realised we could be facing spiritual opposition again. I talked to my friend Shirley, the missionary, and she told me that, years back, she and her husband felt God tell them to give out Gospel tracts in Caistor. During that day, they'd passed the building we were in now. She had put a hand on one of the perimeter fences while she prayed out over the valley. She could still remember the horror of lifting her hand and finding it wet with blood.

We also realised we had a ghost, who would often walk down one particular corridor. He was an old man, wearing a hat. One of our staff met him and talked to him without realising who he was. He asked her about credit cards, and what they were and how they worked. As they were talking, she turned away for a second. When she turned back, he had vanished.

We prayed hard around each of these issues, and that kind of problem seemed to subside.

I had more worldly concerns too, of course. The building was slowly getting done. I was back to working long hours. There were times when I had no staffing, and I needed to face front and get on with it. At one point, I was doing all the baking for the tearoom. I baked in the night, then I'd drive the ten miles to Caistor in the early hours in the morning, delivering it all, and making sure it was all in place for them. Sometimes I would go on to bake a load of quiches in Caistor, ready for them to start the day off. I'd get that done, then I'd run back to Grimsby to get that end opened and ready for the staff coming in.

The next big challenge was to get through the planning for the redevelopment we need to make the business truly viable. This was mainly work on the house attached to the larger premises. I wanted to develop it so that we could offer residential places to our students. It was an old house, Grade 2 listed, but I had hoped that once people had understood what we wanted to do, and why, they'd get behind us and it would end up being straightforward.

I was very wrong.

The building work began, and the council, the architect, the building officers, and the conservation officer all got involved. With every visit and every letter, the thing got more bogged down in their different plans and their different agendas. Everything blocked everything else. Slowly, we ground to a halt.

I couldn't believe it. I was constantly talking to God, refusing to believe the situation, and yet God didn't seem to help. If anything, the tangles were multiplying.

Time passed, and the work was almost at a standstill. My prayers grew agitated.

'Lord, I don't believe this. If you've given me this building and you want me to do this work, then why are we so blocked? That house is supposed to be part of this provision of this building. I don't believe for one minute we can't use it.'

For months, nothing changed. We went on to Christmas 2017, and on into 2018 with the situation gridlocked, bound tight in chains of administration and obscure legalities. I realised I had no choice to put our plans for the house on the back burner while all those experts fought it out.

100

In the first part of 2018 I realised I had been disobedient to God. When we moved in, the place was filled with furniture, all of which came free, rolled in with the deal. We needed it, because, after we'd spent £12,000 on opening the building, we wouldn't have any money to buy new furniture. At that point I promised God that I would give Him 10% of the furniture we'd inherited in this way, and that 10% would go to a Christian organisation.

After a time, nurseries, different people, different organisations had begun to approach us to buy what we had. We had sold bits and pieces on, and the money had kept coming in. It took us off guard and it wasn't till about halfway through that I thought, 'Oh, my goodness me.'

I went into the office, and I said to the staff,

'We've made the biggest mistake possible.'

'What?'

'I promised God that we'd give Him the first 10% of everything in here. And now it's nearly all gone.'

I had to come on my knees before God and say sorry and promise that everything else would now go to God.

We got in contact with Jacob's Well, a Christian charity in Beverley, who set up schools in Africa.

'I've got all sorts of school material. There are desks, chairs, lots of education material. Chemistry equipment, maths books, everything you could think of, going up to twelve years of age. Educational toys. Nursery stuff, the lot. You come and collect it and I'll give you the lot.'

In the meantime, a company had come in to check over all our phone lines. One of their gentlemen asked me.

'What are you doing with all these old computers?'

'We're going to see if we can bring them back on board to use them for students. They don't need anything brand-new. They should be OK.'

'No, no, no,' he said. 'Get rid of those. We've got stuff that comes in that we do up. It's stuff that's been given to us which is far better than this. It's practically new still. We'll give you all that instead.'

They were as good as their word, so we then gave Jacob's Well all our original computers. They took van load after van load from us, and they said they'd never been given such quality as that before. That all went off to a school in Africa.

I felt terribly convicted, and so in the end, we gave a lot more than 10%. So that was one time I was defiant of God, even if it was by accident—and how I put things right.

In late April, just as the sun was coming out and the land was beginning to come into blossom, a Christian TV channel came to see us. They wanted to film a sequence about what we were doing. They sent a small team to put together the report, and the reporter brought his daughter to give her some work experience. He was in mid-interview with me in the house when he felt somebody tapping hard on his shoulder. He stopped speaking and excused himself to the cameraman. He thought it was his daughter, so he turned around to her.

'What do you want?'

'Nothing. Why?'

'You just tapped me on the shoulder.'

'No, I didn't.'

Something supernatural had just happened, and it freaked him out. We couldn't understand what it was, and we carried on with the filming. It went smoothly, and we parted, and I got on with the rest of my day.

The next time I spoke to him, he was shocked, and rather in awe. He told me that the time he had felt the tap on his shoulder was the time his mother had died in Australia. Was that God? An angel? Or a spirit? And why would they use that strange way of speaking into his life? We both agreed on how confusing the world of the spirits can be!

101

The months passed. Heneage Road had settled into a good rhythm. We had more day students, and some great staff and volunteers who were running a very successful mix of day services: crafts, woodwork, music and drama workshops, and gardening. The food bank at Holme Hill was helping many people too. Everything was running well, with just one exception—our building project out at Caistor, where the battles seemed endless.

We got to Christmas and into 2019 with no proper planning progress visible. We had the girls' side of the building work on the house complete, but it had reached the stage where no-one could agree. Things were utterly deadlocked with all the various departments and agencies involved in the planning process, and people were starting to say forward movement was impossible. As we headed out into January, I found it harder and harder to believe that we were so blocked, and that God wasn't helping the work He had called me to.

One cold, grey morning in February, I opened the tearoom up for the builders, then came out and headed for my car. I'd been up most of the night working and praying, and I was exhausted. I tripped, went flying straight across the car park, and fell hard on the sharp gravel. I ripped my trousers, and got blooded all the way down, on my elbows, hands, and knees.

I sat there on the car park floor, with nobody else around, as something finally broke inside me, and I yelled at God.

'This isn't funny. Not at all. Where is my help now? When you said there'd be help for me, where are you now? Why are you giving me this building if I can't use that? I don't believe it, God. What are you going to do about it?'

I was so angry, so frustrated. I had reached the end of the road. I had no idea what do to next.

'God, you've come up all this. I can't do this, so what are you going to do about it? It's over to You. You keep your building.'

I shudder when I look back. This is the way I was talking to the Lord?

I sat there for a while, sorted myself out, picked myself up, stopped my pity party, got in my car, and went back to Grimsby. I opened up Heneage Road, did the day's work, and came back out to Caistor to lock up and find out how the builders were getting on.

As I pulled into the carpark, I noticed a lone car parked there. The driver's door opened. A gentleman got out and stood, looking at me.

He was in his fifties, of average height, quite heavy-set. He had greyish, balding hair, and wore nondescript jumper and jeans.

Then a small boy got out of the passenger side of the car. He was nondescript looking too, perhaps nine years old. He too stood and stared at me.

'Can I help you?' I said, disconcerted.

'Come on,' the man said. 'Let's go inside and have a look.'

He smiled. He had a kind smile.

Something took hold of me. Any more questions seemed too rude. The man seemed so sure of himself that we all three set off walking around the building.

I began by giving them a tour with commentary, but soon I tailed off and let the two of them see for themselves. As we went, the man looked at the walls, the doors, the windows, and the layout. Occasionally he'd glance at the boy, to make sure that he was taking it all in. I noticed how the boy's attention never wavered.

Finally, the man spoke to me.

'I bet the conservation officer said you can't do *this*, you can't do *that*.'

I confirmed that was so. We walked a bit more until he spoke again.

'I bet the planning officer said you can't do *this* because of *this* regulation, *that* regulation.'

I nodded. Bang on.

More walking, and more of the same.

'The conservation officer would have said you can't do this because of this because of that because of the other. Your architect would've thought about this, this, this, and this. And your builder would say—'

He was losing me. But I recognised some of it.

'That's exactly what they were saying!'

He nodded and turned to the boy.

By now I had realised the boy was his son. Distracted, I was thinking about how old he was, and how he must have had his son late in life.

'What sort of mortar do you think is here?' he'd ask the boy. 'And what do you think is in it?'

I was amazed to hear this nine-year-old child list all the things that were in this mortar.

'And what do you think they should do here? And there?'

This nine-year-old had all the answers. What this young lad didn't know about building was unbelievable. He was completely across both the detail of the building, and the background of how it would have been built.

I could see the man was teaching the boy, and that the boy was a more than capable pupil.

'And what do you think this is made of?'

The boy would give him the full details. Which, for a listed building with non-conventional building materials, was incredible.

'This is phenomenal,' I said. 'This is a tremendous help to me. But I've had so many other problems beyond what you've seen here. Could I take your number and get my architect to give you a ring? You both know more than me.'

It turned out he was called Mr. Bones, and he had recently moved to the area from London. He was a building inspector, and his wife was a conservation officer. He and my architect spoke within the week, and lo and behold, amazing, we could move forward. Whatever Mr. Bones had said about all the different regulations cleared the way. For each area, he told them what they needed to do to satisfy the regulations and move on. Everybody agreed at last, and we were off! The end of the building works was finally in sight.

Two Bible verses spring to mind:

'Do not forget to show hospitality to strangers, for by so doing, some people have shown hospitality to angels without knowing it.' (Hebrews 13:2, NIV)

'With man this is impossible, but with God all things are possible.' (Matthew 19:26, NIV)

102

This visit seemed to free everything up. We started day services for mixed sexes later that spring 2019, and I watched in delight as the building work went on apace. Our first four residents arrived in our Caistor house on the Monday before the COVID-19 lockdown in March 2020. Lockdown came and went. Springs Church began services for residents as soon as the pandemic legislation allowed it.

Rock at Caistor has gone from strength to strength. At the time of writing (Christmas 2023) we have seven resident students in Caistor. Our capacity is twelve, and we have done quite a few respite care bookings. To become one of our residents is a very calm, very measured process, with a very slow and careful induction process.

We've had troubles, but we've faced them down, and we go on stronger. I have had it easier than some because I know that if I give God our troubles, then He will walk beside us while we resolve the problem. Over the years, He has proven His faithfulness repeatedly, so I no longer doubt.

Some of the residents come into Grimsby for day services

or enjoy the day services at Caistor. Volunteers and staff help them to work on the land, the community allotment, and the greenhouse. Some of them serve in the shop, some in the tearoom, some in the grounds. There are craftwork, IT, music and puppet workshops—and some of them learn to cook too. The difference having such focus and purpose to their lives is phenomenal, and sometimes I sit back in awe at a Father who has helped me achieve my goal of establishing an enterprise that can care for so many disadvantaged people for the rest of their lives if they want it.

103

I was told when I started Rock that people wouldn't trust me for at least 10 years. The problem is that Grimsby sees a constant flow of new community groups. People notice a need and their heart moves them to do something. They set up and they get going, and they attract some funding. They get a certain amount of money, and what they set up lasts as long as the funding. When that tap gets switched off, the initiative shuts down, and people are left high and dry again. This happens constantly in the town, but we've never done that. Anything we start, we've kept alive. Including the Rock Food bank. Even though it's been quite a slog at times.

I've kept it going, because in the end it's simple.

Jesus said to him, "Feed my sheep"' (John 21:17, ESV).

Starting with that one gift of food from His church at Christmas 2014, we got the food bank up and running out of our own premises in back in 2015, and it's been in operation nonstop ever since. We give bags of food to people who come by, and we also provision the local churches. If they call us and say we have someone who is genuinely in need, we'll provide everything for them. The same for social services.

Similarly, if there is a situation in which people are really struggling, perhaps have nothing in the house, nothing to sleep on, then we can give them furniture from our second-hand shop.

We get people ringing up the office all the time and saying that they haven't been given food. We do benefit checks as people come in to check they are eligible, and this can cause arguments, and we need very clear boundaries to stop people abusing the system. Of course, that can cause disagreements, which can turn nasty. Our staff can get a lot of verbal abuse, especially if the person is on drugs when they turn up, but there are many people who are grateful. So, it's a mixture. We've had no big trouble; I've only once had to call the police, and that was nothing to do with the food bank, more for a fight between some of the service users outside.

I love to be in there, and I love to sit down and talk to the people who come in. It's not always happy though, and there are many ways to help that aren't just with food. One lady came in to talk to me especially. I sat with her, and she poured her heart out, crying all the time. Two days earlier, she'd gone down into the main part of town. She'd walked home through some of the quieter streets, and a guy got hold of her and raped her in one of the alleyways. She'd told nobody, and the only person she felt she could come to was me.

I see that as such an honour. I could comfort her and give the gospel to her as well. She knew the Lord and had been involved with church in her hometown, so I could remind her of the Truth and pray with her. She ended up going to the police in the end, and her attacker got caught, and we could support her through all that.

. . .

Eventually, we saw the need for a food bank wasn't going away. In fact, it was increasing, to where the initiative needed its own premises.

There is an area in Grimsby called the East Marsh. It's known as one of the areas of greatest social need in the country, possibly even Europe, depending on whose figures you look at. That's a cliché in the town, and I hate to look at it in those terms. People always like to look for the bad news, and the endless repetition of those statistics is a self-fulfilling prophecy, but there is truth there too. The area has a concentration of poverty, a high rate of generational unemployment, and many people living there have trouble buying enough food for themselves.

Just before Covid hit us all, back in January 2020, I noticed a suitable building in Garibaldi Street, on the south-west corner of the East Marsh. It was closed and clearly on its way to becoming derelict, but it looked like it had the size enough to work for a serious food bank operation. The problem was that I'd heard it needed at least £100k spending on it.

I still thought we could make it work, and so, when the council decided they wanted to get rid of it, we applied to take it over as another transfer of assets. Again, this was an immense pressure on us, as we'd have to fund the building work ourselves, but I could hear God at my back encouraging us on.

There was one problem: the change in title should have gone through simply, but there were an astounding number of technical hitches and errors, which meant things took a year longer than they needed to.

That gap allowed all the local thugs time to break in. They were probably teenagers, but they did a lot of damage. When we had first looked at it, the building was fine upstairs, and needed no work. By the time the transfer of assets had gone through, and we took ownership, local vandals had got in and completely wrecked it. They had taken out the copper piping, ripped out all the electrical wiring, wrecked the roof, and smashed every single window. Sadly, the council decided it wasn't their responsibility to help us with any of that, and we ended up paying for all of it. Once again, we were offered so much by local companies, with donations helping us with so much of the work.

104

Grimsby has a reputation for being a troubled place, and to some extent, in some areas, that can be true—though I think it's a lot less troubled than a lot of big cities. There is certainly something about the town that makes people want to climb up onto roofs. You can see it early on. The young teens love to scale the fences at my church as a ladder to the flat roof areas. They're happy just to sit up there and chat, drink, and smoke, or perhaps have a little fun blocking the drains or tagging the walls. It's like a clubhouse for them.

As they get older, things get a little more serious. When we first moved into Heneage Road, we'd be in meetings, and we'd see local teenagers skateboarding on our roof and then jumping over to the flats next door. They were risking their own lives, and it was scary to watch.

The real trouble comes a little later. Several times a year, someone older and more serious will get up onto a roof somewhere in town. Sometimes they are drunk, or on drugs, sometimes they're just angry. They rip the tiles off, throw them at the police, make demands, until the police lure them down.

Even in the autumn I was writing this, there was a rooftop protest from a young man which had a serious impact on our building.

It was a Sunday evening, and I was at a service in church when a lady I knew as the mother of one of John's friends came into the service and took me outside. I checked my phone to see thirty missed calls from John. She explained; there was a problem at the food bank, and he had eventually asked his friend to ask her to fish me out of the service!

I headed for Garibaldi Street and found the whole block wrapped in a police cordon. A young man had scaled a building along the block from the food bank, come over to our roof, and got stuck in, ripping tiles off and throwing them down onto the street below. In a few hours, he had caused extensive damage. His one-man protest (I never found out what it was about) cost us many thousands of pounds, which we had to add to the thousands of pounds worth of damage from another incident a couple of months before.

105

You see them on the roofs, but you also see them with knives. Once we were in fully into the Garibaldi Street building, we began to get break-ins, so we had CCTV cameras installed. We put them in the day before a further break-in happened, and so the perpetrators didn't realise they were on camera. We got clear footage of one young man caught red-handed, but the police said they couldn't use the photo in court and so they wouldn't be acting. This went back and forth for a day or so until we gave the photo to the local paper. They printed it and the police arrested the man the following day.

The East Marsh is one of the more difficult areas, and there are constant battles in and around the food bank. People can get very agitated, angry, and physical inside the building and we run into lots of threatening behaviour. Some of this is understandable, some of it, I feel, is not. We're managing food distribution, for free, to a lot of people, and we do our best.

The wider community faces extraordinary pressures. At one point, we were told there were gangs coming over from Manchester. They were getting hold of young teenagers, fifteen- and sixteen-year-olds. They were taking them down to London as drug runners while telling the families they would look after them and make sure there was bread on the table. They would give them money too. But some of those children who didn't do what they were told down in London ended up with their hands cut off.

The police came to tell us about that, and you could see that even they were daunted by the evil they were having to confront. So far, the food bank hasn't had a big problem with violence, but I have to think of the volunteers. Other food banks have had trouble, so I've prepared by making ours like a mini Fort Knox. If anything were to happen, we could close the whole thing off straight away. Even with our security systems, we get people constantly trying to break in. Over time, we've added many measures to keep the building safe, including extensive CCTV, steel shutters, and complicated alarm systems.

All this for a building whose only purpose is to help the surrounding community!

106

The amount of food donated to our food bank is incredible and much needed. In 2023, we gave out 30,810 food parcels with a fair value of £13.50 per parcel. That comes to £415,935 of food donations alone. We work this out on £1.50 per meal, on the low side compared to what they are getting.

We open three days a week and can easily feed 400 people on any one of those days, and the numbers are always climbing. A good 90% of them need food badly. We all want to get the numbers down, but with the economy as it is, everyone is struggling.

We use benefit advisors to go through the benefits and see what else they're entitled to. Recently we're getting new people coming in who are in full-time work, but who are only earning the minimum wage and who therefore can't afford to live. Many people can only find zero hours contracts and are vulnerable in that way. My feeling is the need for the food bank will only grow because of the state of the economy.

We're not able to give people as much as we used to. Our goal is to give them at least three meals a day for three days. We aren't there to feed them for the week, but we are there for crises. So, they get a lot of fruit and vegetables with all sorts of protein. Meat pie, fish, and another meat product. That's three solid meals. Some of our regulars can cook, and that's something we encourage. We've given out a lot of slow cookers and recipe books, and we've recently been putting in little cookery lessons too.

A brief story may give you the sense of what it's like.

There is one man who regularly tries it on. One day he came in and told a tale of such need that the volunteer gave him the extra bag he wanted. The next time he came in, he did the same, and the next volunteer did the same. Soon he'd been doing it for a while and the volunteers had been going along with him, and it turned into a regular thing. Somehow, we all turned a blind eye, despite him every time taking more than other people were getting, until he came in, looked in the bag we gave him, and started complaining. There wasn't enough of this, and he didn't like that, and where was the other that he had last time? How come we thought we could treat him like this?

'I tell you what,' I said. 'Pass that bag over to me.'

He did so.

'Thank you,' I said and walked away.

'Aren't you going to give me it back?'

'No.'

'Eh?'

'You're not happy with the bag, so you don't have to have it.'

'But you've got to give me a bag.'

'No, I haven't. I really haven't. I give you this bag out of the goodness of our hearts, but I don't *have* to give you a bag at all. It's a charity.'

'But I want a bag. Well, can't you give me—OK, I'll have that bag back then.

'No, you won't.'

He started ranting and screaming at me and then eventually calmed down and left.

The next time he came, he asked.

'Is Pam here?'

I don't think she is,' Stephen said.

'I suppose I ought to apologise.'

'Maybe you should.'

And so, he did. Eventually.

A couple more months went by, and I saw he'd come in again.

'Are we friends today, then?' I asked.

He looked at me and smiled.

'Friends, Pam.'

We were back to being fine. Until he got high on drugs, when we went through the same battle again.

It's quite an adventure, greeting some people. You never know where you are with them.

'Are we friends, or are we enemies today?'

'Friends, Pam.'

If you treat people with respect, they treat you with respect.

107

Life at Rock is a road with hills and valleys.

One week I can be in the Houses of Parliament, invited to a gala evening by big business. There are special dinners locally at which I am guest of honour. I was invited to the concert in Buckingham Palace for the Queens' Platinum Jubilee.

The next week I can be haggling with builders over whether we should install acrylic windows or whether we can afford proper glass. Or how on earth we find a reliable cleaner. I can be wondering how we have got to 56 employees and another 50 volunteers and how on earth I'm supposed to get round them all. Or I can be rolling with the punches in the latest battle for funding for our students. (I've noticed this battle coming more and more frequently. It's a sign of the times.)

One thing I've never got complacent about is how quickly and precisely the enemy can strike. The devil is a master of deception, and he's very clever, very subtle, and can come when you least expect it, through the people you have taken into your heart. Sometimes all the troubles arrive at once. It's as though a devil comes and tries to push you down and out. Those moments are the hardest of the hard.

In September 2023, for example, we had a break-in at our Caistor premises in which a tractor and gardening equipment worth around £20,000 were stolen. The residents were very shocked, very scared that the thieves would come back and break into their rooms again. The insurers weren't prepared to cover anything like the full amount of the theft. We comforted the residents, then got down on our knees and prayed for restitution.

In December 2023 we were targeted by a very slick internet fraud scheme and had £60,000 stolen from our bank account. Again, after calling the bank fraud team, we got down on our knees and put it before God.

In both cases the full amount of money was returned to us within weeks.

Especially after the second time, I was so relieved I found I couldn't stop praising God. It was a case of 'Thank you God, Thank you God,' all day long.

In those moments when you cannot see the light and you feel you're in a tunnel, it becomes all about simply believing God and trusting Him and focusing on the truth.

'I am going to come out of this. God knows I was going to go through this. God is here, even though I can't see Him at the moment. God is here and all I have to do is trust God and hold on.'

Those are the hardest times. It's all about standing in your faith. It's so important to keep yourself surrounded by people praying for you and not to be with people who tell you to give up.

It's all about realising the implications of what you are

doing when you step out in God's will. When you're doing things for God and you're making progress, Satan will come against you. Some people don't realise how real Satan is. He's got his demons (and goodness knows what else), and they will do everything they can to stop you. My advice is simple, but deep and long-lasting: always, always clothe yourself in the armour of God.*

---

* *'Therefore put on the full armour of God, so that when the day of evil comes, you may be able to stand your ground, and after you have done everything, to stand. Stand firm then, with the belt of truth buckled around your waist, with the breastplate of righteousness in place, and with your feet fitted with the readiness that comes from the gospel of peace. In addition to all this, take up the shield of faith, with which you can extinguish all the flaming arrows of the evil one. Take the helmet of salvation and the sword of the Spirit, which is the word of God.' (Ephesians 6:13-17, NIV)*

108

One difference in Rock is something many people will never see. We will give people opportunities that other people will say no to. Because of this, we often get our hands burned and many times I think, 'We'll never do this again.' But how many times would Jesus do it to us?

Perhaps someone has done the dirty on you. So what? You've got to make yourself vulnerable again and be willing to take the chance for them to hurt you.

Many of our employees have issues, but we give them work here. Sometimes they need special attention, but I never forget they wouldn't get a job anywhere else. We've done that with many people. But because you work with those people and different people have different capacities, there are a lot of knock-backs, and you get hurt and disappointment.

The cure is always to go back to Scripture and go back to our ethos. We work with people who have learning disabilities and who are disadvantaged, and we are giving those disadvantaged people an opportunity where we can. We have to take care of how we do it, and we've learned from our mistakes.

Sometimes we definitely employ them too soon and maybe sometimes we ought to just give them volunteering opportunities and bring them along like that. We've had to learn on our side too, and when it works, it can work spectacularly well.

One lady springs to mind. She had difficulties with anxiety that stopped her from engaging with the world. She began at Rock by volunteering. Then we gave her a little part-time job which grew into a full-time job, and that was hard at first because her anxiety and social phobias were very strong. She'd be the first to admit she feared everything and everybody and had no confidence in herself whatsoever. Yet today she's managing my second-hand shop in the centre of town.

The part that people don't understand is that we don't work for a profit. I know I could get a lot more money out of that shop. For example, I know if I could put a card machine in there, it would make a big difference to the takings. Or if we could build an internet presence for the shop we'd do better. But that lady doesn't like working with technology, and she would struggle with a card machine or updating a website. So, everything in that shop is cash, and it has almost no profile online.

People have criticised me for that, but the shop covers its costs, it pays her wage, it pays the rent, and it makes a small profit. What is more important, me getting the money? Or what is happening in that lady's life and how she has grown in confidence and her competence? She's gone through lots of problems, and she's had problems with family. We've been there for her, I can trust her 100%, and she's ended up coming to faith, which is priceless. What God has done through that lady and the way she's come on is worth so much more than getting money out of that shop and making it a profitable business.

109

Whenever we have a problem, I give it to God. My process always goes like this:

Step 1 is to work out exactly what the problem is. What, really, is the issue here?

Step 2 is to bring it before God. Sometimes I talk to Him like I would a friend alongside me, sometimes it's more formal, and I'm down on my knees and very serious. The conversation is always along the same lines:

'Here's my problem Lord, I can't see how to solve it. Please Lord, I surrender to You and your almighty power. Will You take this from me and help us come through this?'

Step 3 is to accept that God is now in charge, and that whatever happens is according to His will, and therefore is for the best.

Step 4 is for us then to use all of our God-given talents to solve our end of the problem. God will always, always step in and guide us to a happy ending somehow.

Sometimes people find my familiarity with God disrespectful. They say I'm not reverent enough, that I'm over familiar. I disagree. I'm fully aware of the glory of God, of how taking Him for granted leads to disaster. We see that repeatedly in the Old Testament—and the awe-inspiring power of Jesus in the Book of Revelation is, well, a revelation. I never ever take God for granted!

However, I also see how Jesus called God 'Abba'. This is an old Aramaic word for father, which encompasses affection, closeness, and trust. Abba is the word a child could use to express their childlike trust in a loving daddy. We aren't Jesus, but the Apostle Paul has this to say:

'For you did not receive the spirit of slavery to fall back into fear, but you have received the Spirit of adoption as sons, by whom we cry, "Abba! Father!" (Romans 8:15, ESV)

We are God's adopted children and so we too can also feel a child-like confidence in His love for us.

As the Bible says:

'God chose the foolish things of the world to shame the wise; God chose the weak things of the world to shame the strong.' (1 Corinthians 1:27, NIV)

I'm like a child with a simple faith. I see nothing wrong with chatting to God all day long!

The other criticism people have is when they accuse me of following a "prosperity gospel". This is the idea that we pray in order to get material benefit.

That's absolutely not right.

You might remember how, when I was a child, the wisdom from my parents and the church was 'Keep the pastor poor, keep him humble.'

It's so true that the Bible is packed with verses that reinforce that idea. Here's one from Timothy:

'Those who want to get rich fall into temptation and a trap and into

many foolish and harmful desires that plunge people into ruin and destruction.' (1 Timothy 6:9, NIV)

Yet ... I've mentioned how, even as a young child, I'd think that couldn't be the complete story. I'd look at the wealthy men in the Bible.* Some of them built colossal fortunes. I'd think, well, they were all blessed in God's eyes, how are we so poor? When I think back, I can see how God has always helped me with finances. Why would He bless me so abundantly if money is bad?

So many people don't understand that our money isn't ours. It belongs to God, and we've just been lent it. We are not in charge; God is in charge. He's in charge of our lives, He's in charge of our finances, He's in charge of everything.

The problem many people have when they pray for good finances is that they don't make Jesus the Lord of their lives. Plenty of people accept Jesus into their hearts as their Saviour, but fewer of us accept Him also as our Lord. When you accept him as Lord, He's Lord over everything. He's Lord over your life. He's Lord over whatever you do, He's Lord over your finances. He's Lord over the lot. I've always seen Him as that, and I know God can take everything away from me just in an instant. In what I do at Rock, whatever I do in life, I check with Him for everything.

Over the years, so many people have come up to me and told me an initiative I was beginning wouldn't work because it will cost too much money. So many times, I've been advised I'm taking on too much and I should give up. I stand on the principle that if God has asked you to do something, God will fund it. And if God is not funding it, then you've got a problem, and you might need to look at whether you're trying to do it from

* Solomon, Job and Boaz, to name but three!

your own desires, in your own strength. Has God spoken to you? Is He in it? If so, then OK. He will fund it.

Some people ask how I know that it's not the enemy funding it. That can definitely happen. There are organisations I don't approve of, and they will often try to buy involvement with what we are doing. We have turned down many gifts of money when I've not been happy with the ethics of, or the spiritual influences on, the donor.

In the end, it's simple. I'm always praying around the area of provision for us. When we receive a generous offer from a new donor, before I accept, I will pray around it and test my feelings. It's not until I feel confident and at peace with the person, or the gift, that I know the gift is good. I've got to have that peace to know it's all from God.

There is a wider question. How do we distinguish when we are following our own will rather than God's will? How do we know that it's God leading us, not the enemy pushing us off track? I believe the acid test of whether God is speaking to me is when I act and then I get that unmistakable peace inside.

Sometimes I've had to take that step of faith. That day I had to go to the bank and pay the last mortgage payment on Heneage Road was a big test for me. I knew as soon as I had made that payment, the phone would ring, and I'd have to take on a mortgage at half a million as a very new charity. That's when my faith journey really began!

Even as I was making the payment, I was thinking to myself,

'Am I mad? There's still time to pull out. Still time to be safe.'

Looking back, that was the enemy at work. He's great at whispering into your ear, great at sowing doubt. I hesitated, until I remembered how Duane White had come over to me in front of hundreds of people to give me the message:

'There is a supernatural provision for the vision God placed on your heart. The provision will not come from natural circumstances or man, but from Heaven through people. He is going to give you creative ideas, and He's going to fund what He has put in your heart.'

'No,' I thought. 'I'm not backing out. I know God is in it. So, God will fund it.'

So, I pressed on, and here we are.

I remember when I was young, there was an American preacher I liked. He's still around today but now everybody's against him because he's very much 'I believe it, I receive it.' That's a philosophy that can go wrong, and some people take it to extremes. God has clearly blessed this man financially, but these days, when I catch him talking, all I can think is there's something off with him.

There are so many pastors on TV and YouTube who will tell you that you have to put a seed into this ministry and that ministry. I don't go along with that at all, and I think they take advantage of people. I prefer to believe what Malachi tells us:

'Will a mere mortal rob God? Yet you rob me. But you ask, "How are we robbing you?" In tithes and offerings. You are under a curse—your whole nation—because you are robbing me. Bring the whole tithe into the storehouse, that there may be food in my house. Test me in this,' says the Lord Almighty, 'and see if I will not throw open the floodgates of heaven and pour out so much blessing that there will not be room enough to store it.' (Malachi 3:8-10, NIV)

Most people don't bring their tithes into the storehouse. They don't realise that it's not our money in the first place and that it all, all of it, comes from God, and belongs to God. What's more, they don't understand that you can never out-give God. But it's also about expecting to receive as well as giving.

God said He'll keep the devourer away, and it's expecting to see God in those things. I've had to learn that, even when we can't afford to do it, that's the time you do it.

I can remember that season when I had no money at all. All the way through, I made sure I tithed. God honoured me and I had nothing, but the way God blessed me and took me through, I'll never forget. Even how that money came through my door and how He then challenged me to give it all away. I did so, and then He gave me twice as much and I paid all my bills off. I could have just used the first lot of money to pay some of my bills, but because I did what God told me, all my bills were paid.

I think the trouble is when people get into a state of mind where they see it as a transaction.

'Oh, I'm on the prosperity side now, so I'm going to believe God for this, this, this and this.'

They look at God's promises to bless them, and they put all their hope into that deal, and then they are disappointed when God doesn't give them what they asked for. But they've based it on only part of God's word. They are leaning on the bits of the scriptures that they think will give them what they want instead of looking at the whole thing.

When I was younger, it made no sense to me that God doesn't give us everything that we believe we need.

From the beginning, I knew I couldn't get married once I'd adopted the children. I could see they would need so much of my love and attention. There would be no room for anyone else; how could a marriage possibly have lasted in those circumstances? I knew God was asking me to do a big thing.

As we went on, I found that being a single mother to four adopted children with the background they had wasn't always easy, and sometimes it was far harder than I had ever expected. In those days, I felt so bad. I didn't have a husband, and I didn't have a father for the kids, and for a long time I couldn't understand why. I didn't want to be on my own doing this. It all got a lot easier when I surrendered, and I said to God,

'You're asking me to do this, so You're going to have to be my husband and You're going to have to be a father.'

Even after all that, I can still ask, why did my first marriage fail? Wouldn't it have been easier for me if that had worked out and we'd had kids and a nice, simple family?

The answer is simple. God called me. He called me to adopt that family, and ever since, He has blessed me with an overwhelming gift of total love for those children. I know other people who adopted, and they didn't think of their children as a family. I have never understood that. I lean on how God adopts us human beings into his family. It was clear to me: I was adopting the children into my family and God was the father.

There's still another problem; we expect God to do things quickly, but God's timing isn't always our timing. I had to battle that with the Heneage Road building. Even though I fully accepted the stepping stones idea, the reality of it still took it out of me. Every time I was in there, putting paint on a wall, I would be thinking.

'God, this building isn't what You gave me.'

I suffered because I wanted the end goal there and then. Sometimes God does it straight away, but sometimes we have to wait, and I think because we have to wait, so many people give up.

These days, when someone says I should give up, it's easy to resist. All I ask is, did God give me the vision for this or not? And if He did, then what right have I to give up?

I have to stand in the faith. Life isn't about saying, 'I want this.' It's about saying, 'What do You want me to do, God?'

I don't follow that American preacher any more. I won't follow any man or woman any more. Everyone can fall. They start off well. They may even seem anointed, but then the pressures get to them, the anointing leaves them, and they fall off the perch. I keep a careful eye on Rock and myself for the same reason. I know how careful I have to be. As soon as I start thinking 'This is down to me,' then I've lost it. It's all about keeping your eyes on God. We must remember God has done this; this has nothing to do with you and God can take it away from you, just like that.

Sometimes I see my life as a road.

It's a good road, stretching far ahead, but there are boulders along the way. The boulders are the problems I must face. It's a straight road because I know what God has set before me.

I know what I am called to do. I walk forward, day after day, and every day I cover some distance. As the boulders come up to block me, I seek the Lord and He takes me through. God said He would be with me in everything, and He is.

As I get past the boulders, sometimes they change me.

I have to stay on this road because God has laid it before me. He didn't promise it would be easy, and it soon became clear that there would be attacks from all sides, but He always has the answers, and He will see me through.

In the distance, rising bright in the distance, I see the light of my destination. It shines with glory, like a jewel. Sometimes I see towers, walls, and spires. The gates are pearls, and the walls are pure, transparent gold. The crystal-clear river of the water of life runs down the main street, and there are tall, green, trees on each side.

Sometimes the vision is vague, faded, obscure. There's no detail, just light, beaming, twinkling, sometimes only glowing, ahead. On those days, all I can tell is there is great joy coming.

Sometimes the road leads me through the valleys. It's dark, and it's hard and I feel I'm not going through. Sometimes I go through those desert times and it's dry and I think, 'Where is God? Where is God?'

On the worst days of all, I can see no light. I feel a tunnel close overhead. Those days are all about believing. Believing God and trusting God. Thinking, 'I will come out of this ... God knew I was going to go through this ... God is here ... I can't see Him at the moment, but God is here, and I've got to trust Him, and I've got to hold on.'

It's all about holding on to God. Every day it's all about holding on to the Truth.

In all days, in all seasons, this is my life. I travel down the road. All I know for sure is that God is good, I am called, I am equipped, and the best is yet to come.

When I stand in the Rock premises in Caistor and I take in the magnificent view over the countryside, I'm always careful to keep the truth uppermost in my mind.

'God, You gave me the best. It's not about me. I've done none of this. It's all from You, my own true and eternal Rock.'

It's a truth that lies over all my life, through all the pain, all the darkness, and all the blessing and all the joy. Jesus really does come to give us life in all its fullness.

EPILOGUE

The Light has come in flesh and blood.

As I write these last words, it's a few days before Christmas in 2023. As the vicar at my church said in his sermon this week:

'The incarnation is an incredible picture of God's love. The light comes into the world from the highest majesty to the lowest insignificance and in this we see God coming to us from the cradle to the cross. Could He reach any closer to bring us to home?' (Rev'd Matt Rodgers)

We have a habit in Rock of counting our blessings and making sure we know how God is reaching out to us. Once a week, a member of staff compiles a list of all the ways we have seen God's hand at work, and we pray into it and give thanks. This is the list for the last two weeks. It may give you a sense of what is truly going on, and how much we have to thank God for.

For a while I've been feeling that we should offer free haircuts at the food bank to give people some dignity. It's expensive to get a trim and I can remember how grateful I was after my divorce to be offered an extra hour's overtime which meant I could get my hair trimmed.

I stepped out in faith, and decided to pay one of my staff, who has trained as a hairdresser, to cut hair on a Monday afternoon. This week Rock was given £1,000 specifically for her wage. A local company heard about this, and then paid for and sent us:

•A proper hairdresser's chair
•A large mirror for the wall
•A handheld mirror
•Artificial plants to put in the room
•A barber's cape
•A cutting cape

This same week we were also given:

•250 chickens for Christmas (I told no-one outside Rock we needed them, I prayed, and then a few days later they were offered to us.)

•360 selection boxes of chocolates.

•Over £2,000 of toys.

•An incredible amount of extra food.

•The donations of money were £500, £1,000, £750 and £100

•Three weeks ago, we were victims of a sophisticated financial fraud by an organised gang. They hit us hard, and we lost £60,000 in one day. This week the bank gave us back our £60,000

•One national brand gave us £500 towards new kitchen equipment.

•Another national brand has given us just under £9,000, which will pay for much-needed new doors in the Heneage Road site.

That all happened in one week. Last week we received:

•Gifts and donations of £1,250, £100, £62.50, £100, £50

•48 selection boxes of chocolates.

•An almost unbelievable amount of food donations, too many to itemise.

•Sacks full of brand-new toys

•A visit from a local company who want to give us part of their cold storage building free of charge

•A pallet load of fish cakes

•The bread rolls and treats for the learning disability Christmas party.

•A new metal gate supplied and fitted after a break in at the Caistor site. (The break-in happened a couple of months ago and the gang stole expensive farming and gardening equipment and did extensive damage to our storage facility. We were left with a bill of £20,000. Since then, God has restored all of our loss and more, and this gate is one more part of that.)

•£20,000 worth of food for 2024

In 2023, we worked out that, through all the different areas of Rock, we played our part in supporting 1,300 people per week. God is incredible. It's amazing seeing Him in the small things as well as the big things.

There are Christians who wouldn't see the lists above as evidence of God's provision. I'm different. I see God in everything, and I take God at his word; I can't not do that. I am always amazed at God's provision and goodness. It's so clear that the more we act in God's will, the more we give, then the more God gives us. You simply can't out-give God.

Praise You Father, for You are good.

This isn't the end.

In the future, there will be even more chapters to write of the provision and goodness of God. If you think about how much we want to give to our children, how much more does the Lord want to give to us?

The important thing in moving forward is that we don't take our eyes off Him and that we always remember without Him, none of this would have happened. Every morning, I pray this prayer, taken from a verse in 1st Chronicles:

"Oh, that you would bless me and enlarge my territory! Let your hand be with me and keep me from harm so that I will be free from pain." (1st Chr 4:10, NIV)

It's all about seeing God in the small things and the big things. It's about standing when you don't want to stand. It's about saying 'I can do all things through Christ Jesus' even when everything around you seems to fail.

It's standing in faith when it seems impossible. It's holding tight to the promises of God. But beyond all that, it's being constant and true. Loving a God who wants the very best for us, knowing that if we put our complete faith and trust in Him, He will never let us down.

He is always faithful. All that's left for me is to ask you: Can you dare trust Him?

FIND OUT MORE

If you'd like to know more about Jesus, a good place to begin is Alpha.

Alpha is a community of seekers and sceptics and those who are exploring faith. At its heart is a free, friendly course (one two-hour session per week) which introduces you to the basics of the Christian faith.

Set up by Holy Trinity Brompton church in London in the 1980s. It now runs all over the world and has had tens of millions of people take it.

It encourages discussion about life's deepest matters, and no question is out of bounds. (You can be fantastically rude if you want!)

Most towns in England will have a church that runs Alpha at some point in the year, and it's often possible to find a church that runs it no matter where you are in the world.

Many places even have a version of the course that runs online, so as long as you have internet access you can attend wherever you are.

Find out more at alpha.org

YOUR NOTES